Marrion Wilcox

Señora Villena and Gray

An Oldhaven Romance

Marrion Wilcox

Señora Villena and Gray
An Oldhaven Romance

ISBN/EAN: 9783337007447

Printed in Europe, USA, Canada, Australia, Japan

Cover: Foto ©Thomas Meinert / pixelio.de

More available books at **www.hansebooks.com**

SEÑORA VILLENA

AND

Gray: An Oldhaven Romance

TWO VOLUMES IN ONE

BY THE AUTHOR OF "REAL PEOPLE"

New York
WHITE, STOKES & ALLEN
1887

COPYRIGHT, 1887,
BY MARION WILCOX.
All rights reserved.

PRESS OF TUTTLE MOREHOUSE & TAYLOR, NEW HAVEN.

CONTENTS

SEÑORA VILLENA:

	PAGE
Dr. Vincent and his Sevilla,	1
José María Rodriguez,	9
Señora Villena,	20
Gloria,	34
Medina,	44
Monday. Act I,	53
Tuesday. Act II,	80
Wednesday. Act III,	102
Soirée at Sevilla,	122
The Spanish Session,	148

GRAY: AN OLDHAVEN ROMANCE:

	PAGE
Preface,	3
Part I—By Mr. Penman,	7
Part II—By Mrs. Eaton,	117
Conclusion—By Mr. Penman,	247

SEÑORA VILLENA

Erastro, el corazon que en alta parte
Es puesto por el hado, suerte ó sino,
Quererle derribar por fuerza ó arte,
O diligencia humana, es desatino.

—*Cervantes: La Galatea*

DR. VINCENT AND HIS SEVILLA

> A cada vuelta se mira
> En los ojos de su amor,
> Y en la luz de aquellos soles
> Se le quema el corazon.—*Zorrilla*.

DR. VINCENT and Gloria continued to live in New-York for several years after their marriage.

For a time, that is to say, the mere fact that they were married to each other was in itself sufficient, and it did not occur to either of them to make any change. They lived in the indicative mood, present tense, repeating to each other "I am, thou art, we are," and taking no thought of might, could, would or should.

I like to think of them in the positive, straight-forward, simple part of their conjugation, for their present was almost perfect. To him she was constantly an expression or express image of those hidden thoughts and ideal strivings which he so seldom dared to utter; to her he was still transfigured by virtue of his having once or twice dared for her sake to show the depth and strength and beauty of his nature.

After several years, however, they both had a touch of the subjunctive. This is how it came about: I give their conversation without changing one syllable.

At that time, it should be premised, Gloria was not quite an invalid.

Gloria: Don't you think—somebody—mamita, in fact—thought it might be better—

Vincent: For him?

Gloria: Him! It may be her. It might be better for *it* not to be in the city when it first comes.

Vincent: Very true; and we would be happy in the country ourselves.

Nothing further was said at the time by either. We know their habit of silence, and can easily guess, by the tender and dreamy expression of her face, in what quarter Gloria's thoughts were busied. As for Vincent, he was reflecting how his own earliest association had been with the country, in harmless freedom.

He also showed himself to be an amateur in philosophy, of course: otherwise he would not have been a modern man at leisure.

"Whether it be true or not," he reasoned, "that a child imbibes the love of beauty, and so a useful ambition, from such surroundings, this at least is certain: unless our boy enjoys flowers and all that kind of thing soon after he is born, he will never do it; for after a while he will begin to smoke."

So a transfer was agreed upon without discussion, and they changed their residence to a town sometimes called Oldhaven in the vicinity of New-York.

Surely I may pass quickly over the period of change, inasmuch as they themselves made little ado about it, and may dismiss with a word, also, that season of suspense and anxious expectation in which their vocabulary was limited to I, thou, we, he, she or it.

The close of this period was marked by a burst of happiness which I should be glad to describe if adequate description were possible; but the best experiences of life are known only by their fruits. This best experience will surely teach one to pity, and it may inspire some genial work to which heart and brain contribute equally; but I can only suggest what it meant to Gloria and Vincent by asking the reader to dwell upon the significance of the following transposition of pronouns, and the emphatic position of the first:

He, thou, we, I.

But this list is not complete. I want to show this family of three fully alive in the perfect present; and two pronouns, with the infinite variety of action and suffering which may follow them, are still wanting.

Let me devote a few sentences to the pronouns you and they.

The house which Vincent bought in Oldhaven was not one of those pitiful wooden expedients which stand out-of-doors in the cold, shivering, with nothing over them. No: it was a substantial structure of stone and brick, offering a determined front to the elements. Unpretentious and even rugged externally, within it was secure. We desire an all-the-year-round friendship with such a house; for its thick walls promise warmth in winter and coolness in summer. The expression just used, "a determined front," might be misleading. I therefore hasten to add a point of great importance. The sides of Dr. Vincent's dwelling were neither less nor more attractive than the front; while the rear, vine-covered and ornamented with balconies, was really very pretty.

But after all the best thing about the house was the garden—a pleasant, old-fashioned place, with an abundance of flowers and fruit trees and gravel-walks, with box hedges, and arbors and a sufficient lawn.

Unless I succeed in conveying the impression that these are features of genuine comfort, without one bit of affectation or display, I miss my intention. The exact amount of Vincent's income I do not know; but it was unquestionably much more than enough to keep up this modest style of living. What became of the surplus? If you have any acquaintance among the poor of Oldhaven, you may learn from them.

Perhaps it was the solid strength of the walls of the house which gave to any person visiting at Dr. Vincent's home a sense of security and easy enjoyment; perhaps it was the row of shade-trees, rising like a leafy wall around the limits of the garden and suggesting seclusion in pleasant company; perhaps it was the spirit of generosity which a guest began to breathe in with the air as soon as he arrived, thus unconsciously, as the doctors say, "contracting" generosity, and gaining the conviction that he had a right to his comforts if he made giving his chief luxury. Perhaps; but I think not. I think it was this:

Nobody could tell when Dr. Vincent would play. It might be in season or out of season. "Where is our host?" someone would ask, and Gloria would reply that he had seemed rather quiet and thoughtful, so she supposed that he must have gone to the library. Suddenly an exquisite breath of harmony would be heard, at first so faint and uncertain that it might have been from an Æolian harp, and only the quickest ears would catch it. But when this had grown into a strong melody, all activities ceased throughout the house. The music of Vincent's violin was like the spell which bound the sentinel at the gate and the turnspit in the kitchen of the castle of the Sleeping Beauty.

Those of Vincent's friends who did not allow for Gloria's influence thought it odd that this side of his nature should remain a thing apart from his ordinary life. He never referred to his music nor allowed other people to refer to it. In manner he was cheerful rather than serious, full of delicate humor, not self-absorbed, but ready with thoughtful attention and kind service for his guests.

I think it was this music which made the peculiarity of the place.

As for Gloria's influence, I beg to refer you for further evidence of that to Vincent's own speech and action as recorded in the following pages; but without delay I must mention the tribute which her husband paid to it and to her in naming their home Sevilla. That was as though he had said: Thanks to you, I have here the best of all that is Spanish.

In Sevilla he gathered about himself people who entertained him and each other, not all of one kind, but those who at the same time stimulated and set-off one another. A company, he maintained, should be selected as the *dramatis personæ* are chosen by the playwright — for the sake of contrast and dramatic effect. We might, therefore, go together to Sevilla at almost any season, confidently expecting to find there several people worth taking a good look at; but since June is a pleasant month in the country, and since señora Villena and the Medinas and Teresa Diaz, all of whom we know,* were there during ten days of last June, let us choose that season.

Beside those who have been mentioned, José Maria Rodriguez—not a Cuban, but a Spaniard of the Spaniards, from old Sevilla—was also there.

These people being together in a garden in the pleasant month of June, either mischief or fun was sure to ensue.

And now the present tense has been completed by the addition of those people whom Dr. Vincent could befriend, as the poor, or entertain, as guests. Together these make for him and for Gloria the pronoun *they*.

And the *you?*

You may be any one of the guests you like.

* Characters in "Real People."

JOSÉ MARIA RODRIGUEZ

ONE morning Gloria and Teresa were sitting together in an arbor near the house.

The sisters had no doubt much to say to each other, for they had been together but once before since Gloria had left New-York. Especially the married sister had much to communicate. There was, for instance, the inexhaustible subject of her American acquaintances and her impressions of them, not to mention her husband and the changes in his character since he, an American of English descent, had married a Spaniard. Above all, there was the superb baby to be discussed.

Instead of chatting, however, they were quite silent for a long time, Gloria sewing, Teresa dreaming with her hands crossed. They both had the same subject in mind, and both knew that very well. Finally Gloria decided to come to the point.

Gloria: What are you thinking of, little sister?

Teresa: Nothing at all, in truth.

Gloria: How long have you known señor Rodriguez?

Teresa: How long? I do not know him. Have you forgotten the rules at home?

Gloria: I do not forget. I remember: and that is the very reason why I ask you how long you have known him. If three days, you may be safe still.

Teresa: You know it must be longer. You know he is a business friend of papa dear.

Gloria: If three months, you are in danger—and so is he.

Teresa (languidly): You think I am a flirt still?

Gloria: I know it. You have never cared for any man more than a week, and this Rodriguez you have had chances enough to see—I have not forgotten how we used to manage—ever since last Christmas, when papa took him to the house to dinner.

Teresa: You pretended not to know!

Gloria: I know enough to suspect you, and I have eyes to see that you are not tired of him. But since you have known him so long and are not yet tired of him, it follows that he is the one exception, and that you ——

Teresa: Hush!

Gloria (looking up from her sewing): What is it?

Teresa: He is coming. Shut your eyes once in a while, little sister.

From the window of his bed-room Rodriguez had seen the two ladies enter the arbor. Being a man of the world, he did not follow them immediately, but gave them time to exchange confidences and improved the interval by arranging his plan of action and perfecting his toilet; for in matters of dress and affairs of the heart, Rodriguez was an artist.

The situation was less novel, and therefore less perplexing, to him than it would have been to me or, I venture to say, to the reader. Teresa had been so beautiful and so languid the evening before that he had lost at least half a night's sleep in consequence. That sort of thing could not be allowed to continue. It was imperative that the proper revelation of his sentiments should be made before bed-time; but how? It must be an irresistible appeal, and yet he could not hope to see her alone. But every one will admit that it is more difficult to be irresistible in the presence of a third person.

Such obstacles stimulated the Spaniard's desire and strengthened his resolution. The mirror which reflected a more and more faultless toilet, reflected also a more and more confident expression upon the handsome face of Don José. His person and his plan were ready for use when Teresa cried, "Hush! He is coming."

Gloria greeted her guest cordially and, when he had bowed low to her and then to her sister, made him sit down beside her.

Gloria (secretly admiring his broad shoulders and muscular neck, but not his new coat): We were just speaking about you, señor; and that proves that you will interest us most by telling us about yourself.

Rodriguez: I must obey you, Mrs. Vincent; and the first thing I tell you is this: I am most happy here in your house. I am most happy.

Gloria: What a serious compliment! I shall acknowledge it when I believe it, and I shall believe it when you stay with us a very long time.

Rodriguez: Well, we are serious, we Spaniards. I cannot help it.

Gloria: Serious! You don't know what the word means.

Rodriguez: I do not mean like the Americans: they are terrible! But we are more serious than you Cubans are, you know, and so we miss one half the pleasure of living.

Gloria: If the poor Cubans did not have light hearts, what good thing would be left them? Spain would take away their right to laugh, and sell it for money ——

Teresa (interrupting to divert the conversation from the treacherous ground of Cuba's oppression by Spain): Is Sevilla, your city, so lovely as I hear, señor?

Rodriguez: It is like this place of your sister, which is therefore well named, señorita. It is charming. Even if you were a stranger passing through its streets you would say: there is no other city which is a paradise. You would see through the archway of each house a beautiful court within, with flowering plants and a fountain in the center, where the family meet, and friends come, and the most wonderful stories are told. Ah, but it makes me sad, very sad, to think of this; and I shall return never until I am happy.

Teresa (with mild wonder): You have not been happy there!

Rodriguez (leaning forward and speaking earnestly): That I will tell you, to you, señorita; and I have never told it before. My father came to the United States when a boy to go to school. Here he remained two years. Among his masters in school was an old Spaniard who taught music in the academy. He lived just out of the town in a poor little cottage with his only child, Mercedes, who was most beautiful. At this time she was only twelve and my father he was sixteen. Her father was poor, very poor, and had only the money which he derived from his lessons in town. He was evidently one of those geniuses who never find an audience—never; for although he composed music, heavenly music, no one has ever heard it, with the exception of my father and the favored few who have heard his daughter sing it after his death. It was the love of music which drew these three people together, and my father spent almost all his spare time at the little cottage, either playing the guitar or listening to the old teacher's divine compositions. Then too they became very dear to each other because they were all of one race and all in a foreign land. It was there, even then, that my father lost his heart to Mercedes. He called her his little wife and made the master call him "hijo mio" (my son). When the old musician would fall into melancholy, fearing for his little daughter and wondering what would become of her after his death, then they would embrace and weep together, and my father would swear by all the saints that Mercedes should never want, that she should be his wife and that he would cherish her above all things on earth. Five years afterwards, while at home in Sevilla, my father has received news of the death of the master. He went back to America and married Mercedes; then returned to Spain, where I have been born and where he lived with his beautiful wife in perfect happiness for twelve years.

When Rodriguez had reached this point in his story, his expression and manner underwent a sudden transformation. He had been addressing himself impartially to Gloria and Teresa, receiving encouragement from the former but scarcely a mark of attention from the latter. Now he collected all his forces for a magnetic storm.

A moment before all three members of the little group in the arbor had been conscious of the loveliness of the morning, and in addition Gloria had been conscious of her sewing and Teresa of the fragrance of violets, which was as truly characteristic of her person as indolence was characteristic of her nature. Now Rodriguez had secured the opportunity to speak as his feeling prompted, and that was with such passion that the sisters drew close together and clasped each-other's hands.

He began to speak about his love for his mother; but Teresa read in his face and heard in the tones of his voice a message intended for herself alone. Then he lavished upon his mother such praise as the filial sentiment never suggests; and Teresa saw that he was studying his description of the mother's perfections from her own person. Finally he painted such an enchanting picture of his mother's ideal life, surrounded by all that is admirable in the birth-place and home of Spanish art, that Teresa lost her judgment in contemplation and did not notice that the details of this picture were but copies of her own well-known tastes and fancies.

Do not suppose from this that the passion of Rodriguez was artifice. The slightest touch of sham would have ruined everything, for it would have been instantly detected. It was not artifice, but art. And you may be sure that it was not mere passionate warmth, but that it was fire. I offer proof.

Teresa's eyes were dark, tender and secret things—which I cannot call features without conveying the false impression that anybody and everybody could see them. Anybody and everybody could see that they were large and dark, but nothing more. Rodriguez himself had never seen more than that; but now, as his story progressed, those dreamy eyes became more and more brilliant, until finally they were like flames. Warmth may beget tenderness; but flame answers only to fire.

When Rodriguez saw that light kindled, he was satisfied. In the presence of a third person he had declared his passion, had urged his suit in the most effective manner, and had received encouragement.

That was enough. His artistic sense put a period.

If he had continued to speak in this strain his gladness would have showed itself, Gloria would have noticed both that and her sister's expression and would have discovered the plot. The charm of the situation would have been lost. It cost a real but no apparent effort for him to continue his story, as though that had been from the first his only intention. He did not dare to look at Teresa, but addressed himself exclusively to Gloria.

"When I was little more than ten years old," he said, "my father was called suddenly to New York on business of great importance. He did not take us with him, alas! It was the first separation. I cannot bear to tell the great sorrow that afterwards fell upon me. I had never known anything but joy; and while my father was away my beautiful mother took me closer than ever to herself, so that I was very happy. . . . When he stepped on land, my father, he found me dressed in deep mourning. My mother whom I adored had gone mad and died in four days: and I saw it all. Do you wonder, Mrs. Vincent, that the paradise called

Sevilla was hateful to me until I had learned that such things happen everywhere?"

Gloria put out her hand, which Rodriguez took with profound respect, holding it for a moment in silence and then raising it to his lips. So they became friends.

Then the joy of a hopeful lover asserted itself and would no longer be controlled. Rodriguez began to sing the praise of his host and this new Sevilla which he had founded; and I verily believe that if he had thought of the new baby-carriage he would have praised that also.

"How extremely considerate of him," Gloria thought, "to give the conversation a cheerful turn so promptly, after that sad story."

But I dare not record what they said after that, for they fell to discussing perfumes and perfumery. In that department they were all three very learned and strictly scientific, using terms which I do not understand.

SEÑORA VILLENA

URING the half-hour which Rodriguez, in his bachelor room, devoted to plans for the conquest of one, Concha Casablanca Medina, in her more sumptuous chamber, made her customary preparation to win praise from all the world.

Medina had risen early, put on his stoutest shoes, and joined Vincent in a morning walk to the post-office. He had bidden his wife good-bye as though setting out upon a long and perilous journey. The reader is invited to draw from this circumstance his own conclusions as to the time which had elapsed since that Sunday afternoon when Miguel won "pounds and pounds" of candy by helping his merry aunt to a modest husband.

Concha had on a new dressing-sacque, so she decided to take her morning cup of coffee with señora Villena.

Cup in hand she crossed the hall and stood at her good friend's door and knocked.

"Caramba! Com' quick in!"
Concha turned the knob and entered.
"Oh! 's jou, Conchita?" said the señora. "Why jou knock? I thought 's that leetle moankey."

"What monkey, Coralie?"

"That leetle naygro bo-ee, that leetle moankey," she repeated impatiently. "Jou know, Conchita, he bringer the water, eh?"

"No, I am not the little black boy in buttons," said Concha. "But, good gracious! my dear, what is the matter with you this morning? You look so oddly."

Señora Villena had waked up with a pain in her shoulder, and had immediately begun to think over all the misdeeds and frivolities of her life. She reached the conclusion that she was an old woman, and that the Lord had finally decided to punish her. When Concha entered she was dressed very plainly, her hair arranged not in her usual fashion of *frisé* but drawn down almost over her ears. Seated in a rocking-chair she swayed to and fro as she replied:

"I teller jou, girl, I am now growing to be an old, verie old, an' I must act myself liker wong" (like one). "I dress me verie plain, verie plain."

"Bah!" said Concha. "Nothing of the kind." She had seen her friend melancholy once or twice before.

"But I mean it," persisted the señora. "I mean it for sure. Yes, Conchita, Conchita!"

"Whom do you think I met just before we left town—let me see, day before yesterday? Whom do you think, Coralie?" Concha asked.

"I don' know, my dear," said the señora, indifferently.

"Well, guess. Someone you like," Concha urged.

"No, I cannot guess. I don' care."

"That delightful Monsieur Lafitte," Concha said; "and he told me he saw you at the theater last Wednesday night, and that he had never seen you look so well. He said you had a beautiful costume on, and your diamonds were superb."

While Concha was speaking, a change came gradually over the señora's woeful face. For an instant she tried to resist it, but in vain; for her heart was very much stronger than her head. The change stole upward, lifting her chin perceptibly, then drawing the corners of her mouth with it on its way to her eyes, which it set dancing.

"Don' say, Conchita mia!" she exclaimed "Cáspita! jou know, we had splendid time. Here! Susanne," (calling her French maid from an adjoining room) "com' fixer my hair; taker this plain dress; bringer wong handsome."

She jumped up and, taking Concha by the hand, continued: "My dear, com'. I show jou my new costume. We haver partie to-night, no?—an' we invite Monsieur Lafitte, an' I fixer myself superblie for him." She snapped her fingers and took several waltz-steps, singing "*Les femmes, les femmes.*"

"Not to-night, Coralie," Concha suggested. "We will give that party when we get back to the city."

Another change, this time instantaneous, in the señora's expression. She threw herself into the nearest chair. "Devilo place in the coantry," she moaned. "No fun, no gay! Ah, Conchita, Conchita, I am verie old woman! Válgame Dios!" Then, addressing her trim maid who had brought in a gorgeous skirt, "Taker that away!" she cried. "Don' be so fool, girl! Virgen santísima," she concluded, crossing herself, "Ora pro nobis!"

Concha was laughing so heartily at this

parody of woe that she could scarcely speak; but her quick wit suggested another expedient for overcoming the real melancholy which, she knew, was hidden beneath this grotesque display.

"Do you remember, Coralie," she said, in a breathless way, "that time before I was married, when you got me to write invitations for you to Louis Diaz and Escaso (the little beast!) and lots of others to come to a soirée at your apartments?"

"Toma! often enough," said the señora, without interest.

"But I mean that time—that particular time," Concha said. "On the appointed evening I array myself, I go early to help you receive, I find you dressed to go out!" Here Concha began to act the scene. "You welcome me as though I were unexpected.

"'How jou do, Conchita?' you say.

"'Well, who has accepted? Who is coming?' I ask.

"'Where, my dear?' you say.

"'Why, here, to-night, of course,' I answer.

"'Oh, my dear, I refuser the invitations,' you are good enough to explain; by which you mean that at the last minute you have sent word to everybody but me not to come, as you prefer to go to the theater!"

In spite of herself señora Villena smiled at Concha's perfect imitation of her accent and manner.

"Well," Concha continued, "that showed me that you prefer the theater to a *soirée* at home."

"Why not? I think yes," the señora assented.

"Ea, courage!" cried Concha, drawing up a light table and, after wrapping a lace handkerchief around her wrist, beginning to "dance ballet with my fingers," in her own phrase, upon it. Her fingers being very white and tapering, ending in pointed nails, which had just been polished to a dazzling brightness, and the handkerchief falling short of being a skirt, but still falling somewhat,—it was a pretty invocation to the "Muse of the many twinkling feet."

"Courage!" Concha repeated, making all her fingers race from the sides of the table to the edge nearest her auditor. "Here comes the whole *corps-de-ballet* to the foot-lights." She hummed a Spanish dance and made the *corps* keep time with simple steps; then, "Here comes the *première danseuse*," she said. The subordinates disappeared, and from the background came her index and middle fingers alone, whirling, spinning, pirouetting, now kneeling for applause, now defying criticism in that right-angle position which always suggests the question "How?" and sometimes the disapproving "Why?" Next, her left hand ran out from the side-scenes, and knelt for the first dancer to mount and posture on his arm. "That is the maître," said Concha; "he is very strong."

"Brava! Encore! Otra vez!" cried the señora, and drew a ring, one of many, from her hand. "Here, Conchita mia, jou taker that."

"I have no fingers at present, as you have seen; and anklets are not in fashion," Concha laughingly replied. Then, to drive the thought of giving from her friend's mind, she quickly added: "I tell you what we will do. We will have a play here."

"Eh? What jou say, bébé?"

"I say, we will give a play here, at Dr. Vincent's," Concha replied in a convincing tone.

"A play! theater! in this Old—I don' know how you call—Oldhaven!"

"No, not in the town: right here where we are."

"Oh, bébé!"—in a reproachful voice. "Where the stage, eh? Where the orchestre?"

"I will take care for all that. Promise to help me! Will you promise?"

The señora promised and believed: so Concha was in for it.

That is how the idea started—in a chance suggestion.

A most happy chance, I shall always think; for the little play-seed fell into rich, warm soil, when it took root immediately.

And the soil was favorable to this particular seed rather than to any other. Have you never noticed that the Spanish-American has one passion and one talent: the passion for observing manners and the talent for imitation? When we of Puritan lineage win through plodding study and bitter experience an uncommon knowledge and appreciation of our fellow-men, we call that knowledge and appreciation by a name which the philosophers use— "insight;" but the Spaniard is born a member of the Appreciative Union. I do not think that great philosophers use or that all great philosophers understand that term.

I shall devote a number of pages to showing how rapidly the little play-seed grew in the mellow soil and the tropical climate of an Appreciative Union.

First of all Concha went to seek Vincent, and found him just returned with Medina from that walk which the one called a constitutional, and the other a journey.

It took twenty words and twenty-five gestures for Concha to state her intention and convince both her host and her husband of its feasibility.

Of course she did not stoop to details: it is such a woman's prerogative to inspire, and it is the simple duty of all men to execute for her.

The twenty-fifth gesture was the one which convinced her husband. She went away with him and left Vincent thinking.

"It is not so easy," Vincent thought; "and it is not so hard. For me alone it would be impossible; for them without me—or somebody who has rules—it would become grotesque. I am the stupid whom they need to check their extravagance now and then. I am to them like the *quantum sufficit* of heaviness which every genius should have, to keep him from becoming a crank. I am their ballast: that is all I am."

So he continued to charge himself with stupidity; and if it were not for the cleverness of his argument, the genuine conviction in his mind might raise a corresponding belief in my own, as I watch him now.

Presently his thoughts came back to the matter proposed.

"It is only one step in advance," he reasoned. "It is after all only the natural thing for them. Here they are—all born appreciators, mimics, actors. They get at the essence of the characters of people by intuition; they are forever acting the history of some acquaintance, so that I know their friends better than my own. My wife even imitates me to my face, and her imitation is more like me than I am. Only one thing more is needed: to prune the luxuriant growth of their fancies. They think of too many things at once, that's the trouble. If they come together untrimmed, they will make a thicket and not a garden."

Here Vincent began to walk up and down the wide, cool hallway where Concha had met him. He stared at the most familiar objects, because he really was not noticing them.

"Yes, one thing more is needed," he said, half aloud : "They must have a common plan of action, of course. That is, we must arrange a plot beforehand. But we can manage that, easily enough."

His manner while he was considering the question of the plot showed easy confidence; but presently he stopped before a painting which he did not especially like.

"By Jove! another thing," he exclaimed aloud. "Where? If we use one parlor for the stage and another for the auditorium, I shall have to change that mountain-scene. It would never do in the parlor."

He had in fact made a false start. The picture which he did not like represented a mountain-side; and, unconsciously influenced by that, he had planned a scene in which Teresa, as a shepherdess, should be climbing something and be in peril somehow and be rescued by Rodriguez, as sportsman, with one of Vincent's birdguns slung over his shoulder.

"Pshaw! What shall we use for the stage?" he repeated aloud.

"That so, bo-ee!" a merry voice answered; and señora Villena, as she carefully descended the polished stairs, greeted him with: "Goo-morning! That so; jes what I tell Concha. Where the stage?"

A good laugh blew away such light first-thoughts as shepherdess and sportsman; but nothing more substantial offered itself immediately to take their place.

After he had accompanied señora Villena into the garden, where he soon left her with Gloria and the others, Vincent went to his study. Little good that did him.

He sat at his desk, pen in hand and writing-pad before him, looking very serious and thinking about shepherdesses dressed as queens or Japanese girls or raving beauties, with sportsmen to match, as kings or minstrels or rich old gentlemen. It was no use: he could not deceive even himself.

More than ever persuaded that he was stupid, he put down his pen and went out to join his guests.

It was ten steps from the back piazza to

the arbor, where they all were met. Vincent took five steps toward them, and then said:

"Here is the stage!"

Gloria saw him coming and arose; Rodriguez, who was nearest, heard him and turned around.

"Here is the stage—right here," Dr. Vincent repeated.

Then explanations followed. Concha broached her plan, and all applauded.

"It come to me like *that*," Vincent said; "I mean about the stage. Here we have the very thing. This arbor in the center ——. But let us begin at the beginning. Scene: A garden in the rear of Vincent's house. Right, a flight of steps and piazza. Left, a tennis-ground and high stone wall ——."

"Where the wall? I don' see," señora Villena interrupted.

"There isn't any wall now," said Vincent; "but we will put something to answer the same purpose. We can make so much play out of a wall. To continue, then: A high stone wall on the left. In the background, flowers and shrubbery. The interior of the arbor is visible to spectators, but not from piazza."

"Who are the spectators?" Medina asked.

"Why, all of us who are not acting, of course," Concha explained.

"I could see you from where I was in the arbor just now," Gloria objected.

"But, my dear," said Vincent, "if you had been sitting on the other side, which will do just as well for the play, you could not have seen me, or I you."

"And you, sir, have the play ready?" asked Rodriguez.

"No," said Vincent, "not yet; but I begin to believe that the way to get it is to keep my eyes open. And Medina, who is a great poet, will help me over the hard places."

So in appreciative unison they favored the growth of this little dramatic plant until luncheon time.

These things and others which are to follow were said and done because señora Villena woke with a pain in her shoulder.

GLORIA

HEN they sat down to lunch, Vincent found at his place a sheet of blotting-paper, folded like a napkin.

"What does this mean?" he asked.

Gloria answered sweetly from her end of the table: "Oh, you have become a literary man so suddenly, my dear Carangol" (her pet-name for him), "I fancied you might prefer it to dry your lips."

"I have n't been able to write even the first word yet, my dear," Vincent said; "so if you please I will take a napkin as usual."

"Gloria, you are a meace!" Concha cried. "I could bite you for being such a sweet meace!"

"Excuse me, — what is that word 'meace'?" asked Rodriguez. "Is it English? I believe not, for it seems from the connection in which you use it to signify so much that is complimentary."

"Not English; no, indeed," said Concha. "It is my own word, and yours, señor, if you like it."

"I have thought," Medina ventured, "that 'meace' took its *m* from mouse, its *ea* from neat, and its *ce* from nice: so that it meant a nice, neat, mouse."

Señora Villena clicked with her tongue and shook her head impatiently. "Fly from here on the second, straight!" she commanded. "Jou can spell, bo-ee, after all? Don' say, bo-ee. Caramba!"

The theatrical exaggeration of scorn with which this was delivered raised a great laugh, which all found not less appetizing than the first course of luncheon, being served at that moment.

What was said for a brief space after that, I do not record. It makes little difference what one says between soup and fish: everybody laughs instead of replying.

But in justice to Medina I must state that he had had in mind a derivation for the pet name, Carangol, which Gloria had given her husband, and that he decided not to make it public in that company, which welcomed light-hearted humor, but abhorred labored wit.

When they had reached that stage in

the progress of the meal when appetite lingers, but is patient, the conversation became so general, so rapid in its movement and so sudden in its changes, that if I am to give even a small portion of it I must not stop to describe attitudes or to distinguish between "he said" and "he exclaimed."

Concha: I think that Miss Kelt is beautiful. Do you, señor?

Rodriguez: She has beautiful hair.

Concha: You do not think her beautiful, but you will not contradict me.

Rodriguez: Have you ever seen her dance, señora?

Medina: Rodriguez means that she is stiff. He is a polite Socrates, our friend from Sevilla: he suggests his disagreement in some fine, indirect way, and makes us convince ourselves.

Teresa: Where did the Carters live when you first knew them, my brother?

Vincent: In rooms in Fiftieth-street. The rooms looked as though some one had gone away, taking with him everything he wanted; but that was not Carter's fault.

Gloria: Mrs. Carter's?

Vincent: No: a rich old uncle's, who let them remain poor. After his death Carter moved out of town, and I don't know of a pleasanter home than that he has now.

Señora Villena: Eh? Mr. Carter is that fonny fellow, no? He hass call 'Don Juan' 'Mr. John,' no?

Vincent: He is more than funny: he is fine. He notices things like this: When he was poor he kept a school for children. One day a little scholar, a boy of six years, came running up to him, dancing with delight, clapping his hands and crying: 'Mother is dead! I am so glad, for I am going away into the country!'

Medina: I passed the famous Richard Blake on the street several days ago.

Gloria: Indeed! How was he looking? Did you speak to him?

Medina: No, señora. He gave me, to tell the truth, rather a surly nod—like this (imitating). I did not care to speak to him. But, on thinking it over, I decided that he was not angry with me, or scorning me for some fault I was at the time conscious of having committed. No; more probably his foot pained him, because his boot-maker had made a misfit, because the boot-maker's son had taken Blake's last to carve into an image of St. Stephen, like the picture in his spelling-book. Blake gave me a surly nod because Stephen was stoned.

Vincent: Ah, Medina, you are my man. You are engaged.

Medina: For what?

Vincent: To write our play. You can wind the characters up in a plot with complications reaching back to the Garden of Eden.

Rodriguez: I have heard my English friend Mr. Silverspoon speak of this Blake. He has said that Mr. Blake is an eccentric, and too serious, too earnest, but a worthy man—oh, yes, very *solide*. And his wife—charming!

Teresa: Margery Blake! Yes, she is delicious.

Medina: The idea of Jack Silverspoon calling another man eccentric! That is too good.

Gloria (to Rodriguez): Did the original Mr. Silverspoon tell you Mr. Blake's strange history, señor?

Rodriguez: No, señora, he has not. It is true he once began; but he very soon thought of something different, and—you know how he is—he forgot the story to finish it. It is, I think, that Mr. Blake has had a quarrel, or something so, with his wife, no?

Gloria: A quarrel? Not that, señor; but he separated from her without quarreling—the cold-blooded wretch! And Margery behaved like an angel!

Vincent: A rather frisky angel, my dear.

Señora Villena: What those things of the steam-boat—na, na!—how jou call?— from the side of the steam-boat? Peddles?

Vincent: Paddle-wheels?

Señora Villena: Tha's it, bo-ee! Good for him an' for her. Caramba! (filling in the sense with vigorous gestures) I giver them one good beating: no leetle—so!— liker that peddle-wheels. Tha' so: I do.

Gloria (to Rodriguez): I am sorry you did not make Mr. Silverspoon finish telling you, señor. He met the Blakes when they were separated—that is, they were together and yet separated. It was very strange; and the whole story is so romantic. Mr. Silverspoon is an intimate friend of the Carters, you know, and he met them both at Mr. Carter's house. His acquaintance began then, at the most interesting time.

Rodriguez: I shall be glad that he has not completed, señora, if you will therefore be so kind and tell me this history.

Gloria: I warn you beforehand that it is not natural, like certain "realistic" novels, but surprising, like—like—

Medina: Like fact.

Rodriguez: I am prepared for the worst, señora: I sometimes read the newspaper. But excuse me for mentioning that in connection with fact, señor, and with your friends' experience, señora.

Gloria: Part of it did come out in the papers, but not the best part. All of our good friends here know from the hero and heroine themselves——

Vincent: Gloria! you are my good angel, as usual.

Gloria: What is it, Carangolito mio?

Vincent: Why, the plot! you have suggested it. Don't you see? Scene: not my garden, but Carter's. Persons represented: Mr. and Mrs. Carter, Blake and Mrs. Blake, and Silverspoon. Rodriguez, you know Jack best: you will do him——

Teresa: To perfection.

Gloria: A doubtful compliment, little sister.

Vincent: Oh, Jack is a good fellow.

Compare him with Professor Jump, for instance. The professor is a fool who pretends to be clever, while Silverspoon is a clever man pretending to be a fool. I can fancy Jack saying to him: Professor, I am your inferior and humble servant; for I am only a make-believe fool, while you are the genuine article! I almost wish, for the sake of the contrast, that I could use the professor; but after all what a good contrast in Carter and Blake! Carter wears a holiday countenance from the first of January to the thirty-first of December; Blake from the thirty-first of December to the first of January. Now, we need some other characters. Let me see. There is Miss Kelt, for example.

Concha (smiling at Rodriguez): Miss Kelt has been pronounced stiff by a polite Socrates. You may have ugly people on the stage, Dr. Vincent, but not stiff ones —never!

Vincent: And, besides, she really was not there, at Carter's. Let's stick to facts pretty closely. I must get to work while the enthusiasm lasts. Gloria, send my tea to the library.

Gloria: Tea! You will drink tea this afternoon?

Vincent: Well, you know I am not used to this sort of thing, and perhaps a gentle stimulant——

Señora Villena (filling a glass with sherry): Here, bo-ee, jou drinker that.

Vincent pledged his guests in the sherry, and then excused himself and went immediately to his library.

The others sat at table until the middle of the afternoon, the gentlemen smoking, all telling stories, all laughing, all discussing *opéra bouffe* and singing their favorite passages. Finally Gloria put a guitar in Medina's hands.

Meantime Vincent was seated at his desk. His face was much less serious than it had been in the morning, and the writing-pad was being rapidly used up. He wrote what he had seen, what he had heard, and what he himself thought about it all.

When Gloria had gone out to get the guitar for Medina, she had sent "that leetle moankey" to the library with a cup of tea and a very short note—in fact, three words, scrawled in pencil on a half-sheet of scented note-paper.

Those three words I cannot tell you, for they were of a language which has no grammar. Vincent read them over several times, and forgot to drink his tea until it had become cold.

Gloria was a meace.

MEDINA

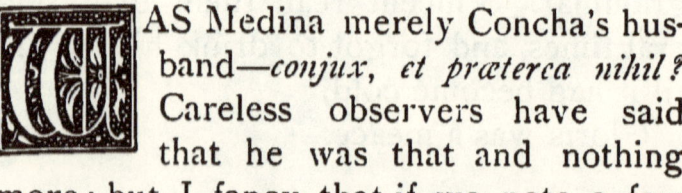AS Medina merely Concha's husband—*conjux, et præterea nihil?* Careless observers have said that he was that and nothing more; but I fancy that if we note a few characteristic acts we shall reach a somewhat different conclusion.

When he composed a song about Cuba (or, more probably, he had in mind Puerto Rico, his native island) he insisted in that song that although his old home was, like other localities, sometimes visited by storm-wind and dull winter's night, yet bathed in summer's warmth should memory hold it continually. So then, he was an idealist.

When Miguel had asked him how much candy his information about Concha's preference was worth, Medina replied, "All the candy in the world": a thoroughly ideal conception.

Now, the German idealists,—those who have excellent taste in the matter of beer but cannot discriminate between sentiment and sentimentalism, and those who eat lemons in order to prolong a life of destructive criticism—we know. We also know the English idealist, who runs and rows a great deal to expand his chest, who reads Greek a little and who calls himself ill if his complexion is a shade less brilliant than his sister's. These types we all know; but what is a Spanish idealist?

Does the reader remember—or, better, has he seen—that group of gentlemen with coat-collars turned up, hugging the stove in the office of the Spanish hotel? They have not what we call an object in life: they have an enthusiasm, or nothing. Medina was one of those before he saw Concha.

"I have known only one man whose life was perfect," he used to say. "That man was a cobbler who lived near my plantation in Puerto Rico. While he was at work in his little shop he would sing. A voice! —— like Brignoli's (poor, dear Brignoli!) The neighbors would flock together to listen outside his window. Managers of opera companies visiting the island would hear about him and offer him great sums: he paid no attention to them.

I myself have proposed to give him money for training his magnificent voice. He replied: 'Señor, I sing because I am at work. If you like to hear me, send me your boots to mend.' I could get no other answer. That cobbler was the one happy man."

Since his marriage Medina had told this anecdote only once. Then he said:

"I have known only two men whose lives were perfect. One of these was a cobbler and the other is myself."

He saw that this alteration spoiled the story, and therefore ceased repeating it.

The enthusiasm awakened by Concha had drawn him away from the stove. Inspired by her he had already achieved more than some of us ever win through steady pursuit of our "object in life." He had laid his hand upon happiness.

The idealist had found and gained his ideal.

The Spanish idealist is the man who seeks a woman like Concha. The class is quite large.

Inspired by Concha he had written much verse, and had even allowed some of it to be printed in literary papers; but after an editor or compositor of one of these had changed his "darkness and the rain," so that it read "hackmen in the rain" he swore horribly and published nothing further. None the less he was still stimulated to the point of production by his wife and continued to compose songs for her.

I do not wonder at his persistence, for if she liked his new songs, accompanied with those soft chords of the guitar which are to the voice what cream is to food—making almost anything good—she would sing with him; and if she did not like the song she would go to him and, taking away the guitar, would herself take its place. That is criticism worth having.

It is plain that he was something more than Concha's husband: he was also her lover.

Vincent had been steadily at work. Late into the night and again the next morning, after his walk to the post-office which he never omitted, he had been writing rapidly. In the afternoon of the second day he called Medina to his aid.

"You must help me assign the parts," he said.

Medina: What! You have written your play without reference to the actors?

Vincent: On the contrary, I have had them in mind; but there are some difficulties.

Medina: For example?

Vincent: For example, Silverspoon. Of course Rodriguez must take that part because he knows Jack best. But Silverspoon speaks such extreme English, while Rodriguez has scarcely learned American, and makes even that " walk Spanish."

Medina: Trust him to imitate —— or couldn't you show by the spelling?

Vincent: I never could see the point of misspelling English words to show that the English do not pronounce them as we do.

Medina: Perhaps not as a rule. Well, I will go over the part with him. Have you done Jack to the life?

Vincent: Tried to. There's another trouble: Jack has a way of jumping around, you know; and Rodriguez is dignified.

Medina: Rodriguez is an athlete and will be glad of the chance to show his strength.

Vincent: Bravo! Medina. You are thorough enough to be a Scot. You crack the very bones of a subject to get at its marrow. Then there's another thing: Who can do Rose?

Medina: Rose?

Vincent: Oh, don't you know? Rose was the nurse the Carters had at the time. We couldn't leave her out: she was quite an important character. Besides, their baby was just about the age ours is now.

Medina: I don't quite see what to do with Rose. Let me look at the manuscript.

They read the part together; then

Vincent (with hesitation): Do you think Teresa ——

Medina: Teresa as an Irish servant girl!

Vincent: But pretty, you know; and just by way of burlesque, I think she will consent.

Medina: Teresa likes to surprise people now and then. She reminds me of an inactive volcano. Perhaps she will.

Vincent (walking to and fro in the library): Then comes the hardest question. You know Carter's grouty old neighbor—the mysterious old fellow?

Medina: Certainly. Well?

Vincent: Well, you see, you are to be Blake and Rodriguez to be Silverspoon and I to be Carter: that uses up all the men in the company.

Medina: But you have not provided a part for señora Villena. She is a finished actress: she will play the neighbor, although he was a man.

Vincent: His being a man does not trouble me, but he was *old*—that's the rub. The señora will never submit to that. It is too near the fact—to her the one terrible fact, that so much of her natural share of fun is in the past.

Medina: I will get your wife and Concha to persuade her.

Medina found Gloria and Concha together on the piazza. When he had stated the difficulty Concha began to laugh, and to explain her merriment told them how she had found señora Villena very melancholy, and how she had persuaded her that she was not old by suggesting first a *soirée* and then a play.

Gloria was thoughtful for an instant; then she said: Concha, you go and talk to Coralie. You can manage her best. Señor ——

Medina: Command me, señora.

Gloria: You come with me to direct some envelopes.

The word *soirée* had been spoken: that

was enough. Gloria said to herself: "Here is my chance to start something, too—as well as Concha." Quiet and dainty ladies are perhaps not jealous of a friend's success, but they are certainly watchful.

So she and Medina wrote invitations and addresses for half-an-hour. In selecting her guests she tried to follow out her husband's idea of bringing together people who would improve each other by contrast, but in addition to that she prepared a surprise.

"These three are to go out of town," she said, handing Medina the envelopes. "There are the stamps—in that little box at your elbow. You must not tell anyone that I have invited a single soul except the Oldhaveners. Promise! Now how many have we done? Twenty? One more, for Mr. and Mrs. Penman. There! A thousand thanks, señor. Now I will send them off before Mr. Vincent comes out."

The invitations were for Thursday evening of the following week. Like the wind, falling upon the placid surface of a sheltered mirror-lake and troubling it for a brief space, so these cards of invitation, addressed in Medina's roundest hand, disturbed the surface of society in Oldhaven, which is a quiet town of the reflecting and reflective order of towns.

MONDAY

Tan imposible sería dejar de amarla, como hacer que estas aguas no mojasen, ni el sol con sus peinados cabellos no nos alumbrase.—*Cervantes.*

Y eleven o'clock on Monday morning everything was ready. The rôles had been learned, the difficult passages rehearsed, and the costumes prepared. Even the weather had been ordered to correspond with their intent, and a bright Monday gave assurance of a bright week.

All that they had sent for had arrived, except the audience.

"Cá, no, I do not do that!" the señora Villena had declared. "Acter myself for no public an' dresser me liker yentelman for nobodie—for jes jou! Caramba! I teller jou, no!"

But Vincent had scruples against inviting mere acquaintances to look on while the private history of friends was being represented.

"We don't need anyone beside ourselves, my dear Coralie," Concha said. "Suppose we should send out tickets every time we talk about people we know! This is only a better way of doing what we do so often for our own amusement."

"But of course I have invited my own family," Gloria said; "and they make quite an audience in themselves."

"Tha's right, bébé, jou doer that, or they never forgive you—never!" cried señora Villena, as usual failing to catch the tense of the verb.

"And they know the story already, so there's no harm," said Vincent.

Before twelve o'clock these spectators arrived from the station in two carriages. Little Alfredo led the procession from the front gate to the house; next came fat señora Diaz, trying in vain to check him with hand and voice; next came the still fatter grandmother leaning on the arm of cousin Louis, the musician. You see it was very warm: therefore the mamita had ventured out of doors. Last of all came Isabelita Diaz rather pensively, wishing that Manuel had become a member of the family so that he might have been invited. "Papa dear" had not merely declined, but he had refused, to join the party.

You should have heard the cries of joy when these guests were welcomed at the door, the gentlemen embracing each other not less ardently than did the ladies: all caressing, admiring, questioning together —all except Fredo. He was standing on a chair and making faces at "that leetle moankey." Fredo was completely fascinated by the shining buttons and no less shining black face of the serving boy. When the mother and mamita went up stairs he remained behind, and great was his disappointment when buttons offered to go away. Jumping down from the chair, he seized him by the sleeve.

"Where are you going?" he asked.

"Mus' be goin' now," said the negro impatiently.

"Where?"

"Oh, sugar an' molasses pills!" Buttons resented being treated like a strange animal.

"Sugaranmolassespill," Fredo repeated, doubtfully. "And where is that? Is it far from here?" Buttons disdained to reply, and departed in a very stately manner.

"Sugaranmolassespill," Fredo repeated to himself, and then ran upstairs. "Mamma!" he cried, "what is sugaranmolassespill?"

"Eh! What is that, Fredo?"

"Sugaranmolassespill! That black thing said it. What does it mean?"

Señora Diaz thoughtfully put her finger to her lips, repeating: "Sugaranmolasses—How you say, Fredo?"

"Pill, pill, sugaranmolassespill!"

"I don't know. We will go and ask the mamita."

Together they went into an adjoining room, where the mamita was resting after the fatigue of her walk from the carriage to the second story.

"Mamita," said señora Diaz, "Fredo says the servant called him—How do you say, Fredo?"

"No, no, mamma, I will tell the mamita. It was thus." With many gestures he described the scene.

When he had pronounced the long word, "Eh!" said the mamita, "say it again more slowly."

Fredo repeated.

"I don't know. Molaspil? Maybe it is an animal."

"It would seem to be a place," suggested señora Diaz.

"I don't know, my dear, I am sure. I fear that the servant has said some bad words in English. Never say it again, Alfredo. You may sit down, my daughter and grandson"—for they had remained standing, as a mark of respect.

Towards the end of the afternoon these five spectators were seated in comfortable chairs, placed under a small maple-tree and facing the arbor which has been mentioned, and prepared themselves to be entertained by the seven actors. This they did by consulting the following programme:

The Neighbor.

A COMEDY IN THREE DAYS.

CHARACTERS.

PAUL CARTER. A Gentleman of Leisure. *Dr. Vincent.*
GLADYS CARTER. His Wife. *Mrs. Vincent.*
RICHARD MASON BLAKE. An Amateur Botanist.
                                            Señor Medina.
MARGERY BLAKE. His Wife. *Señora Medina.*
JACK SILVERSPOON. An Eccentric English Artist,
        Friend of Mr. and Mrs. Carter. *Señor Rodriguez.*
ROSE. A Nurse. *Señorita Teresa Diaz.*
HOLE-IN-THE-GROUND. The Neighbor. *Señora Villena.*

Scene: Garden in the rear of Carter's house. In the center is an arbor. Right, a flight of steps and piazza. Left, a high stone wall—not a real stone wall, but a very good imitation in wood. Between arbor and wall, a lawn-tennis ground. In the background, flowers and shrubbery. The interior of arbor is visible from auditorium, that is, from the maple-tree, but not from piazza.

A querulous voice is heard from behind the wall, but no one is visible. Then an ash-barrel is thrown over the wall. A short silence. Then Neighbor looks over the wall.

Neighbor: I be even with that Scotchman! —— Caramba! Somone coming! (Disappears.)

"Mamita!" Alfredo cried. "Do you see, eh, mamita? The señora Villena, with the hat of a man on, eh?"

"Ssh!" said mamita. "It is a play."

(Carter enters, in smoking-jacket and slippers, with Blake, disguised as gardener.)

Carter: And here, you see, I keep my rose-geraniums. I flatter myself that there is not a finer lot of plants in the State. Now, my man —— By the way, what's your name?

Blake: Schuldheiss, sir.

Carter: "Schuld" what?

Blake: Schuldheiss, sir.

Carter (genially): That will never do to call you by. That is too long. What is your first name?

Blake: Karl, sir.

Carter: Good! I'll call you Karl. Now then, Karl, you understand the care of flowers perfectly, I suppose?

Blake: Yes, sir, I ought to. I studied with —— I mean I worked for the Herr Professor of Botany at my home in Germany.

Carter: It seems to me you speak English remarkably well for a German. How long have you been in this country?

Blake: Two years, sir; but I studied English at school.

Carter (aside, rubbing his hands): This is highly satisfactory. This is splendid. He is trustworthy, hardworking, good-natured, intelligent—extremely intelligent. In a word he is a German. (Turning to Blake. Aloud.) I am right glad I advertised for a German, Karl. The last gardener I had was a Scot, who kept the place beautifully, to be sure; but stingy! —— Why, he used to scold my wife whenever she picked a flower, and order me off the grass! But as for you, Karl—I can read character. I am never deceived by appearances. — You are trustworthy, good-natured, intelligent ——

Blake: Sir!

Carter: Yes; you need not try to deny it. You are all that I asked for in my advertisement. I can see it plainly. You are intelligent ——

(Mrs. Carter [Gloria] comes out of house. She stands on piazza, holding telegram in hand.)

Mrs. Carter: Paul! Paul! she will be here to-morrow!

Carter: One moment, my dear. (To Blake.) Now, to begin with, go to the tool-house, get some twine and tie up the carnations.

(Blake goes out behind arbor.)

Carter: Whom were you speaking about, my dear?

Mrs. Carter: Why, Margery Blake, of course. Are you not glad she's coming? It will be such a good rest for her. I wonder if she will be as handsome as she was when we were at school together. What a beast her husband must be.

Carter: I am glad your friend is coming to stay with us. (Pauses and seems thoughtful.) I wonder ——

Mrs. Carter (quickly): I know! I know what you are going to say. You are wondering if the poor thing has any hope or spirit left in her.

Carter: No, not exactly that. I am trying to imagine what Hole-in-the Ground has thrown over the wall this morning.

(Blake enters, bearing ash-barrel.)

Blake: I found this among the carnations, sir. Several of them were crushed.

Mrs. Carter: What a shame! If I were in your place, Mr. Carter, I should employ a mounted policeman to protect us from that old brute, that old bear!

Carter: Tut, tut! my dear. (To Blake.) So, our agreeable neighbor has sent us an ash-barrel this morning, has he? You must not mind little things like that, Karl. Sometimes he testifies his affection by the gift of a large bouquet of dock-weeds. We have come to expect something of that sort once or twice each day, and really I fancy we should feel badly if our neighbor's little attentions should be discontinued. The thing began when your predecessor, the Scotch gardener, was here; and I guess he must have provoked old Hole-in-the-Ground in some way.

Blake: What kind of a man is he, sir?

Carter: People say he is a miser, and some say he is crazy. But as we never see him we don't believe he is a person at all: so we call him Hole-in-the-Ground.

(Neighbor puts his head above wall and shakes his fist at Carter, without being seen. Carter puts arm around Mrs. Carter's waist and draws her away. They walk up and down stage, without paying attention to Blake, during following conversation.)

Carter: It is the only imperfection in our otherwise perfect happiness, isn't it, Gladys?—and we may afford to overlook such a trifling annoyance, mayn't we, dear?

Mrs. Carter (doubtfully): Perhaps we may.

Carter: Yes, ours is certainly the ideal existence. We have surrounded ourselves with all those things which make life beautiful. We have a comfortable house

Mrs. Carter: And you have your garden.

Carter: You share the benefit of that. And you have your baby.

Mrs. Carter: Don't you share the benefit of that?

Carter (doubtfully): Yes. (With conviction.) Yes, oh, yes! And you have me.

Mrs. Carter: And you have me, I am sure!

Carter: But to my mind the crowning charm of our situation is that we live well within our means, so that we can give freely to those who need assistance. Ah! my dear, there's no pleasure equal to that —to be able to give freely.

Mrs. Carter: That is the reason why I keep a puddle for the robins to bathe in, don't you see? I give the poor robins a free bath—give it freely. It is a great pleasure.

Carter: I suspect you of making fun of me.

Mrs. Carter: Not at all! Think how fortunate we are compared with poor Margery Blake!

(Blake, hearing this name, lets ash-barrel fall.)

Blake (aside): What!

Carter: Are you sure, my dear, that Mr. Blake is so much to blame in this matter?

Mrs. Carter: You are never willing to blame anybody, Paul! I am out of patience with you! If Mr. Blake is not to blame, then of course she must be. Somebody has done wrong; and it is a great wrong which separates husband from wife.

Carter: Perhaps not. It may be only a great mistake.

(Blake sighs and takes up ash-barrel.)

Carter: Remember, my dear, we have never met this Mr. Blake, and we have no right to judge him without knowing the man and hearing his side of the question. Hello! Here comes Silverspoon!

Mrs. Carter: Here comes mamma's boobly-pink-palms-precious-treasure!

(Teresa, as Rose, in a snow-white apron and a wonderfully crisp cap, comes forward from background, pushing baby-carriage, and Silverspoon [Rodriguez] hastening after her.)

Silverspoon (speaking with strong English accent): Maiden, stay! Hasten not, fair maid. (To baby.) Innocent creature, will you have a flower? Oh, but you must not eat it! (To Rose.) Does the baby eat flowers?

Rose (aside, looking at Silverspoon): Ach, isn't he swate!

(Silverspoon catches sight of ash-barrel and grasps Carter's arm.)

Silverspoon: There's another!

Carter: What do you mean?

Silverspoon: I mean, my dear fellow, what I mean; and I say, there's another!

Carter: An ash-barrel. What of it?

Silverspoon: An ash-barrel, did you call it?

Carter: Yes.

(Silverspoon goes up to ash-barrel and looks at it with head on one side.)

Silverspoon: Quaint, antique, lovely, odd! How pleased the queen will be!

Mrs. Carter: Why, Mr. Silverspoon, what do you mean?

Silverspoon: My dear Mrs. Carter, all my life I have been trying, trying,—working, you understand—to think of something to present to my gracious sovereign that would give her pleasure. I have traveled almost the world over, vainly seeking some curiosity worthy of her royal highness, and have failed up to this time. Worn out with travel in ancient countries, I land here in America, and behold! I immediately find it. I tell you, my dear sir, (to Carter) my fortune is made! But let me whisper it, for fear some roguish person might catch at the idea and carry it out and so ruin my hopes. I mean to make a collection of ash-barrels and send them to the queen.

Carter: And what will the queen do with them?

Silverspoon: Do with them! What do you think she will do them? Put apple jelly in them? Why, man, they will be on exhibition at the Tower of London!

Carter: Carry this 'thing of beauty' over there, Karl, and set it against the wall, where Mr. Silverspoon may see it whenever he comes.

(Blake goes out as directed. Places barrel against the wall at the left.)

Mrs. Carter: I am so glad you are to be on hand, Mr. Silverspoon, to help entertain an unfortunate school friend of mine who is coming to stay with us. Perhaps you read in the papers something about the separation of Mr. and Mrs. Richard Blake of New-York.

Silverspoon: No, I have never read an American newspaper since one of them had the impertinence—the beastly assurance—to make fun of a picture of mine,—and a good picture, Mrs. Carter.

Mrs. Carter: I have no doubt of it—I

mean that the picture was charming. Well, it is but right that you should know about our expected guest. Let us sit down, and Paul and I will tell you.

(They enter the arbor. Rose goes out, glancing fondly at Silverspoon.)

Mrs. Carter: There were many guests that evening. Cravats were white and dresses were sleeveless. It was the last of Mrs. Richard Blake's Wednesday evenings at home.

Silverspoon: This is going to be interesting.

Mrs. Carter: Supper was served at twelve o'clock. The supper-room was large, but not too large to accommodate the brilliant company of society people. In the center was a round table of polished oak. Twenty guests were seated at this, and as many more at smaller tables——

Carter (interrupting): You see we have the particulars from a person who was present. Mrs. Blake was said to be the most charming hostess in the world. People came to enjoy her quite as much as to enjoy the feast she provided.

Silverspoon: Of course.

Carter: No, not of course, for her suppers were said to be something exquisite.

Silverspoon: Let us fancy that we are present. See the gleam and sparkle of silver and crystal; see that pyramid of roses rising from a bed of violets; see those silent waiters, who, more efficient than the genii of the Arabian Nights, will bring you everything you desire without putting you to the trouble of rubbing a lamp or a ring. That is what makes such an occasion memorable. For the time every desire of which you are conscious is being gratified.

Mrs. Carter: See Mrs. Blake, the hostess! She is very young—scarcely more than twenty; she is gay; if you have any good point she will discover it and make the most of it while you are at her house; she fascinates you by her self-confidence and her confidence in you; she collects about herself the merriest spirits of the metropolis, and lo! when they are met she is the merriest of them all; she has black eyes which see everything and read motives easily; she thinks quickly and moves quickly, without fear of mistake; and if she does make a mistake, it passes for something clever.

Silverspoon: Splendid! And to think

that she is going to be here! Please go on. What happened?

Carter: One of the guests sprang to his feet and called out: 'A toast! My friends, I propose a toast!'

Silverspoon: Let us play it out! Here, you, Carter, be Blake; and Mrs. Carter, be Mrs. Blake; and I shall be the guests.

Mrs. Carter: But it is not a laughing matter, Mr. Silverspoon. How can you make light of anything so serious?

Silverspoon: I? Not for worlds! My dear madame, we will play it out seriously. Now then, I am the guest proposing the toast. (Rises.) Old friends' young wives! Their graces in this wine we—a— we pledge! (Applauds.) And now I am the other guests applauding.

Carter: As you suggest, the toast to the ladies was greeted with loud applause, and the guests all looked to Mr. Blake, the host, to respond. We have never seen Mr. Blake, but we have heard of him as a very polished man — a wit and a scholar, especially fond of botany, who had spent most of his life abroad.

Silverspoon: What did Blake say?

Carter: Not one word!

Silverspoon: Beastly!

Carter: This silence was like a wet blanket. The company began to feel very uncomfortably, and the gentleman who had proposed the toast, trying to restore the genial tone, cried: 'What! Moody to-night, Richard! Riding a dark horse —black care mounted behind you and that sort of thing? Confess and receive absolution. What is it? Come, make a clean breast and we'll forgive you.' But this sally was a flat failure, and worse. People shifted uneasily in their chairs. Some looked down with nervous smiles, others anxiously studied the face of their host, who arose slowly and glared at the unfortunate guest before beginning to speak.

(Neighbor cautiously surveys the group in arbor with expression of great interest in what is being said. Silverspoon accompanies Carter's narrative with pantomime.)

Carter: Mr. Blake said: 'I shall tell you why I do not respond to the toast which has just been offered. Perhaps you noticed'—here he pointed to his wine-glass which was filled to the brim—'that I did not drink the health of old friends' young wives. I did not, because my glass is filled not with wine but with my books'—

Silverspoon: Eh?

Carter: 'So is yours and yours and yours,' continued Blake, calling the guests by name; 'and so are all your glasses filled, and you are all drinking my books to the health of my wife and each others' wives and sweethearts!'

Mrs. Carter: His wife went up to him and laid her hand on his arm. 'You are not well, Richard,' she said; but he continued without appearing to notice her: 'You thought you were drinking port, doctor, and you, madame, supposed that to be champagne; that is my Chaucer, sir, and that is a set of Dumas, madame.' And so he went on——

Carter: Staring his guests in the face, with diabolical frankness, like this: 'I am sick of lying. I must speak the truth and I can't make the truth distinct enough to satisfy myself. I am ruined! I have pledged my library at last, and these things are bought with it. I have no longer the ability to amuse you. I have therefore no longer any claim upon you and you have no claim upon me. This is brutal, but I mean it. Let us go our several ways.'

Mrs. Carter: Ugh! The brute! Every time I think of it it makes me furious!

Carter: I must say for my part, I admire plain speaking like that—under the circumstances. It is honest and downright. He said just what he meant and left no room for misunderstanding. His wife was ruining him by her extravagance. He had warned her and pointed out the consequences without effect. What could he do? He stopped short before it was too late, left her enough for her comfortable maintenance, and went out to seek his fortune like a man, without asking favors of anyone.

Mrs. Carter: And I say it was harsh and cruel! She was young, undeveloped, totally without training or experience—except for a short experience of frivolous society. He ought at least to have given her a longer trial.

Carter: Then it would have been too late. She would have been reduced to poverty.

Mrs. Carter: But——

Carter: Excuse me, my dear, but I really—it is evident that we cannot agree on that subject—I really must see how the new gardener is getting along.

Mrs. Carter: Then I'll go with you. Mr. Silverspoon, won't you accompany us?

Silverspoon: Ah, thank you, thank you, no. You see, my dear Mrs. Carter, there might be another precious art-object coming over the wall, and I would not miss it for the wealth of the Indies.

(Carter goes out. Silverspoon detains Mrs. Carter.)

Silverspoon: Allow me one question, Mrs. Carter. Is she pretty?

Mrs. Carter: She was beautiful when I last saw her.

Silverspoon: What has become of the husband?

Mrs. Carter: Nobody seems to know. You will do your best to entertain the poor thing, I am sure. We count upon you.

Silverspoon: Never fear! You will see altogether too much of me, perhaps.

Mrs. Carter: Impossible!

(Mrs. Carter goes out.)

Silverspoon: Extraordinary and highly interesting!

(Takes out sketch-book from pocket and begins to draw.)

Silverspoon: I suppose these people think

I am nothing but a fool—— Believe I'll just take advantage of being alone to have a whiff.

(Fills and lights his pipe.)

Silverspoon: Now for my part I say there's no such fool as your desperately serious man—like that Blake they were talking about, for instance. What an ass! I could have told him better. I'd have told him about this pipe—how it was hot at first, and when I smoked twice as often as usual to correct that fault it became bitter—and how I was about to give it up when all of a sudden it became sweet. Blake threw his pipe away instead of seasoning it.

(Mrs. Blake [Concha] in traveling costume, comes out on piazza. Standing there, she looks about without perceiving Silverspoon.

Mrs. Blake: It would serve me right if they were not at home.

(Comes down steps. Goes to arbor and sees Silverspoon, who is holding pencil at arm's length to measure the object which he is sketching. Silverspoon rises and bows.)

Mrs. Blake: I am looking for Mrs. Carter. Are you, perhaps——

Silverspoon: Mrs. Carter is not here, madame, but I am.

Mrs. Blake (cordially, putting out her hand): I am so glad to meet you. You know Gladys and I were very intimate and she has written me all about you, so I feel as though we were old friends. What a lovely home you have! And I suppose—— (Hesitates.) Have you any children?

Silverspoon (aside): What can she mean?

Mrs. Blake: Oh, yes: now I remember. You have one.

Silverspoon (aside): What can she mean? (Aloud): Aw—you are the lady Mrs. Carter was expecting?

Mrs. Blake (astonished): Yes. I came to-day—a day sooner than I said—to give you all a surprise.

Silverspoon: You have!

Mrs. Blake: I hope Mrs. Carter is well. Do you think she will be here soon?

Silverspoon (collects sketching materials): Won't you sit down a moment and I'll go and find her.

Mrs. Blake: How kind of you!—Such lovely weather——

Silverspoon (at entrance to arbor): Did you say the weather was lovely? Did you remark that the weather was fine? Yes, lovely! (Waves sketch-book wildly.) It makes me feel like a child again at home in England, running bareheaded through the meadows.

(Mrs. Carter enters and stands laughing at Silverspoon. Does not see Mrs. Blake, who is in arbor.)

Silverspoon: Oh, how fresh the air is! See me! Do I not look young, light and happy? (Springs into air.) See how gay I am! I am picking wild flowers! Shall I pick some for you, madame?

Mrs. Carter: 'Madame!" (Hastens towards the arbor and sees Mrs. Blake.) Why, Margery!

(Mrs. Blake and Mrs. Carter embrace.)

Mrs. Carter (to Silverspoon): What were you doing?

Silverspoon (very quietly): Only trying to entertain Mrs. Blake as you told me to.

Mrs. Carter: My dear child, where on earth did you come from? I am so glad to see you. Do you know, we must have misread your telegram, for we thought you were coming to-morrow. Please excuse the mistake. You must be tired. Come with me this instant and take off your bonnet. I am so anxious for you to meet my husband. He will be here presently. He is at the other end of the garden——

Mrs. Blake: Who—is—this? (Points to Silverspoon.)

Silverspoon (bows): Mr. Silverspoon, artist.

Mrs. Carter: Our friend, Mr. Silverspoon,—Mrs. Blake—Pray excuse me—I judged from what I saw that you had become acquainted.

Mrs. Blake: But—I—thought—*this*—was—your husband.

Mrs. Carter: Here he comes.

(Carter and Blake come in. Blake is carrying ferns in pots. Puts them down between arbor and piazza, and kneels with back to arbor, to press earth about their roots.)

Mrs. Carter: Paul! Paul! Come here! Here is Margery.

(Blake starts; glances over his shoulder, but does not see Mrs. Blake, who is still in arbor. Mrs. Blake comes out from arbor. She and Carter shake hands cordially.)

Carter: Welcome to our home, Mrs. Blake!

(Blake rises and turns around. Sees his

wife. Immediately turns his back and busies himself about plants again.)

Blake (aside): She here! She will never know me in these clothes.

Mrs. Blake: I thought to surprise you, Mr. Carter; but I think I am the most surprised person present, thanks to Mr. Silverspoon.

Carter: What have you been up to, Jack?

Silverspoon: Nothing. Only entertaining Mrs. Blake by playing the fool.

Carter (laughs): Sorry I was not here to see, old man.

Mrs. Carter: Now you must come right into the house with me, Margery. I know you must be fatigued, and meeting so many people you never saw before is——

(Mrs. Blake and Mrs. Carter pass from arbor to piazza. As they pass the gardener, Mrs. Blake glances at him.)

Mrs. Blake (aside): My husband!

(Mrs. Blake and Mrs. Carter go into the house. Carter crosses to speak to Blake. Silverspoon is left standing alone by the arbor.)

Silverspoon: Gad! I hope the husband will never come back. (Bows, to signify that the first act is concluded; then comes forward to help Alfredo descend from the lowest branch of the maple-tree, where that young critic had climbed during the performance, saying that he always preferred the gallery.)

TUESDAY

HEN, on the following day, the five spectators had taken their places, they saw Mrs. Carter sewing in the arbor while Mr. Carter and Mrs. Blake were playing tennis—a game which Concha, in her own character and upon her usual high heels, had always scorned.

"In tennis-shoes Concha is completely disguised," said cousin Louis, the musician.

Mrs. Blake: Forty—fifteen!

Carter: No. That was out!

(A tennis ball, struck wildly, flies over wall.)

Carter: Oh! That was the very last!

Mrs. Blake: Then I suppose we will have to stop playing. Just when I was sure of a game! Have you not *one* more?

Carter: Not a single one. Old Hole-in-the-Ground has got them all finally. A whole dozen this summer already!

Mrs. Blake (draws near to Carter. Mysteriously): Do you think he would hear if I said something?

Carter: No.

Mrs. Blake: Then I won't say it.—Why don't you go over after them?

Carter: I have not strictly the right to. That would be trespass; and it is too small a matter to quarrel about—the loss of a few tennis-balls.

Mrs. Blake: You say you have never seen him?

Carter: Never distinctly or near at hand. He is a mysterious person;—lives all alone—at least with a house-keeper as old and almost as strange as himself—goes and comes in the night ——

Mrs. Blake: Goes and comes?

Carter: Goes out of town, I suppose, and always at night. We see a livery carriage at the door; it drives away; that is all. A few days—sometimes a week or a month—afterwards, he returns in the same fashion. Otherwise I don't believe he goes out at all.

(Mrs. Blake crosses tennis-court to wall, where ash-barrel is still standing.)

Mrs. Blake: I want to look over.

Carter: Not for worlds!

Mrs. Blake: Why not?

Carter (hesitating): That would spoil all the fun. The fact is, I enjoy this mystery and would not dispel it for anything.

Mrs. Blake: Please! (Insisting.) Please help me up Mr. Silverspoon's 'thing of beauty.'

Carter: Promise not to tell me what you see?

Mrs. Blake: Yes.

(Carter assists Mrs. Blake to mount ash-barrel. Standing there she looks over wall and makes signs to someone on other side.)

Carter: What is it?

Mrs. Blake: I promised not to tell. It is more mysterious than imagination can picture. It is awful! Help me down.

(Carter gives Mrs. Blake his hand. They walk slowly towards arbor.)

Mrs. Blake: Have you really never seen your neighbor's garden?

Carter: Of course I have formerly; but not since Hole-in-the-Ground has lived there. He took the place less than a year ago—or, rather, it has always belonged to him, I believe, but he had leased it ever since we have lived here, and he only returned last year.

Mrs. Blake: I warn you not to try to see him. Well, since we must stop playing, I think I will sit with your wife.

Carter: And I'll go see about the plants.

Mrs. Carter: Paul!—I shall punish the new gardener as a foe to my domestic happiness if you spend all your time with him. He must be an extraordinary person.

Carter: Your observation hits the mark as usual, my dear. He is a treasure! So intelligent! He knows the botany by heart.

(Carter goes towards background. Mrs. Carter hastens after him.)

Mrs. Carter: I hate myself! I am ugly and a perfect fiend!

Carter: My dear!

Mrs. Carter: You need not deny it. That will not do any good. I have my glass: I can see. Besides, I was brought up to believe that I was the ugliest thing in the universe. When I had dressed to go out in the evening and tried my best to look well, the first thing I'd hear from my brothers when I came down stairs would be this:—'Gladys, you are a fright!'

Carter: Excitement is extremely becoming to you, my dear. I can scarcely keep my hands off you. This is my answer.

(Carter takes a small mirror from his pocket and holds this before Mrs. Carter's face. She dashes it to the ground.)

Mrs. Carter: I might as well break it that way as by looking into it!

Carter: It is not broken. Look again. You have good taste, child: you cannot help admiring yourself.

(Carter holds glass before his wife's face until the latter looks better pleased.)

Mrs. Carter: Promise not to speak to Karl?

Carter: May I not watch him weed the beets?

(Carter goes out.)

Mrs. Carter (aside): I must and I shall and I will get rid of that Karl in one way or another!

(Mrs. Carter and Mrs. Blake seated together in arbor.)

Mrs. Carter: My dear Margery, I have an idea. It came to me just now, when I was cutting down these skirts for Babelkins. See them. Aren't they pretty? It seems a shame to spoil them, and I hate to put her into short clothes. She will never be so cunning again.

Mrs. Blake: They are exquisite, my dear. Why don't you save them for ——

(Mrs. Carter puts her hand over Mrs. Blake's mouth.)

Mrs. Blake: What is this famous idea?

Mrs. Carter: You know what a nice girl that nurse girl of mine is,—rather green, perhaps, but decidedly pretty,— and you hear what a nice man the gardener is. Now, I have been thinking what a splendid couple they would make. So I've made up my mind that I am going to throw them together as much as I can and see whether I can't make a match. Don't you think it is a charmingly romantic idea?

Mrs. Blake: No! Not at all! Not in the least degree!

Mrs. Carter: Pray why not?

Mrs. Blake: Why not! Because I think they are very ill suited indeed!

Mrs. Carter: Why, Margery! What do you mean? In what way are they ill suited?

Mrs. Blake: In what way! Why in every way! He is a thousand times——The idea is perfectly preposterous!

Mrs. Carter: Well, Margery, I think you talk without having any foundation for your remarks. Do you think she is too nice for him? Why, you don't know how nice he is, Margery dear. You have not seen so much of him ——

Mrs. Blake: Not seen so much of him! That makes no difference. Anybody could see in one instant that he is a thousand times too good for her!

Mrs. Carter: The more you praise him, the more I become convinced that I must get him out of the way. You must see it yourself, dear Margery. Paul is completely taken up with the man. I have no benefit of my husband any longer! Now, if I can only make Karl spend the greater part of his time in courting Rose——

Mrs. Blake: The greater part of his time courting Rose!

Mrs. Carter: Why, yes, don't you see?

Mrs. Blake: I see that Mr. Carter would be angry, and very likely would send poor Karl away!

Mrs. Carter: All the better, don't you see? I am sorry you disapprove, for I was just about to send Rose with a message to Karl.

Mrs. Blake: But your husband has just gone to speak to him. Why did you not send the message by him?

Mrs. Carter: Because, for one thing, I did not want Paul to know that I had given this order, and, as I was saying, I *did* want to throw Karl and Rose together.

Mrs. Blake (majestically): No, Gladys! Rather than place a poor, innocent young girl in such an embarrassing position, I will take the message myself. (Aside.) Just the opportunity I have been waiting for.

Mrs. Carter: How can you suggest such a thing? I cannot think of allowing my guest to take so much trouble. I will go. (Starts to go.)

Mrs. Blake: Gladys!

Mrs. Carter: Margery!

Mrs. Blake: Perhaps I am mistaken about—about Karl.

Mrs. Carter: Well?

Mrs. Blake: If so, I should have opportunity to change my opinion. Let me go and see him now. I will talk with him, and if I find that he is only a superior gardener,—I am sure Rose is very nice and I will help you to,—I will enter into your plan.

Mrs. Carter: My dear Margery! How kind and good of you!

Mrs. Blake: What is the message?

Mrs. Carter: To remove that unsightly ash-barrel. You see I do not want Paul to know. He might insist on keeping it —on Mr. Silverspoon's account.

Mrs. Blake (kisses her): Very well, my dear. (Going; then turning back.) And, Gladys, I can't make up my mind from seeing him once, perhaps; so you will help me to see him as often as you can, won't you?

Mrs. Carter: Certainly. Now I must go into the house to get a pattern.

(Mrs. Carter goes into house. As Mrs. Blake goes towards background, Blake comes forward with rake in his hand. They meet. Blake turns aside. Mrs. Blake stops.)

Blake (takes off his hat): Can I do anything for you, Miss?

Mrs. Blake: Richard!

Blake: Karl, Miss.

Mrs. Blake: Karl, Mrs. Carter—begs you to—to remove the ash-barrel.

Blake: All right, Miss. (Starts to go.)

Mrs. Blake: May I go with you, Ri—— Karl?

(Blake goes across tennis-ground to wall. Mrs. Blake follows. Blake puts down rake and takes up ash-barrel.)

Mrs. Blake: Karl.

Blake (impatiently): Well, Miss?

Mrs. Blake: Let me carry this for you, Karl?

(Takes up rake.)

Blake (savagely): Yes.

Mrs. Blake: Oh, Richard! Why do you keep up this disguise with me? I thought the time for disguises had passed, since you have let me see the whole bitter truth. Can't you forgive me, Richard?

Blake: I have forgiven you. I do not even blame you. It was my own fault that I did not restrain you. There is no use of talking about it now. The fact cannot be altered; and it might be a great deal worse. I left you sufficient means to live at your ease—in the only way you could live ——

(Mrs. Blake makes gesture of protest.)

Blake: As for me, I am content and happy enough in this work. (Bitterly.) You remember my old taste for horticulture.

Mrs. Blake: Oh, forgive me, forgive me, Richard! You have not forgiven me, or you would say that you love me. You are cold, cold to me, because you think only of my past folly. Believe me,

I had rather live in the most abject poverty with you than in luxury without you. Oh, you must believe me!

Blake: I cannot believe that. No; the course I have taken is the only one for your happiness and for my own. If I should listen to you now, and try again to meet your wishes, the old story would be repeated. I am no longer able to satisfy your demand for costly amusements. I have left you enough for one: it is too little for both of us.

Mrs. Blake: Then let me be a servant also! Anything—I would do anything to help you—husband!

Blake: I do not believe it.

(Blake turns sharply and goes out. Mrs. Blake, in great distress, leans against the wall, covering her face with her hands. Neighbor peers cautiously over wall. Does not at first see Mrs. Blake. Then coughs, to call her attention. Mrs. Blake, startled, looks up.)

Neighbor: Hear every word of it.

Mrs. Blake: And you are ashamed?

Neighbor: No. Ashamed? No.

Mrs. Blake (going): Then you are no better than your reputation.

Neighbor: Perhapsly. Com' here.

(Mrs. Blake pauses.)
Neighbor: Jou mean it?
Mrs. Blake: Do I mean what?
Neighbor: Want him back?
Mrs. Blake: Yes, of course I desire to be reconciled with my very own husband. But what is that to you? What right have you to interfere?
Neighbor: Jou do it.
Mrs. Blake: Do what? What shall I do?
Neighbor: What jou say.
Mrs. Blake: Descend to his level and work as he does?
Neighbor (nods vigorously): Jes. Servant.
Mrs. Blake: Do you mean to tell me that I am really to go out to work as a servant girl?—Where?
Neighbor: My house.
Mrs. Blake: Ugh!
Neighbor: Piece of advice. Cá, somebodie com'! (Disappears.)
Mrs. Blake: Go to that house? Never! I work as a servant? (Looks at her hands. Shrugs her shoulders. Then bitterly.) What difference does it make whether my hands are fine or not, if he does not care! (Sudden idea.) If I could make him jealous—(Another idea.) Silverspoon!

(Mrs. Carter comes from house.)

Mrs. Carter: Well, Margery, what do you think of him?

Mrs. Blake (having Silverspoon in mind): He is a refreshing original. I don't wonder that you are so fond of him.

(Mrs. Carter is offended.)

Mrs. Blake: Oh, forgive me, Gladys dear! I was thinking of something else. Come, I will go into the house with you. I know you have something to do, and you must not make a stranger of me.

(Mrs. Carter and Mrs. Blake go into house. Blake comes forward from background alone, working.)

Blake: How familiar everything here seems; yet it is impossible that I should remember. I was only five or six years old when I was taken away; and, besides, most of the features of the scene must have changed since that time. Of course that ugly wall was not there, for this garden was part of my father's estate. My father!—What a strange thing for a father to do! To let me remain in ignorance of my parentage—supposing myself to be an orphan—under the care of a guardian until I became of age, and then to permit me to travel about all over the world, for years, supposing that I had no home! Incredible! I should not believe it possible—if I did not know it to be true. And all this time my father has been alive, living alone, friendless, hating the world, and, I fear, hated by the world,—kind to me alone; making himself a miser so that I might have abundance. Now I return to my birthplace, a ruined man, ashamed to make myself or my wants known to my father. Appeal to him now!—He would think that my necessity and not my affection led me to him. And then, such an evil-tempered old gentleman he turns out to be! How would such a man receive me? I must wait, at least until I have learned more about him. But yet, if he had not always watched over me like a guardian spirit, how could he have known the moment of my need and sent me word in the nick of time that he was living and would welcome me at the old home?

(Falls to work energetically; then suddenly stops, as though struck by an idea.)

Blake: Is Margery's being here an accident or the work of that providence living on the other side of the wall? How did it happen that the Carters invited her to visit them at this particular time? The thought of such a thing never entered my head, or of course I should not have applied for this position. And yet I can't say that I am altogether sorry. She will naturally keep my secret, and in a few days she will go away and leave me in peace. If she stayed longer she'd drive me crazy! She fascinates me. In spite of everything, I worship her; and if she should give me the least reason to hope that she is capable of anything but frivolity —— —— I was harsh with her yesterday.

(Picks a bouquet.)

Blake: Some of her favorite flowers: for that reason she will know they come from me. I'll leave them here, where she will find them.

(Puts flowers on bench in arbor. Mrs. Blake and Silverspoon come out of house and walk towards the arbor, the former with small sewing-basket in her hand, the latter with book and sketch-book.)

Mrs. Blake: Let us sit here, Mr. Silverspoon, and you may read aloud while I embroider.

(Enters arbor, Silverspoon following. Mrs. Blake opens her work and begins to sew.)

Silverspoon: No, I will not read aloud.
Mrs. Blake: What?
Silverspoon: I say I will not read.
Mrs. Blake: Why?
Silverspoon: Because I have something much better to do.
Mrs. Blake: Well, then, you may sketch me if you like; and if it is a good likeness you may keep it.
Silverspoon: Do you mean it?
Mrs. Blake: Most certainly. Am I sitting right? Pose me.
Silverspoon (takes up the bunch of flowers): Now please put down your embroidery and hold these flowers and ——
Mrs. Blake: Why, where did they come from? Heliotropes — my favorite flower!
Silverspoon (with a lofty air): They were sent me.
Mrs. Blake: Sent to you!
Silverspoon: I said so.
Mrs. Blake: For pity's sake, by whom?
Silverspoon: I don't know, I am sure. One of the many persons who admire me intensely. But, my dear Mrs. Blake, allow me to pose you. Please don't pay any attention to these flowers. I assure you it is an every-day occurrence.

Mrs. Blake: I do not believe they are yours at all. Where did you find them?

Silverspoon: 'Find them'! I tell you they were sent to me. In fact, when I heard you exclaim, I half accused you of being the donor.

Mrs. Blake: Dear Mr. Silverspoon, if you tell me where you found them, I will give you a *boutonnière* for yourself.

Silverspoon: And I tell you, my dear, dear Mrs. Blake, that they were sent me.

Mrs. Blake: I don't believe it; and to show you that I do not, I am going to keep them all myself.

Silverspoon (shedding imaginary tears): Very well. If you rob me of my rights, I shall try to bear it like a man.

Mrs. Blake: Come! Please pose me. See how nice I look with these flowers—so! (Striking an attitude.)

Silverspoon: Charming! If you will only stand just so, I shall have you on paper in about four minutes.

Mrs. Blake: How fearful that will be! I think I shall move.

Silverspoon: I beg of you, my dear Mrs. Blake, do not move. If you stand so for only five seconds longer, I will tell you who sent you the flowers.

Blake (looking up from his work, aside): What is the fool going to say?

Mrs. Blake: So they were sent to *me*. Oh, I know!—Mr. Carter?

Silverspoon: No, fair lady. It was I.

Blake: Oh!

(Silverspoon and Mrs. Blake look around.)

Silverspoon: He must be ill, poor fellow.

Blake: Ah! (Goes out.)

Mrs. Blake: Thank you, Mr. Silverspoon. I am glad to know who sent them. Karl!

(Blake turns back. Mrs. Blake goes to him.)

Mrs. Blake: Karl, I am very anxious to keep these a long while. What is the best way to preserve them?

Blake (gruffly): Don't keep them at all!

Mrs. Blake: It is not a success! I can't flirt with Mr. Silverspoon!

Blake: No, decidedly it is not a success.

Silverspoon: You cannot flirt with Mr. Silverspoon! I don't see why you need tell the gardener!

(Blake goes out.)

Silverspoon: What do you mean?

Mrs. Blake: I mean that I have been trying my best to flirt with you and have not succeeded.

Silverspoon: Is it my fault? I am sorry. Won't you try it again?

Mrs. Blake: It would not do any good, now that Karl has gone away.

Silverspoon: Karl! The gardener! In Heaven's name, what has Karl to do with it?

Mrs. Blake: I wanted to make him jealous, don't you know?

Silverspoon: You wanted to make the gardener jealous! He! Gardener! Jealous—of me!

Mrs. Blake: Yes, jealous—of you. Don't you see?

Silverspoon: Don't I see? No, I confess I do not see. I protest! (Reflecting.) I think I shall have to tell you a secret.

Mrs. Blake: Do.

Silverspoon: I am not so much of a fool as I appear. Sometimes I may be taken seriously.

Mrs. Blake: Oh, if you are serious you must go away. Fly!

Silverspoon: Really? But——

Mrs. Blake: Not one word! Go!

(Silverspoon goes out. Mrs. Blake goes

quickly to the wall and throws the bouquet over.)

Mrs. Blake: Now I must go after them. He sent me flowers. He does love me. I will show him what I can do! And I think a cap and apron will be very becoming.

(Neighbor puts head above wall.)

Neighbor: Well?

Mrs. Blake: Well.

Neighbor: Jou going to do it?

Mrs. Blake: Yes. Will you make me work very hard?

Neighbor: Verie hard. Oh, jes, verie much!

Mrs. Blake: I am coming, anyhow.

Neighbor: When?

Mrs. Blake: This evening.

(Neighbor puts finger to his lips and disappears. Mrs. Carter comes in.)

Mrs. Carter: Alone! I thought I heard you talking with someone.

Mrs. Blake: Mr. Silverspoon has just gone away.

Mrs. Carter: Ah! What a nice, surprising man he is, is he not, Margery?

Mrs. Blake: Very.

Mrs. Carter: How thoughtful you are to-day, dear child. (Puts arm around

Mrs. Blake.) There, dear, don't think about it. It will all come out right in the end. Your husband will see his mistake——

Mrs. Blake: My husband has not made any mistake. It was all my own fault!

Mrs. Carter: There, there, dear. Do not think about it. The best way to dispel one's own grief is to interest oneself in plans for the happiness of others. For instance, Rose and Karl—Have you made up your mind to assist me to bring them together?

Mrs. Blake: Never!

Mrs. Carter (reproachfully): Why, Margery!

Mrs. Blake: Karl is my husband! Karl is Richard Blake! Karl is the most shamefully abused and — abused and — abused mortal! And all by me!

Mrs. Carter: Karl your husband! What is he doing here—in this disguise?

Mrs. Blake: I cannot imagine; but this I know, dear Gladys: instead of helping you to bring Karl and Rose together, you must help me to bring Karl and Margery together. Oh, how clearly I see my mistake now! What you have told me of your own happy life—so simple, so generous, so noble—is like a revelation to me. It shows me my own folly and my own selfishness.

(They enter the house.)

"Our Spanish women," said cousin Louis, the musician, speaking with confidence, as the only man in the audience, "are frivolous in minor points, but in matters of importance they are obedient and dependent. Are there many such untamed creatures—such little tyrants—as this Margery Blake? I should think the Americans who marry them could do nothing afterwards."

WEDNESDAY

T the close of the second act Rodriguez, going to his room to dress for dinner, had passed Medina in the hall.

"Do you not think the audience a very cold—a very unresponsive?" he had asked. "They have not thrown one thing at us."

"Wait till to-morrow," Medina had said. "They are beginning to feel at home. Being out-doors, they have not quite known what to make of it. When they feel the liberty of the theater, look out for your head! You deserve a broken one for your cockney English and your capers." It is perhaps necessary to explain that this was a compliment.

The audience did feel at home when for the third time they took their chairs under the maple-tree.

(Silverspoon is seen walking alone up and down the tennis-ground.)

Silverspoon: What a bore! She has

gone away, and gone away thinking me a fool. Gad, but I caught it from her yesterday! But I hadn't done anything. Perhaps she doesn't like me because I am near-sighted. And she went and told the gardener—that was the worst of it. This comes of being what people call funny. And just look at that! (Points to ash-barrel.) Carter had that put back for my sake. He takes me seriously!

(Mrs. Blake, dressed in cap and apron, sitting on wall, throws an apple at him. Silverspoon is startled, but does not look around. Rose, carrying baby in her arms, comes in, conceals herself behind the arbor and observes them.)

Silverspoon: The old devil! Firing apples at me—me—as though he did not know my preference for ash-barrels!

(Mrs. Blake throws another apple.)

Silverspoon: Hello! Hello! I say, back there, if you don't stop that, I'll come and —come and pull your nose off!

(Silverspoon continues to walk. Another apple. He turns angrily, sees Mrs. Blake, and does not recognize her.)

Silverspoon (aside): Oh! Deuced good-looking! (Aloud.) Was it you who threw the apples? I thought it was that old d—that old gentleman who lives over there. Pray forgive me for the language I employed. If I had known it was you, I would not have said I would pull your nose off. No, indeed, not for worlds. Your nose is very well where it is, and you are not an old devil by any means.

(Mrs. Blake replies by gesture only.)

Silverspoon: Oh, I say, don't be too rough on a fellow for a simple mistake. Pray forgive me.

(Mrs. Blake repeats gesture.)

Silverspoon: Ah, I see! Deaf and dumb! What a beauty! What a splendid nose!—it must be a great comfort to you. If I did not know that Mrs. Blake had gone away—I wish I were not as blind as a bat! She looks so much like her that I must keep up the same flirtation. (Takes out sketch-book.) I must draw her—not draw her from the wall, but on the wall. I must——

(Begins to sketch her. She makes gesture to stop him. He offers to put up sketch-book. She nods and offers flower. He takes it and puts it in button-hole.)

Silverspoon: How sweet of her! Lovely creature!

Rose (aside): Isn't he illegant!

(Mrs. Blake shakes her head violently and makes motions.)

Silverspoon: Not for me? Not for me? Ah, I know what I'll do. (Takes out sketch-book and writes.) Not for me? (Shows what he has written to her. She nods.)

Silverspoon: For Mr. Carter? (Writes as before. She shakes her head and makes gestures.)

Silverspoon: Does she mean sewing? Mrs. Carter? (Writes as before. She shakes her head.)

Silverspoon: Ah, I see. Stupid of me! That gesture means holding the baby, of course. (Writes as before.) For Rose and the baby? No! What is a poor fellow to do? There's nobody left—except Karl! (Writes as before. She assents.) Karl? It isn't! It cannot be! The beast! That infernal gardener interferes in every affair with the women that I begin! It will be so with the queen. When I present those ash-barrels to her majesty, Karl will be there to get all the credit and all the smiles!

(Gesture by Mrs. Blake.)

Silverspoon: Now what does she mean? Does she want to see the villain? (Writes as before. She assents.) Just my luck! Well—(Sighs deeply. Exit.)

Mrs. Blake: How stupid men are! How they deceive themselves! They swear they adore us—and really fancy they do—when it is not us at all! Every hair of our head is precious. (Puts hand to head.) This style ten dollars! The very hem of our gown is sacred; but a little rouge and a few artificial freckles transform us into servant girls!

(Blake comes in with Silverspoon. Mrs. Blake motions latter to retire. Silverspoon goes out, followed by Rose.)

Blake: Margery!

Mrs. Blake: Sally, sir.

Blake: What do you mean; and what is the meaning of this peculiar costume?

Mrs. Blake (imitating Blake's manner): The course I have taken is the only one for your happiness and for my own. I have left you in the enjoyment of your chosen occupation. As for me, I am content and happy enough in this work. You remember my old taste for—masquerades.

Blake: Explain! Explain!

Mrs. Blake (earnestly): You said you did not believe me capable of any sacrifice. I mean to prove to you that I am.

Would you do second work for me—for my sake?

Blake (laughs): No.

Mrs. Blake: Well?

Blake: Margery, you are adorable! (Looks around.) There is nobody to see. Jump down and I'll kiss you.

Mrs. Blake: Oh, no! I have not proved it yet. That will take time; and besides

---

Blake: And, besides, I am as poor as ever. Is that what you were going to say?

Mrs. Blake: Nothing of the kind! But that reminds me—since you want to make more money—I was sent with a message from master. Master wants to know if you can spare any time to work for him.

Blake: For him?

Mrs. Blake: For him.

Blake: Judging from what I have heard, he must be a disagreeable person.

Mrs. Blake: Oh, we must not mind a good beating once in a while. And just think what fun we'll have! While I am scrubbing the kitchen floor, you will come in with the potatoes—charming! And Saturday nights you will go out to the drunk store and come home—delicious!

And when your garden-clothes get over-ripe, what bliss to patch them!

(Mrs. Blake disappears. Blake resumes his work. Silverspoon enters, followed by Rose; and their by-play excites great commotion among the audience. Cousin Louis and Isabelita, watching Rodriguez, clap their hands and shout "Bravo! Bravo!" But the mother and mamita are watching Teresa and their eyes are stormy. "Ei! What is the girl thinking about! Can she not behave! Shame! Oxte! Teresa, Teresita!" they cry to each other and to her.)

Silverspoon (aside): Woe! Shall I never escape from this torment? (Aloud.) What do you mean by following me, creature?

Rose: Crater, indade! It's mesel' as knows the manin' uv a glance uv the oi, loike, an' yersel' as has tould me a swate sacret wid that same bright pair ——

Silverspoon: Sweet secret! Oh!

Rose: He gives a side glance and looks down: look out! as the poet says.

Silverspoon: Confusion and torments!

Rose: Faith! I saw ye an' yer thricks wid writin' and talkin' tinder. (Imitates.) 'What a beauty!'

"The Americans call those things 'serants'! The satire is just," shouted cousin Louis. "Brava, Teresa! Bravo, Rodriguez!"

Silverspoon: What in the world can I do? If I go that way (pointing to the house)—the Carters will see me in this ridiculous scrape. If I go that way (pointing to the wall) she will have me in a corner. If I take refuge in the arbor she will surround me. I might set my back against the wall and bid her defiance—but no! Hole-in-the-Ground would be sure to hear. I would climb a tree—but that would spoil my crease. Oh, what shall I do?

Rose: My! how modest. Would it help ye any ter see me on ther wall, shakin' me hid an' movin' me hands loike her? There! just hould on ter that (gives Silverspoon the baby) whilst I climb. (Sitting on wall.) Up I am, sur! Och! hould its hid up sthraight — the poor helpless infant! An' pull the skirts down! Don't ye go puttin' yer hand on ter the soft spot, man aloive!

Silverspoon: Heaven defend me! What shall I do! Sound the fire-alarm? Put the baby in the ash-barrel? Something must be done, and quickly, too.—— My good girl, please come down?

(Rose shakes her head and makes gestures in imitation of Mrs. Blake. Mother and mamita have decided that this is not the place to say and do what Teresa's conduct calls for. They have also decided what they will say and do to both Teresa and Rodriguez at a more convenient season. They are silent and terrible. Isabelita and Fredo are hysterical with laughter. Cousin Louis is waving his chair.)

Silverspoon: What? I beg pardon, I did not hear. There's a dear, good girl, come down, come down!

(Rose repeats gesture.)

Silverspoon (aside): She expects me to say something flattering: if it is what she can't understand it will answer the purpose quite as well. I must think up some quotation. (Reflects a moment; then quotes.) 'Spirit of merciful interpretation, angel of forgiveness that hearkenest as if forever to some sweet choir of far-off, female intercessions: do thou, angel that hearkenest, do ye, choir that intercede, join together to drive away that dark spirit, born amid the gathering mists of remorse, that strides after me in pursuit from forgotten days, overhanging and overshadowing my head.'

Cousin Louis sits down again. His face wears an expression of grief. "Bah!" says to he Isabelita, "that is not good. That is strained, overdone! Bah!" Isabelita nods assent. Only Fredo continues to laugh.

In the midst of Silverspoon's apostrophe, Mr. and Mrs. Carter come in. Mrs. Carter, about to start forward, is restrained by Mr. Carter.

Mrs. Carter: My poor baby! (Hastens to Silverspoon.) Rose!—Mr. Silverspoon!—Are you all crazy? (Takes baby from Silverspoon.) Mamma's poor, wee one!

Carter: What a pity to interrupt him, my dear!

Mrs. Carter: 'Interrupt,' indeed! Rose!

Silverspoon: Pray, do not be angry with her, Mrs. Carter. It was all my fault. You see—you see—I—in fact, I wanted to draw her, and I was speaking to her when you came in in order to give her the right expression, don't you know?

Carter: The expression was admirable, my boy,—especially of her feet.

Mrs. Carter: If you gentlemen think it proper to joke about such conduct, I do not!

(Carter holds the pocket-mirror before Mrs. Carter's face.)

Rose (sobbing): Please, ma'am ——

Silverspoon: I promise you, dear, dear Mrs. Carter, it shall not occur again if I can help it —— never!

Carter: Come! let it pass this time, my dear.

Mrs. Carter: Well, then, I suppose I must forgive you this time, Rose. Here! take baby and ——

(Mrs. Carter walks aside with Rose, giving instructions in an undertone. Isabelita whispers to cousin Louis: "See what a perfect actress Gloria is! She understands small points. Her mantilla is put on unbecomingly, to show that she has been in a temper.")

Carter (pokes Silverspoon in the ribs): Pretty girl, eh?—You sly dog!

Silverspoon: No! Upon my word. This was not that sort of thing at all!

Carter (incredulously): Tut, tut, man! Tut, tut.

(Rose goes out with baby.)

Mrs. Carter: I am so lonely without Margery! It is something terrible!

Silverspoon: Terrible! I don't think I quite understand where she is gone.

Carter: I don't think *I* quite understand where she is gone.

Mrs. Carter: Perhaps not. She was a high-spirited girl!

Silverspoon: Very! Where did you say —did I understand ——

Mrs. Carter: She seemed the one thing needed to make our life here perfect bliss.

Silverspoon: She did!

(Silverspoon goes to the arbor, takes from his pocket a large poster, folded; unfolds this and fastens it to the arbor with a pen-knife. On this poster is a vigorous sketch of Mrs. Blake and printed in large letters, the following:

Strayed or Stolen!

FROM OUR MIDST, A CHARMING YOUNG PERSON.

FINDER WILL BE LIBERALLY REWARDED, AND NO QUESTIONS ASKED.

It was the original poster, which Vincent had begged of Carter when the latter had first told him the story.)

Carter: Come, my dear. Acknowledge that our life is perfect bliss without Mrs. Blake.

Mrs. Carter: What would you say if you should lose Karl?

Carter: Lose Karl! What do you mean! Have you any reason to think —— Karl! What is this talk I hear! Are you dissatisfied with me?

Blake: No, sir.

Carter: And you are willing to stay?

Blake (with hesitation): I shan't go before you agree to it.

Carter: Oh, well; that is satisfactory, I am sure. (To Mrs. Carter.) My dear, instead of falling into the melancholy vein, suppose we have a game of tennis. Oh, I forgot! There are no balls!

(A number of tennis-balls thrown over the wall. Fredo roars and rolls over on the ground in his delight. The others are patient.)

Silverspoon: A miracle! Another wonder! In America they have snow-storms in mid-summer, and each snow-flake is a regulation tennis-ball!

Carter: Many thanks, neighbor!

(Carter goes to arbor; sees Silverspoon's poster and beckons Mrs. Carter.)

Mrs. Carter: Tear it down! This is going altogether too far!

Carter: Ignore it, my dear.

(Mrs. Carter puts out her hand to tear down the poster. Carter restrains her.)

Carter: Oh, no —— please!

Mrs. Carter: There! I know! I have always known that I was ugly and plain and homely and ——

(Carter puts mirror before her face.)

Mrs. Carter: Not *very* good-looking.

Carter: Here are the rackets. Now, my dear, you and Jack ——

Silverspoon: Oh, I forgot!

Mrs. Carter: Don't tell me that you have an engagement. I won't consent to give you up also!

Silverspoon: No, I forgot to tell you.

Mrs. Carter: What?

Silverspoon: There is a stunner over there.

Carter: A stunner—over there?

Silverspoon: A beauty. A lovely maiden who sits on the wall and wants to see Karl.

Carter: What! Rose?

Silverspoon: No; another. She has golden hair and the most exquisite nose! I started to converse with her, but she would not have it and sent me away. There was only one trouble.
Carter: What?
Silverspoon: She was deaf. And one other.
Mrs. Carter: What?
Silverspoon: She was dumb. Otherwise charming.
(Mrs. Blake comes in from piazza.)
Silverspoon: Here she is again! (Hastens up to her and takes out sketch-book.) I will write it for you, poor thing.
Mrs. Blake: Poor thing yourself, sir. (Drops a courtesy.) Master's compliments to Mr. and Mrs. Carter, and he is coming, ma'am.
Silverspoon: Another miracle!
Carter: Why! That is Mrs. Blake, or

Silverspoon: If it is Mrs. Blake, I——
Mrs. Carter: Who is your master, my good girl?
Mrs. Blake: That I don't know, ma'am, but here he comes himself, ma'am.
(Neighbor comes in. It is the first time that señora Villena has put on her full

costume, for previously she had shown but her head and shoulders above the wall. Now, she has avoided the indelicacy of dressing " liker yentleman " in all respects by devising a rough coat with skirts which reach to the top of her dainty French shoes. In her right hand, brilliant with diamond rings,—all she possesses being put on for the grand occasion—she grasps a heavy, knotted stick. In her left is a similar stick which she uses as a crutch.)

Blake (aside): My father! Alas! how feeble and worn!

The play could not go on for a time. The señora's grave manner and ridiculous costume; Medina's voice shaken on the word "father" and breaking on "alas"—it was too much. Actors and audience—even mother and mamita—shouted and screamed.

Neighbor (to the audience): Don't be so fool! Jour servant, madame. Jour servant, yentlemen.

Carter: I am very glad to meet our neighbor finally.

Mrs. Carter: We are very glad, indeed.

Silverspoon: Indeed.

Carter: Welcome back, Mrs. Blake!

Silverspoon: It *is* Mrs. Blake! If I had known that it was you on the wall ——

Mrs. Blake (imitating Silverspoon): ' Deuced good-looking! .... How sweet of her! .... Not for me? .... For Karl? .... It isn't!'

(Mrs. Carter leads neighbor to seat in arbor.)

Carter: Why did you leave us so suddenly? We were in despair.

(Mrs. Blake points to poster,—"No questions asked.")

Neighbor: Silence, friends! Shut op, bo-ee! (To cousin Louis.) I shall ex-explainer everything myself. I am man of few words, but I do—I shall explainer everything.

(Blake draws nearer. All very attentive.)

Neighbor: Thirty-five year sago, I marry a beautiful wife. I lover her! I lover her! We have wong chil'. Wen this chil' wass less than wong year, my wife die. I can never say so before. Even now the memory of that —— cá! it maker me sad. From that time I hate the world an' see nobodie—not wong persong! I maker the rebellion from my soul an' my heart with the good God an' man. An' the most estranger thing wass this: that I cannot bear to see that chil'. I hater him: he reminder me too much of the mother. After a few year I sender that bo-ee away to a friend who taker good care of him an' teller him I am dead, an' his mother too. By-an'-by he grow to be a man, an' a fine man—*solide.* He don' know, but all the time I watcher him. Wen he wass marry, I am there. I don' say nothing: nobodie see me in that church. Wen I seer him so happy, I wass crazy to embracer him! All the love I have had for the mother, I giver that to him then. I want to taker him home with me and keeper him always. But I say, No! Wat he would thinker of me? Wat he would thinker of me who leaver him so,—who everyone hate? I cannot speaker to him.

Blake: Father!
Carter: Karl!
Silverspoon: The husband!
Neighbor: Pay attengtion! . . . Wen he iss in trouble I sender to him, but he will not com'.

Blake: And I was ——

Neighbor (imposing silence with a gesture): Then I have been sad for long time, till I see this leetle girl (takes Mrs. Blake's hand)—so sweet!—in her cap an' her apron.

Blake: And I was only restrained by the fear lest you should think my poverty, and not affection ——

Neighbor: Cá, let us finish this trouble, this sadness, an' all be yolly! Hurry op an' haver good time!

(Blake and Neighbor embrace. Neighbor takes Mrs. Blake's hand and gives her to Blake.)

Neighbor: Taker her an' be good bo-ee! Don' quarrel no more. Leaver happy. (To Mr. and Mrs. Carter.) We be good friends, no?—an' to prover that ——

Mrs. Carter: We will have the wall taken away.

Señora Villena's triumph was complete. Everyone praised her, and Vincent thanked her for saving the day and redeeming the play.

"Have I done my part well?" Teresa asked her mother when they were alone in the latter's room. "It was so extravagant! But did you like my acting?"

"That was not acting: that was behavior," said the mother, very sternly.

Then Teresa was forced to tell how Rodriguez had declared his passion in Gloria's presence but without exciting her suspicion. "And I am sure," she concluded, "that the burlesque this afternoon was a complete blind, just because it was so exaggerated. Nobody but you understood me. He did not—I know that."

"But what he did in Gloria's presence, my child, was done with grace and delicacy."

"Ah, darling little mother! You cannot expect me to equal him!"

THE invitations which Medina had addressed were for the day following that on which the play was finished. You may know from this that Gloria was full of fears. What if it should prove an anticlimax?

At half-past eight in the evening Vincent, his hands clasped behind his back, was walking up and down the brilliantly-lighted, empty but expectant rooms of the ground floor. Presently cousin Louis came down stairs and joined him.

"Well, our good host," said the latter, "I suppose they will be here——Why! How is this?" he asked, noticing that Vincent was not in full dress. "You have put on a morning coat since dinner?"

"There will be one or two guests to keep me company in this bad form, as you will see," said Vincent. "I'm sorry; for the rooms will be warm and this coat is heavy. What do you think of those flowers in the corner? Aren't they too close together? I think I'll call the gardener"

Louis Diaz laughed. "You remind me of Carter," he said. "And, by the way, did you not put a good deal of yourself and your own traits into that character of Paul Carter?"

"But I know Carter," said Vincent, "and I set down what I knew. However, on second thought, you are right," he corrected himself; "for I had to add some points where my information was defective. I thought I reasoned out what was probable for him and in him—the unknown from the known; but very likely, as you say, I was only studying myself then. His way of living is so like my own."

"Is his wife economical, as you represent her? I only know them socially—not intimately."

"There I confess I took a suggestion from Gloria. Gloria is not exactly economical, but—well, I will tell you what she said to me the other day. We were out shopping together and I offered to give her a piece of jewelry which she admired.

"'Oh, I have that,' she said.

"'You have it!' I said. 'Then what is

it doing here in the shop? Oh! you have ordered it and Mr. —— has neglected to send it. Let me speak to him.'

"'No, no,' she said, 'I would rather have Mr. —— keep it for me.'

"'And why?'

"'Well, I saw it a good while ago and asked the price. Then I saved up my pocket-money until I had enough to buy it. Then of course it belonged to me if I wanted to go and get it; but by that time I thought I'd let Mr. —— keep it for me. And I think so still.'"

"Hm!" said cousin Louis, critically.

"I am interested to know what will become of that money she has saved up," continued Vincent; "and I have put more than usual into her purse this week just to see if she will let Mr. —— keep that bracelet (it was a bracelet) when she has enough and to spare."

The fair subject of their conversation entered the parlors a moment later, and soon the entire family were met. Then the ladies put their hands upon each other to adjust things, while the gentlemen, being unable to imagine the slightest change for the better in such toilettes, applauded uncritically.

Such a time is favorable for hearing terms of endearment: and what a range is given to expression by adding a few letters at the end of a Spanish word! If you would tell how close is the union in a family, what more can you say than this: A Spanish father has been known to call his baby "papa", while the baby was calling its grandmother "mamita" (little mother). Both extremes of age are flattered and drawn as near together as possible. And have you noticed that Isabelita, being the oldest sister and unmarried—too old to be unmarried, others beside herself have said, —is always called *little* Isabel, while the youngest, Teresa, is named without diminutive? I do not mean that this is an inflexible rule. It is largely a question of taste. Señora Villena's way, when not in one of the rare fits of melancholy, was to fancy that she herself and all her especial friends had not outgrown the taste for dolls.

"An' that bébé," she was saying to Gloria, "that bébé he is asleep so conning." Suddenly her face expressed mortal terror. "Bébé!" she cried, "there are a mice in the wall!"

Gloria's ear had caught the same sound

but interpreted it differently. "Someone is coming up the gravel walk. That is what you hear," she said.

The first guests were arriving.

These proved to be monsieur and madame Dindome, who taught music, one singing, the other the piano. They brought with them their daughter Marie, an exceedingly pretty girl with a fine voice, who kissed the hostess at least six times, laughing continually at nothing, speaking half English, half French, with many antics which may have been natural or may have been for the benefit of the strange gentlemen present. Monsieur Dindome wore a full-dress suit, with the exception of a large flat shield-cravat which hung down half-way to meet the low-cut waistcoat, leaving a wide margin of shirt-front. Upon his feet were cloth gaiters.

When cousin Louis saw that cravat he commended Vincent for putting on a morning coat.

The next arrivals were Mr. and Mrs. Horace Penman, and with them Miss Slyme. They deserve more than a word in passing, for Mr. Penman has often been pointed out to strangers as a typical Oldhavener. He was a tall, thin man of very erect figure and grave countenance. He had lived temperately and worked deliberately; so that now, at sixty or sixty-five, he was active and would cure a headache by exercise rather than take medicine. But he would tell you that he was an old man. He was a lawyer with a good practice—enough, at least, to keep him from the bench. He was intensely respectable. To those whom he had often met and whose family history he knew, he showed himself friendly or even cordial; but with recent or slight acquaintances his manner was coldly indifferent. We may take ourselves out of the class of slight acquaintances and know the man's real nature by dwelling for a moment upon what he said to John Eaton, about twenty years ago.

John Eaton, as Mr. Penman's most intimate friend, had asked him why he did not marry one of the Misses Slyme. Everybody knew, he had said, that he had been engaged to them, or one of them, for years.

"That is it," Mr. Penman replied. "Engaged to both of them! I can't make up my mind to prefer one to the other.

They are precisely alike and they are inseparable. And certainly I cannot ask them to settle it between themselves. Each would draw back and say: 'After you, dear sister.'!

"But even if that difficulty were removed, I should hesitate to take this important step through fear of the disease."

"Disease!" echoed John Eaton.

"Yes, a disease which counts its victims by thousands and hundreds of thousands. Guess what it is from this description of its symptoms: An active and public-spirited young man becomes suddenly recluse in his habits. From being an ornament to society he becomes indifferent to the charms of ladies and shuns parties of his male friends. He is no longer elegant in dress; he is no longer a good fellow. His enthusiasms and his idealism are gradually and surely converted into a humdrum anxiety for steady advancement and safe investments. He keeps accounts at home and allows himself just enough pleasure and recreation to keep his health good, he says.

"Such are the first symptoms of this disease. You smile and think these slight matters; but mark the awful intensity of that which follows. In one short year this young man disappears from view,— at least he is never seen except when hurrying between his home and his place of business, his doctor's or his apothecary's. He might almost as well be dead. His face is haggard and unshaven; his eyes are heavy and seem unused to more light than is admitted into the sick-room; if one succeeds in stopping him on the street as he flies along, he looks self-conscious, bashful, timid, and quickly excuses himself on the plea of engagement.

"His case would seem to be desperate. But no: he recovers after a month some of his old genial ways and happy looks. His friends take courage, and hope all may yet be well,—when, lo! the same symptoms reappear in the same order, the crisis must again be passed,—and so on, and so on, again and again perhaps."

"I can guess!" cried Eaton. "It is the devoted-husband disease."

"Guessed, my friend," said Mr. Penman; "and now you know all the reasons why I postpone marriage."

He married Miss Gertrude Slyme two years ago, but the sisters are still inseparable and both happy in a quiet way.

Now we know more about Mr. Penman than anyone else does, excepting his intimates.

Again the door-bell rang, and Mr. and Mrs. Green entered. Mr. Green came in limping, and when asked the cause gave the following explanation:

"Nothing but a slight piece of carelessness on the part of one of my servants, in leaving a dust-brush on the stairs. Mrs. Green had gone down just before me, but of course did not pick it up, as she could not soil her hands with a household article. Never mind: the bruise is slight. Well, madam," he continued, addressing his wife, "have you made up your mind as yet?"

"About what, Mr. Green?"

"As to whether you will go to England with me next week."

"Really I have not decided; and I think it improper to discuss family matters in public."

"My dear Mrs. Green, you know my principle. I will not quarrel at home. Home is the place to be at peace. What I say, when we disagree, I want everybody to hear. Did I not inform you yesterday afternoon that you were to give me your answer here at Mrs. Vincent's? If you do not decide by the time you have finished drinking that glass of lemonade or punch, whichever it may be, I decide for you."

While this dialogue was proceeding, the assembled guests were silent, not knowing whether it was jest or earnest. Mr. Green walked away to the other side of the room. After everybody had begun to speak again he returned and, standing at a short distance from Mrs. Green, said, in a voice so loud as to call the general attention:

"Well, madam, have you made up your mind?"

"Yes. I will go."

"We sail on Wednesday," he said, and then devoted himself to the rest of the company.

Inasmuch as this episode has lifted the domestic curtain, we may as well understand the situation.

Mrs. Green, when still Miss Chester, after being engaged several times came to the conclusion that life was sad and that she might never change her name. She was of a frivolous disposition, inclined to be gay and passionately fond of society, in which she had moved among the best people. She was not pretty, but very aristocratic in appearance.

Mr. Green had opened a successful school for boys in Oldhaven. He was a very religious and fairly learned man, unpretentious, and of a happy, contented nature, thinking little of the world outside his own library. He was a just man, but not stern.

Now, the back windows of his house looked out upon the grounds of Miss Chester's father. From the garden Miss Chester heard him calling to the maid: "Mary, be good enough to ask the cook what vegetables she has for Professor Green's dinner."

"How polite he is to his servants!" Miss Chester said to herself; and her second thought was: "Is he good-looking?"

Soon afterwards she saw him at the window. He was quite good-looking.

Once she saw him with a small basket on his arm enter a hovel in the outskirts of the town. "He is of a religious, charitable disposition," she said.

From that day Miss Chester arrayed

herself in a plain black, but becoming, gown. She allowed herself but one ornament: a huge black cross, hung by a silk ribbon about her neck. She sang hymns with the windows wide open and attended church twice on Sundays. She even did the marketing for the household, and each day chanced to be at the market when Mr. Green was making his purchases. After discovering that he taught in the Sunday school she also took a class. At a teachers' meeting they became acquainted.

"One so simple, domestic and religious," thought Mr. Green, "would make a true helpmate." In an hour of blindness he asked, and was given—he little knew what.

Three weeks after their marriage Mrs. Green laid aside the simple black gown and the goodness. Once more she was a gay society woman. Green was forced to care for the house and lead as lonely a life as before. As years went by he found himself more and more successful, more and more lonely: for the children of this marriage were like the mother. In a word, the just man became stern.

One day Mrs. Vincent, when calling on

Mrs. Green, happened to meet Mr. Green at the door.

"Is your wife at home, professor?"

After lifting his hat and ringing the bell he answered: "I really do not know, madam, but will inquire."

When the servant appeared, "John," he said, "is Mrs. Green at home?"

"No, sir; she has been in Saratoga for a week."

Without evincing any surprise, Mr. Green asked: "Do you know when she returns?"

"Yes, sir; this evening."

An ingenious method, this of Mr. Green. He maintained peace at home by adjusting all differences with his wife in public.

But we must hasten to note other guests, who now arrive so thick and fast, that only a word can be given to each.

Miss Brown, who wore smoked glasses and wrote for children's papers, came in alone. Miss Reba Thomas, who read humorous poems with a decided lisp, came in with Miss Knox, who had a talent for laughing. Mr. Donald Livingstone— the elegant, the handsome, the wealthy

Mr. Livingstone, respected by everybody present except Mr. Penman, who had his suspicions—entered with dignity. I do not remember who came for a time after that: youngish men whom one distinguishes as good dancers or indifferent dancers, and young ladies only remembered as the young lady in pink, or the young lady in white with pink. But what would a party be without them?

Last of all came, in response to the three invitations which Gloria had secretly sent out of town, Mr. and Mrs. Blake,. Mr. and Mrs. Carter and Mr. Silverspoon. Silverspoon had made the trip from New-York in company with the Blakes, and they had found the Carters at the Elm House when they reached Oldhaven.

Gloria and Medina, who alone had expected them, drew together and watched the effect of the surprise upon the others.

"Look at your husband!" said Medina. "An author confronted by the creatures of his imagination, who demand to know what right he had to make one good and another evil—or, what is a great deal worse, one interesting and the other insipid."

"Look at señor Rodriguez!" said Gloria. "He thinks Mr. Silverspoon is his own reflection walking out of a mirror. And see! Coralie has put out her hands to ward him off, as though he were a piece of furniture about to fall on her. Mrs. Carter does not wear her hair so high as I thought."

Medina laughed. "And I have no doubt," he said, "that Concha is comparing the real Madame Margery with her counterfeit of yesterday, and that Louis Diaz is revising his judgment."

Not long afterward Teresa was saying to her mother: "How much señor Rodriguez flattered Mr. Silverspoon!"

The mamita, who was seated behind them in a great arm-chair, leaned forward and said: "That the Silverspoon? Ah! His face very cross; but his hands and feet aristocratic—and his voice, also. Oh, yes, he may be a gentleman." The mamita prided herself upon knowing only Spanish people.

Silverspoon became conscious that three generations were looking at him with interest, and came forward to pay his respects to them. The mother and Teresa greeted him cordially and gave him permission to sit with them; but the mamita, after acknowledging his bow politely enough, secluded herself in her memories and leaned farther back in her arm-chair.

On the opposite side of the same room Rodriguez was standing by Mrs. Green.

"Who is that beautiful girl with the dark eyes over there,—the one sitting with two stout ladies?" she asked him. "I have caught you looking in her direction once or twice, and I cannot blame you."

"That, Mrs. Green, is the señorita Teresa Diaz, of New-York."

"You speak as though you knew her: perhaps you can tell me about the thin young man who is with them. I noticed that she seemed very glad when he went up to them."

"Oh, yes, madame; that is one of my friends. He is a very successful artist."

"Is he engaged to the young lady?"

Rodriguez looked for a moment at the unconscious subjects of this dialogue before replying: "I cannot tell you that, madame."

Cousin Louis liked to corner men at

parties and converse with them. "I prefer to get the good of these affairs," he would say, "by taking people at their best. I talk with the men and I look at the women." The truth was, he liked to lead in conversation.

He and Mr. Penman were standing together.

"I think, sir, that I once heard you play the piano in Boston," Mr. Penman was saying. "The concert to which I refer was excellent in its way, and especially the soloist seemed to me to show much skill. You must pardon me, as I am near-sighted and I have a poor memory for names, but I think —— let me see, it was in December, five years ago."

"I did play several times in Boston that winter," said cousin Louis; "and I should be very happy to think that I gained your approval. Ah! perhaps we can fix the occasion. What selections did I—or the soloist, whoever he was—play that evening?"

"Hum," said Mr. Penman, taking off his glasses and appearing to reflect. He was a learned man, and accustomed to being consulted as authority in the law and general literature. I think, therefore, that he hesitated to say "I don't know music," not through affectation but through force of habit. It took half a minute to remember that he did not know.

In less than half a minute cousin Louis saw the point and changed the subject. "Speaking of art matters," he said, "reminds me of that English artist who came in just now. Probably you have not met him. No, not that gentleman: that is Mr. Rodriguez. On the other side—there, talking to Miss Diaz."

Mr. Penman put up his glasses and looked steadily at Silverspoon. "No, I don't know him," he said.

It seemed to cousin Louis that the tone in which this was said implied an additional, "Don't care to;" and he felt himself challenged to interest Mr. Penman.

"Well," he continued, "there is a man who is at the same time rude and very refined. I say nothing of his rudeness, for that is the first thing to strike a stranger; but I will give you an instance of his refined way of putting things. When he first came to New-York his taste was offended by the generally filthy state of the streets, and especially by the custom of leaving barrels filled with ashes and all sorts of rubbish on the sidewalks. But in speaking to New-Yorkers, instead of openly criticising, he called attention to the disgraceful practice by pretending to admire these ash-barrels as art-objects; and he did this with so much humor that 'Mr. Silverspoon's ash-barrel' is become a synonym for irony. And, by the way, this is quite a coincidence! Another man who is much politer than Jack Silverspoon, and who avoids expressing his disapproval flatly, is the one you looked at first—there, with some lady I do not know."

"Mrs. Green," said Mr. Penman.

"Now, he has this system in its perfection. You can see at a glance that he is a strong-willed and hot-tempered man, this José Rodriguez; but he never contradicts: he suggests his dissent in some subtle way. If one is clever enough to see and understand the suggestion, then that is sufficient; if one is not clever enough, what good would contradiction do such a person? Rodriguez and Silverspoon are great friends, and that may explain their having the same practice."

"Great friends?" said Mr. Penman, interrogatively. "They do not look it."

"I thought I must be mistaken," said Louis, "but if you also notice a peculiar expression—perhaps a hostile expression—in Rodriguez's face, I think I can account for it." At that instant he saw Silverspoon lean forward and in an undertone say something to Teresa at which she blushed and smiled, rewarding him with a brilliant glance and a murmured reply.

"The dark man looks decidedly hostile, I should say," Mr. Penman observed.

With his usual rapidity of judgment cousin Louis drew his conclusions and decided upon his own course of action.

On the other side of the hall was a large room which had been set apart for dancing. Mr. Carter was there, chatting with Mrs. Blake and passing comments upon the dancers.

"There's an extraordinary couple!" said Mrs. Blake. "Concha Medina engaged in fascinating an old gentleman in cloth gaiters. She takes the strangest fancies!"

"I have met her partner before," said Carter. "He isn't so old as he looks, I fancy; and as you see, he is a good dancer.

He is a Frenchman—Dindon, Dindome, or something like that. Quite a character, they say."

"Suppose we see for ourselves. I will call Concha, if I can catch her eye," said Mrs. Blake; and, presently succeeding in this attempt, Concha joined them and presented Monsieur Dindome.

"You will forgive my interrupting your dance, my dear Concha," said Mrs. Blake, feeling that some excuse was necessary, "when you hear what I have to tell you. You know we have been seeing a good deal of Jack Silverspoon lately."

"Yes," said Concha, expectantly.

"Well, he confessed to me that at one time he was quite attentive to Teresa Diaz."

"One of a thousand!" said Concha. "If you want to surprise me, my dear, mention somebody who has not been attentive to Teresa."

"Monsieur Dindome, for instance."

"Pardon me, madame," said that gentleman. "I haf observed her befo I haf seen you"—including both the ladies in an impressive flourish and bow.

Passing cousin Louis in the hall soon afterward, Concha said:

"Something for a censor to enjoy! Mr. Silverspoon has been attentive to Teresa."

Cousin Louis was on his way to seek Vincent. He found him engaged in complimenting madame Dindome upon the appearance of her daughter, Marie, and congratulating Mrs. Penman and Miss Slyme upon the rugged health which their husband and brother-in-law seemed to enjoy.

Drawing him aside, he said earnestly: "My dear friend, I have reason to fear that there is trouble ahead."

"What! Is the punch giving out? No wonder: such a warm evening. I will go and order more."

"Not that. Have you noticed Rodriguez?"

"By Jove! Thank you for reminding me. I have been neglecting him. Where is he? I shall introduce him to that pretty little Marie Dindome."

"And I go with you," said cousin Louis, taking Vincent's arm. "Slowly, please. I have something to say to you as we go."

Gloria had found opportunity for a short confidential chat with Mrs. Blake.

"And Richard is so sensitive and so proud, my dear!" the latter was saying. "He positively refused to be dependent upon his father; and, what do you think! he has begun to invent things—all sorts of things for pulling up weeds without bending over, and then using them for I forget what. He has even found a use for me. He says I stimulate him (sometimes he says *irritate*) to such a degree that he invents something before he knows it. He struck twelve the other day."

"Why, Margery, what do you mean?"

"Oh, that is his way of saying that he has done his best, like a clock. You see, I was in a temper, and he invented something which will make us rich again. I do not exactly understand what it is; but Richard says everybody will want it."

"You must be very happy."

"Happy! I am growing stout at the mere thought of it; and if this invention succeeds, I fear I shall soon have an impertinent figure."

Gloria rose, saying: "Now I must leave you, Margery; but promise me not to stir for two minutes, and I will bring you a charming gentleman."

"Whom?"

"Señor Rodriguez."

As they walked arm in arm through the rooms, cousin Louis told Vincent what he had seen and what he thought about it.

"Has anyone beside yourself noticed this?" Vincent asked.

"Yes, Concha Medina."

"In that case," said Vincent, "there must be something in it."

The object of their search was not in the parlors, and they were about to pass into the hall when Mrs. Green stopped them.

"Dr. Vincent," she said, "if you see that Spanish gentleman you introduced to me please tell him I have something to say to him, and I will be right here. He left me quite abruptly to speak to that gentleman who is engaged to Miss Diaz, and then they went out together."

Vincent promised, and with Louis Diaz walked rapidly through the hall and stood in the doorway.

Two men were near them on the piazza, and appeared to be disputing some point.

"Not now," they heard one of the men say in Silverspoon's voice; "we must not disturb the festivities. After they have all gone away we will leave together. Alone?—or would you prefer——"

They did not hear the end of the sentence; for, with a common impulse, they had stepped back into the hall.

"The sort of thing," said Vincent, "that they would not like anybody to hear; and I am afraid it is a thing shameful to hear and shameful to speak."

"Oh, no; the duel, as between gentlemen, is not shameful," said cousin Louis.

At this moment Gloria met them.

"I have been looking everywhere for señor Rodriguez," she said. "I want to take him to Margery."

"And I have promised to take him to Mrs. Green," said her husband. "Suppose we stand here: the draught is pleasant."

"Poor martyr—in that heavy coat!"

"Cousin Gloria," said Louis, "if you mean to stand here, I insist upon getting you a wrap."

"Mamita has one for me: ask her," said Gloria; then, when he was out of hearing: "Carangol, I am trying to do all I can for poor Rodriguez. Mamma found fault with little Teresa for acting that absurd part you made her take, and she has been so ashamed that she has not looked at him since. He does not understand—thinks she has given him up—and feels dreadfully: I can see it."

"Oh! oh!" said Vincent. "Another cause of war."

Fortunately he was not called upon to explain this expression, for cousin Louis returned with a lace shawl, while from the piazza came Rodriguez and Silverspoon.

"Here you are at last!" cried Gloria. "Why, you both look as guilty as though you had stolen away to have a cigar!" She claimed Rodriguez for Mrs. Blake, and took him away with her.

As soon as her back was turned, Vincent laid his hand on Silverspoon's arm, saying very earnestly: "Don't do anything unworthy of you — anything foolish."

"And I tell you, my dear sir," said the other, "that I never felt more like it in my life."

THE SPANISH SESSION

En punto á cantar no cabe término medio: ó buen cantar ó buen callar, que quien canta bien, parece ángel que á Dios alaba, y quien canta mal, asnico que rebuzna.—*Trueba.*

IT was half-past two o'clock when the last of the Oldhaven guests took their departure. From the lateness of the hour (almost unprecedented in the annals of conservative Oldhaven society) I judge that they had enjoyed themselves. The Carters, the Blakes and Silverspoon had been privately commanded to remain.

"Because," Gloria had said to one, "because!—you shall see." To another she had explained: "Now that the conversation and dancing and supper and conversation and conversation are over, let us have some fun."

"The Spanish session will begin," Vincent had said with marked emphasis to Rodriguez; "and you, señor, are at present a member of my household—my family. If you acknowledge my authority you must stay with us."

"But, as I have assured you, sir, I have made with Mr. Silverspoon an engagement."

"Jack will stay also."

And so, at three o'clock, the Spanish session began.

Not formally appointed, but born to rule such a company, señora Villena led on merriment to madness among the guests. She hurried to and fro, exhorting and stimulating everybody to "doer something liker carnival."

It was like a carnival: friends calling out to one another across the rooms, everybody talking at once, dancing, laughing, singing, gesticulating. The very spirit of extravagant fun was there, as master of revels, directing the strangest things to be done. Those estimable Oldhaven people who had gone could upon occasion attain to cheerfulness; but tempers so tamed and disciplined as theirs could not reach this pitch of harmless revelry.

Tell you in detail what was done? No, I cannot: everything was done too quickly. An instantaneous photograph? Well, perhaps if we seize the quietest instant we may get an impression.

Exhausted by her efforts señora Villena has thrown herself into a chair; but no, not exhausted, for she is speaking with all her usual animation to Concha, who is offering her a glass of wine.

"Bébé, that Mr. Penyentleman he is magnifique, superb, solide! My dear, he taker fancy to me!"

The trifle of disorder in Concha's costume makes her enchanting.

Cousin Louis is at the piano, improvising something like a devil's dance, but glancing over his shoulder to make sure that Rodriguez and Silverspoon have not slipped out.

Gloria has given her hand to Rodriguez, and together they are trying to invent new dance-steps to suit this music. It is impossible, but their failure is a pretty thing to watch.

So Teresa thinks; but you could not tell that she is looking at them. She appears to be listening to her mother's advice.

The mamita is clapping her hands to encourage Gloria. The steps of that dance are Spanish.

Vincent is between Silverspoon and Medina. The latter is saying:

"Like some dry tobacco in a box on my table. The box says, 'Always Moist.' I keep it as a model lie."

At the same instant Silverspoon is saying in his heart: "Mrs. Vincent has the lost arms of Venus; and she moves like a flame."

The other figures are indistinct: that is, I cannot remember. But I do remember that an instant later señora Villena was on her feet, and that her *aide*, Concha, was throwing a handful of small candies at Mr. Carter because he looked too quiet. Of course no person has more than a general idea of what happened for a while after that.

But Vincent had it in mind to say a few significant words to señora Diaz and Teresa. He had never before interfered in a matter of this kind; but here, he reflected, was an obvious mistake and misunderstanding drawing the most serious consequences after it. There was no time to be lost. Moreover he was himself (as having assigned the part of Rose to Teresa) the author of this misunderstanding. With a view to making opportunity for saying what was needful, he said in an undertone to Medina: "Now is the time for that story you promised," and then seated himself by señora Diaz.

Medina stepped out into the center of the room and cried aloud, "Silence!" and señora Villena repeated "Silence!" and others caught up the sound, so that "Silence! Silence!" everyone cried in mockery of the word.

When finally all were looking at him, and only whispers and titters were heard, Medina spoke.

"My good friends and grown-up children," he said, "our host has commanded me to tell you a story in the Spanish style. Some of you already know the originals of the characters I shall introduce; but if you do not all feel, by the time I have finished, that you know them, blame my invention, and not the Spanish style. I call it

Ochanda and Amador

I

"'Doña Cármen!'

"'What is the matter with you, señor Bozmediano? Dios mio! what has happened?'

"'Ah, dear friend! Give me some claret with water, or I shall die!'

"'Instantly, señor .... Here, drink the wine quickly! Do not fear: it is the good red wine which you have always at my apartment. And now tell me, what is it?'

"'Ah, doña Cármen, qué horror!—That girl!'

"'Ochanda?'

"'Yes, señora. I have met her! More wine! If I see her again, I die! I am coming up the stairs to my apartment above; as I pass your door I see her floating down; she looks at me—like this! Ave-María Purísima!'

"'But she will not harm you—a great, strong gentleman such as you.'

"'Yes—I say, yes! With her eyes! I know there is a devil in each of them! They flash fire; they are two evil flames! I shall be scorched and shriveled and burned to a crisp! To-day I ran after a humpback on Broadway and touched his hump for good luck; but it has done no good! That girl has looked at me!'

"'Do you believe she is crazy?'

"'I know it. She never speaks.'

"'That is true. And she eats hardly

anything, although our table is the best in New-York—for a boarding-house.'

"'Ora pro nobis!'

"'All this is true; yet I do not believe she is crazy.'

"'A beautiful young girl who neither speaks nor eats, and who paces the floor of her room the whole day long—for I hear her! Of course she is mad!'

"'Listen! Three months ago she comes here with her sister and brother-in-law, the señor de Velasco. She has left behind her in Habana her lover.'

"'Eh? Ah!'

"'She wishes to return. She is not allowed. She says to herself, I will! She refuses to enjoy; to speak, to eat, to go to the theater. She thinks they will be forced to permit her to return to her lover. Is it true?'

"'Your wisdom, doña Cármen, is superior even to your wine: to praise it more highly would be impossible . . . . But where did she learn the evil eye?'

"'Caramba! Nothing of the kind. You have lived too long in this cold city: you have forgotten how Spanish eyes look!'

"'Impossible, señora; for I have been

your neighbor. And now ——. But let me first make sure that she is not in the hall. Adios, doña Cármen!'

"'Vaya usted con Dios, señor Bozmediano.'

II

"'Señora de Velasco.'

"'Oh, señor don Amador!'

"'I come, señora, with the greatest respect to request your permission to pay my addresses to the señorita Ochanda, your sister.'

"'Hum!'

"'I have already, as you are doubtless aware, been so fortunate as to secure the consent of your husband.'

"'Very true. He has told me.'

"'To you, señora, I present an especial petition. I beg, not only for your consent, but also for your assistance.'

"'I fear your attempt is a hopeless one. But you are the friend of my husband, señor: tell me in what way I can aid you.'

"'A thousand thanks, señora! Now that I may count upon your good will, I am confident of success!

"'Oh, as to my good-will, you might

have anticipated that. To say nothing of our friendship for you, the attentions of that military gentleman who takes his meals here have become annoying. We know nothing about him, except that he is an officer, a captain. What is his name?'

"'Brady. But he is not a real officer—not a soldier. He is captain of a professional base-ball nine, and has taken board here in order to learn the Spanish language, his nine having an engagement to play in Habana next year. I trust, señora, that he has not made himself offensive in any way!'

"'Oh, no! Pray do not look so fierce. You alarm me! What I said was merely to intimate that we feel genuine anxiety for our sister and would welcome the protecting friendship of someone in whom we repose entire confidence. But have you considered the difficulties?'

"'Yes, señora.'

"'That, in the first place, we took her away from home in order to break off an unfortunate attachment?'

"'I am aware of that, señora.'

"'That she resents our wise interference and pines for the worthless fellow?'

"'Yes, señora.'

"'That she attempts to force our compliance with her childish whim by steadily refusing to speak or eat or take part in any entertainment? She shocks even the widow doña Cármen, and frightens the fat señor Bozmediano almost to death.'

"'I have been a sorrowful witness of all that, señora; still I am not without hope. Pardon me if what I say is too direct and blunt; but since you have graciously promised to assist me, it is but right that I should plainly speak my mind. She does not love the gentleman in Habana.'

"'What makes you think so?'

"'When she has refused something especially nice at table, I have read in her expression the desire to eat it. When we have been speaking together about some fine bit of acting at the theater, I have seen an eager look come into her face for an instant.'

"'She is shamming, you think?'

"'I should prefer to have you tell me, after I have added one other point. Genuine love softens the disposition: now, have you noticed more tenderness in her manner since she formed this attachment, or less than ever before? — I mean of course toward those who had not been instrumental in thwarting her.'

"'Very much less.'

"'Well, then ——. But I must again beg you to forgive my bluntness. Do you not see that she makes a display of her grief? These are not the effects of genuine love. What name would you yourself give to it?'

"'Obstinacy.'

"'A word which I should not dare to use in speaking of your sister, señora. Now allow me to tell you my plan. It is of course absolutely necessary that she should let me speak to her and pay her those little attentions which — without which a woman's natural defenses protect her heart completely.'

"'What can you do! We have tried everything—threats, surprises, her favorite amusements. Nothing will move her to speak.'

"'Well, the passion to which you have given a name is strong; but the passion of curiosity is still stronger. See, señora, these envelopes ——'

"'What a large one!'

"'That is the outside one. Within that is one somewhat smaller, and then another still smaller, and so on. In all, there are ten envelopes, one enclosed within another. The last is quite small, as you may imagine. Now the outside envelope is, as you see, addressed to a friend of mine in San Francisco. When he opens it he will find another, sealed, stamped, marked 'confidential' and addressed to your sister in your care. She opens this, only to find enclosed a smaller envelope, sealed, stamped, marked 'confidential' and addressed to a friend of mine in Liverpool. So, in course of time, she receives a letter from Liverpool, in all respects similar to that which had come from San Francisco, except that the envelope is smaller, the stamp and postmark foreign, and the enclosure another envelope addressed to a friend of mine in Paris. And so on to the last and innermost envelope, which, when it finally is returned to her, after zig-zagging across the water and the continent, will be found to contain ——'

" 'What ?'

" 'The envelopes are all sealed at present, señora; but when the time comes you shall see.'

" 'Oh, please tell me now !'

" 'It is something which I cannot well

describe. . . . . But I should have explained that I have five sets of envelopes like this; so arranged, however, that each set follows a different and separate course. Thus, one set begins, as I have told you, at San Francisco, another at Dublin, and so on; while the innermost envelope of one set will be forwarded from Sevilla, of another, from Habana, and so on. She will, therefore, receive one of these mysterious letters every day or two.'

"'And my part! What am I to do?'

"'If you will be so kind, señora, see that they are handed to her while we sit at table.'"

III

"*First Letter.*

"Ochanda found it placed on the table beside her napkin, glanced at the postmark 'New Orleans' and at the unfamiliar handwriting, but did not open it.

"*Second Letter.*

"When Ochanda took her place at table on the following day, she found, in addition to the first letter which she had disregarded, a second. She noticed that the handwriting was the same, while the second bore the postmark 'London.' She opened both of them. The first contained an envelope, sealed, stamped, marked 'confidential' and addressed to M. Lafitte, &c., Paris; the enclosure of the second was similar in all respects, save in its being addressed to Samuel Barnes, Esq., San Francisco. She left them on the table when she arose, after taking a few spoonfuls of soup. Her brother-in-law mailed them.

"The fat señor Bozmediano noticed that don Amador had been gazing earnestly at Ochanda, so when she had left the room he said to him in a whisper: 'You also fear that girl; but never mind, she is gone now, and we may enjoy our dinner!'

"*Third Letter.*

"Ochanda opened it, and finding only an enclosure for 'Herr Dr. Schmidt, Leipzig,' looked angry, and handed this to her brother-in-law.

"*Fourth Letter.*

"This came from Sevilla; and don Amador saw those wonderful black eyes sparkle. Ochanda herself posted the enclosed envelope, leaving the house for that purpose for the first time in several weeks.

"*Fifth Letter.*

"Ochanda glanced at the postmark 'Chicago' and looked perplexed. That evening she actually spoke to her sister. 'How long does it take to go from Sevilla to Chicago?' she asked; and when her sister had told her, she looked more perplexed than ever. When putting away some linen, the sister found in Ochanda's bureau a sheet of paper on which five names and addresses were written.

"*Sixth Letter.*

"The sister said to Ochanda, 'Little sister, will you have the goodness to explain your receiving from all parts of the world letters addressed in gentlemen's handwriting and marked confidential!'

"*Seventh Letter.*

"Again Ochanda spoke. 'Little sister,' she asked, 'can *you* explain?'

"*Eighth Letter.*

"Ochanda listened attentively while don Amador described to her sister the methods of an imaginary secret society of dynamiters. Among other things he said: "It has branches or chapters in all civilized countries, and of course these chapters communicate with each other. But in order to keep the membership secret, an ingenious device is resorted to. Some innocent person is selected to transmit their reports, messages and explosives, and of course this cat's-paw is changed frequently enough to prevent all risk of detection.'

"*Ninth Letter.*

"Ochanda was afraid to touch it, and said to her brother-in-law: 'Will you please open this for me?'

"*Tenth Letter.*

"It was passed around the table, for everybody's inspection. Don Amador studied the address long and earnestly.

"'Can you tell anything as to the writer from the writing?' the sister asked.

"'Yes: not with absolute certainty, but —yes, I can tell his occupation and age.'

"'What?' Ochanda asked; but immediately added, 'Excuse me,' and left the room.

"*Fifteenth Letter*.

"Everyone in the house was given opportunity to wonder and to guess.

"'If this continues,' said don Amador, 'we shall all become Yankees.'

"*Twentieth Letter*.

"Ochanda had become, in a totally new sense, the center of interest. Nobody thought her insane, or even obstinate: the thoughts of all had taken a new turn. A more entertaining topic of conversation had been provided. What was to be the conclusion of all this? Who or what was persecuting this innocent and charming young girl? It was more exciting than a play.

"'The letters are rapidly decreasing in size,' don Amador suggested: 'perhaps they will soon disappear altogether.'

"Of all the boarders he was the most fertile in suggestions and the most ingenious in putting the mysterious case in new lights: so then, in importance he was second only to Ochanda, and associated with her in the minds of all.

"In her mind, also? Not yet, perhaps. She had begun to act like other people, probably because her thought-center was shifted from Habana to the uncertain source or sources of those letters.

IV

"'Welcome to my apartment, señor Bozmediano. Will you have some of the red wine?'

"'Ah, doña Cármen, doña Cármen! With you only do I feel safe and at ease in this house.'

"'It is scarcely polite to observe to a lady—even to an old lady who has had a husband who is with the angels—that you feel safe in her company.'

"'Ah, little Cármen, you know well that my heart is wholly your own!'

"Bah! If I had not money ——. Here is the good wine, señor. Drink! We are too old to dispute.'

"'Dispute, indeed! Ah, no: we leave that to the little don Amador and that blood-thirsty young man from Habana. Would that he had remained at home, that we might have some peace! Ay Dios mio! he is terrible.'

"'Never fear! He will go home soon enough.'

"'He will kill the little Amador first— or some of us!'

"'Not he: he blusters and swaggers too much!'

"'But who would have thought that the little Amador himself had sent those letters? Now, how he contrived to be here and to send letters from Sevilla and San Francisco at the same time is what I should like to know.'

"'Cá, Bozmediano, you are little better than a fool! It amazes me that I have patience to receive your calls.'

"'Dear little Cármen! We are too old to quarrel: give me therefore the least bit more of the good claret.'

"'In one point only you are sensible: you drink the wholesome red wine. Bozmediano, I tell you, if ever you take to drinking white wine, I put you out! . . . But it was truly odd that don Amador should have addressed one of those letters to the old lover of Ochanda, not knowing that he was even acquainted with her. He might at least have asked the man's name, since he knew it was someone in Habana.'

"'Oh, señora! No, no, not the little Amador. He is not inquisitive: he is a gentleman.'

"'Bozmediano, when I think to put you out, you say something which makes me respect you . . . . And to think that Ochanda forwarded that letter, and that the scamp of a lover opened the little one inside to see what stranger was writing to his sweetheart! And to think that he saw something in the little last envelope which made him very angry —— and that he will tell nobody what it was! I could scream with disappointment!'

"'Tell me this, little Cármen: How does it happen that the other four little envelopes which came last were quite empty, while this one which fell into that terrible man's hands contained something so important?'

"'Tell me this, señor: Was it necessary to put something in each of the last envelopes? Would the little don Amador have to ask her five times—or give her five things, whatever it was? Caramba! I shall not sleep to-night for trying to think what it could have been! Can you not see that Ochanda is madly in love with don Amador, and that his little finger is worth the whole body of that blustering rascal who opens confidential letters, and does not tell what is in them? He will go back to Habana very quickly, I promise you—if, indeed, he has not run away already .... But that message, that message—or whatever it was—in the little envelope! The little Amador has told the little Ochanda what it was: for see how radiantly happy she is!'

" 'Then it must have been a question: the one question which can produce such a result.'

" 'Oh, must have been!—must have been! That is not enough: I need to know what it was—not must have been!'

" 'It was—shall I tell you what it was? Ah, little Cármen, do you forget how often I also have asked, implored? Cruel little Cármen!'

" 'Cá, now I put you out!' "

*　　*　　*　　*　　*　　*

While Medina had been speaking, Vincent had improved the opportunity; and his timely suggestion to señora Diaz had been, in substance, this: Both Gloria and I have the highest esteem for Rodriguez. To Teresa he had whispered: "Rodriguez thinks that he has offended you, and is most unhappy in consequence."

Cousin Louis was still seated at the piano,—a position which suggested his unquestionable superiority in the matter of music, and so lent authority to whatever he might say, from the eminence of the piano-stool, upon any matter which chanced to be under discussion.

"Your story about Spaniards," he said when the applause which rewarded Medina had subsided; and then repeated when he had secured attention, "your story, Medina, suggests the experience of a young Cuban in whom I am interested. He came to New-York about two months ago, with the idea of seeking his fortune. It was a crazy thing to do, for he did not know a word of English; but there was no chance for him at home. His father, an old friend of mine, lives near Espiritu Santo. He is a planter: you know the rest—ruined by the low price of sugar. This boy had never seen a city—not even Habana—until he was eighteen years old. What do you call such fellows in New England, Vincent?

Hayseeds? Well, he is the Cuban variety of country lout. A perfect greenhorn! He started out alone the other day to buy a cravat, and walked along the street, looking in the shop windows. When he saw what he wanted he went into the shop, took a clerk by the coat-collar, led him out of the door and pointed to the cravat which had struck his fancy. After narrowly escaping arrest as a lunatic, he got the cravat, put it on in the shop and then made his way to a restaurant. The waiter brought him a long printed bill of fare, of which he could not read one word, but with assurance he pointed to the first item. The waiter nodded, went away and presently returned with mock-turtle soup. 'Ah, it is not so difficult to get along in this country', thought Perico; and when he had finished his mock-turtle soup smiled at the waiter and put his finger on the second item of the *menu*. 'Very good, sir,' said the waiter, and brought a dish of tomato soup. Perico was hungry, and managed to finish this also. 'Now for something solid', he said to himself, pointing to the third and fourth items. '*Very* good indeed, sir!' said the waiter, and brought vegetable soup and ox-tail soup. Perico would not let it appear that he had made a mistake; so tasted each of these. 'I have begun at the liquid end of this list', Perico reflected; 'but I cannot eat so much as the Americans. I shall at once call for the most substantial dish'—and he pointed to the last item on the bill of fare. In obedience to this command the waiter brought him toothpicks."

"Iss he a lean, or iss he a fat?" asked señora Villena.

"He belongs to the fat order: a big-chested fellow with splendid physique," answered cousin Louis; and then explained, for the benefit of the Americans present: "We divide all Cubans who come here into two classes. In one class we put the smoke-dried, indifferent people, who never amount to anything. They are the lean—sometimes we call them threads. In the other class we put the wide-awake, strong, capable people. They are the fat. The average American thinks that there is only one class—the class we call 'lean'—in all the West Indies. You ask him, 'What is a West Indian?' He answers, 'A Cuban'. 'And what is a Cuban?' 'Oh, a yellow-skinned mortal who inhales strong cigars before breakfast'. But I have seen, even in Cuba, such arms and chests as a professional athlete might envy. This Perico is one of that kind. He is a great, honest, simple-minded lad, with a neck like a bull—and a voice! He has been begging me piteously to train it for him; but I do not understand the voice. I know only this instrument,"—striking a chord on the piano.

"The poor boy!" said Concha. "Is his voice really so fine?"

"Magnificent possibilities!" exclaimed cousin Louis. "If he has a good master now, we, for our part, shall have a Cuban Brignoli in New-York. But without training now, he will contract bad habits, and that will be the end of it. He has no money, and I, as you all know, am poor."

Gloria had drawn near to cousin Louis, and was thoughtfully turning over a pile of sheet-music on the piano. "Play this song of Gounod," she said, leaning over his shoulder to put the music before him, and as she did so asking in a whisper: "Would two hundred dollars do any good —to begin with?"

In the same tone he answered: "Quite

enough", and then began to play the accompaniment to "*Ah! si vous saviez*", while Medina sang that exquisite entreaty in a fashion to delight a musician but to shock a linguist. Has there ever lived a Spaniard who could pronounce French correctly?

Then he sang something of his own composition which he called

A Serenade to Nobody

> She sleeps, she sleeps, my lady fair,
>   Yet ever in my sight;
> A throbbing star is in her hair
>   And her robe is the soft moonlight.
> Dear, gentle winds that come and go,
>   Bear her my note of love;
> I am her servant here below
>   And she is my queen above.
>
> Her fragrant breath is on my face,
>   Yet far away she seems;
> And though I'm held in her embrace,
>   I am not in her dreams.
> Dear, gentle winds, that to and fro
>   Bear goblin, sprite and elf,
> Be pleased to say, (she'll never know)
>   My love is the night itself!

When this song was finished cousin Louis swung around to face his audience and said, with a very happy light in his eyes: "My friends—and especially my dear Vincent—if ever I am rich enough to marry, I shall look for a wife who will be content to economize in the matter of bracelets in order to send a great melodious voice to speak of beauty to all men in the chosen language of beauty." Only Vincent and Gloria understood this reference to bracelets and realized that Perico had found a patroness, but no one dared to question: cousin Louis had spoken from the piano-stool.

While Medina was singing Vincent watched Teresa most narrowly. He saw that she lifted her eyes to meet those of Rodriguez; he saw that Rodriguez construed this as permission to approach her; he saw that señora Diaz did not disapprove. Going to the window he drew aside the curtain, raised the sash and threw the blinds wide open.

"See!" he said.

"The dawn!" cried Concha.

The fragrant air of morning poured in through the open window, bringing with it that incomparable suggestion of the young life of a summer's day. How quickly they all responded to that pure and tender suggestion, in silence drawing together before the window and gazing out upon the smooth lawn with its clusters of bright flowers! They heard the leaves of the little maple-tree near the arbor whispering as a gentle breeze stirred them. A branch of honeysuckle, heavy with dew and laden with bloom, broke away from its fastening at the lintel and, slowly swaying to and fro before their faces, sank downward and lay outstretched on the turf.

Rodriguez and Teresa were standing behind the mother. For an instant their hands met.

Medina was the first to speak, unconsciously trying to analyze the charm of the scene. "There is not the broad sunshine which we love," he said: "there is also not one shadow."

"Hush!" said señora Villena, her finger at her lips.

"Where is your husband?" Mrs. Blake asked Gloria, in a whisper.

"Calla, Hush!" the señora repeated. "The leetle birds they begin to wake op!"

No, these were not bird-voices, but tones infinitely more sweet. We like to deceive ourselves, and sometimes we ask Nature to sympathize in our moods. Nature has no heart but that which beats in the breast of the man who loves her. That silent company of men and women who loved Nature heard her many voices, warmed and made significant by the heart which puts its own meaning into them. Vincent's warm and generous heart or that of the old violin?—for such a violin is no part of stockish nature: it has a heart, put into it by its maker and kept alive in it by generations of masters who have told it their secrets in passionate confidence. I cannot determine whether it was the master or the violin which interpreted to them the thrill of dawn, for I cannot separate such a master from such an instrument. Ask cousin Louis: he is a musician.

Cousin Louis? He would not have answered any question whatever then. Even after this music ceased he heard nothing else, he saw nothing at all. Although Vincent had said to him before leaving the room: " I put you in charge: keep them in view!" he did not notice that Rodriguez and Silverspoon had paid their respects to the hostess and gone away together until Teresa put her hand on his arm.

"Do you know why the señor is leaving the house at this hour?" she asked.

"Leaving! How long ago?"

"An instant. He and Mr. Silverspoon must be in the hall still."

Cousin Louis hurried out and found the two gentlemen just passing out of the front door. Waiting only to put on his hat and throw a light coat over his shoulders, he soon overtook them. He was contriving an apology for this intrusion when Rodriguez turned an unmistakably happy face upon him and exclaimed:

"I have wanted very much to see you, señor, to ask your permission and assistance in a certain matter. This is most fortunate!"

"My dear fellow, you do not need assistance," said Silverspoon. "You should have seen the look she gave me when I praised you this evening."

"So that was what you were saying to Teresa!" cousin Louis exclaimed.

"Certainly. Won't you walk down to the hotel with us?" Louis eagerly consented; so they locked arms and proceeded together.

"I asked our friend Rodriguez to give me a chance for a good quiet talk," Silverspoon began to say, after a moment of silence; but cousin Louis interrupted.

"*You* asked *him!*" he exclaimed. "Oh, I had not thought of that."

"Yes, I asked him. Why, what's up?" said the Englishman.

"Oh, nothing. Only I thought—no matter now what I thought! And then I saw and heard several things to confirm my suspicion—never mind what. And certainly Rodriguez did look angry—but let that pass. If *you* made the appointment with *him*, that changes the face of matters." It occurred to cousin Louis that Vincent would try not to laugh when he should hear how he had been misled, and the thought was annoying.

"Can't say I understand you altogether," said Silverspoon; "but I fancy my head is not so clear as it might be. I have been spending the evening with some friends. But on one subject I entertain positive convictions. I am absolutely sure that I am the happiest Englishman in America. This is what I wanted to tell you, Rodriguez; and now that I have you both by the arm so that you can't get away from me until I have finished, listen! One year ago, when I was at home, I wrote a question on a bit of paper and put it in the hand of the sweetest girl in Warwickshire. Yesterday I got her answer. Now I am going to tell you about her until I am satisfied."

But I must not report what was said about the sweetest girl in Warwickshire, for Rodriguez's path to Teresa has been cleared of fancied obstacles, and my purpose has been to describe only those entertainments which were planned in consequence of señora Villena's having waked one morning with a pain in her shoulder.

THE END

GRAY: AN OLDHAVEN ROMANCE

Not in Utopia, subterranean Fields,
Or some secreted Island, Heaven knows where!
But in the very world, which is the world
Of all of us,—the place where in the end
We find our happiness, or not at all!
—*Wordsworth.*

PREFACE

THERE are to be found in Oldhaven two types of character which can be studied nowhere else, I think, to greater advantage. One type is that of the self-respecting, studious, yet easy-going townsman, whose aspect is grave but who has nevertheless a keen sense of the humorous and whimsical; who has conservative views upon every subject; whose muscles are exercised and whose charities are dispensed with regularity; for although his circulation is slow, his conscience is active. Such a man is Mr. Horace Penman, who has been mentioned in the foregoing pages. Mr. Penman dislikes foreigners, excepting those whose acquaintance he has made. All those whom he has met socially (as, for example, Mrs. Vincent and her friends) he finds charming; but they, he persists in believing, are exceptions to the rule. In this the man's character comes out very clearly; for while his rule is narrow his practice is liberal. His opinions in their severity bear the stamp of the law; but he will make, one at a time, so many equitable distinctions that no person who knows him well thinks him severe. The impression which he makes upon slight acquaintance, however, is commonly unfavorable. Mrs. Rutherfurd Davenport, one of the prettiest brides in Oldhaven, in the course of her comments upon Mr. Penman said to me the other day: " People who know a great deal can't impart it, and yet they can let people know that they know a great deal."

The second type is that of the woman who is intellectual, but who has no regular occupation for her mind. Her intellectuality is question of taste, not of profit. She is therefore not thoroughly intellectual, but retains in great measure the mere womanly dependence and impulsiveness. With a facility which is sometimes astounding she captures the outposts of various sciences and gets a reading knowledge of various languages; but she is herself never mastered and reduced to habits of orderly thinking by the spirit of genuine learning. She is a woman; she is also somewhat of a scholar; but much more woman than scholar. She is surprising. Do not fancy that through any knowledge you may have of either women or scholars you will be enabled to form an idea of what she will do next. Such a woman, but lifted by her beauty and social influence above the bonnets of the class to which she belongs, is Mrs. Winthrop Eaton.

These people, Mr. Penman and Mrs. Eaton, have been in my mind for a long time. Little by little they have told me about themselves and about other people whom they know. Little by little their story has become so distinct that it now seems part of my own experience; but I could not, if I tried, tell it in my own words. Inevitably I should fall into their manner of expression. It seems best, therefore, that with this brief explanation I should step back and let them in their own fashion impart to you their several and very different views of the same matter.

Part I—By Mr. PENMAN

OSKAWASK IN THE YEAR 1855.

"IF the house is an apology for a dwelling-place, at least it occupies an humbly apologetic position. A sandy hill-side slopes down to a sluggish, weedy little stream, and just beyond this stream stands the house in question.

"'After you, sir or madame,' says this humble dwelling to the brook; and so, year after year, it has waited for the stream to pass in front of it. At least I can see no better reason why the dwelling should stand in this boggy, low place."

Meditating in this fashion, I, Horace Penman, paused for a moment before the humble cottage at the foot of the sandy hill and beside the weedy stream.

"What sort of man is the owner?" I asked myself. "Has a traveler a fair prospect of being received and sheltered for the night here?"

It was the 9th of November, in the year 1855. Night was drawing on, a storm was gathering in the west and I knew that the nearest tavern was ten miles distant.

I was on my way from Oldhaven to Boston, traveling, as was most agreeable in the bracing air of late autumn, on horseback.

As the result of my reflections I dismounted, threw the bridle over a picket of the tumble-down fence separating the front yard from the highway, and advanced toward the rambling, unpainted house. As I placed my foot upon the lower step, the door was opened before me, and in the doorway stood a man of middle age—a tall, lean figure, slouching forward. Rusty, faded homespun trousers, supported by a single suspender from the left shoulder, heavy boots, coarse shirt, open at the neck—such were the garments of the man in the doorway. He looked at me with a marked absence of interest.

"Good evening," I said. "Could you take me in for the night?"

He shut a large jack-knife which he was holding in his right hand and put it into his pocket. This was done very slowly. Then he examined a piece of soft pine which he held in his left hand. This he did very attentively.

"Good evening," I began to repeat, raising my voice.

"Waal," drawled the person thus urged, "I don' know. I guess I'll go an' ask Israel."

"Jonathan!" piped a shrill voice from within the house, "Jonathan, ask the gentleman to come in to the fire."

I did not wait for a second invitation, but crossed the threshold and made the best of my way in the direction indicated by the shrill voice.

"Jonathan Slyme, I am surprised at you for letting the gentleman stand in the cold!" exclaimed a little woman whom I found seated before an open wood fire.

"Why, Saray," supplicated her husband, "I was a-goin' ter ask him ter come in. I jes kinder thought I might as well ask Israel first."

A brief silence followed this remark. Sarah and Jonathan looked at one another, and the stranger glanced about the room.

The room was long and narrow and low, scantily furnished with six or eight rude chairs and an extension table which was set with half-a-dozen plates and dishes of different patterns. The bare floor was very uneven. There were two curtainless windows at the end nearest the highway, and at each of these a young woman was seated, bent over her sewing. The generous hearth, before which their mother sat, was piled high with logs, great and small, through which the bright flame was climbing upward, curling about the ends which showed marks of the axe, fastening upon projecting bits of dried bark, leaping from lower to upper, gaining the topmost log, and then shooting straight upward in spears of white light. Is there anyone who doubts that this royal adornment may supply the place of all those objects with which we, now in the day of registers and radiators, strive to beautify our rooms?

"Israel is coming right back, and then we can ask him, Jonathan," said Sarah. "Sit down, sir. He is gone to fetch in some more logs. He is the greatest hand to make a fire!"

This was said with so much pride that I saw my advantage in humoring her by talking about this Israel, whoever he might be.

"So, madame, have I to thank him for this very agreeable blaze?" I asked, rubbing my hands and holding them out towards it with sincere appreciation.

"Yes, sir, my son Israel does everything good that is done around here," she replied, with a look of contempt directed towards her unprosperous husband. He, however, far from resenting this thrust, nodded slowly several times, repeating: "Yaas, I guess he dews pretty much all the good as is done around here, in Oskawask," whereupon he leaned his rounded shoulders against the mantel-shelf, thrust his hand slowly into the depths of his pocket and, after fumbling in a way which showed that the object sought was one of many things in that ample receptacle, produced the jack-knife, opened its single large blade and fell to work upon the piece of pine which he still held.

This seemed a favorable omen. He accepted the traveler's presence and turned his attention again to the interrupted employment. It was clear enough to me now that Jonathan accepted things as they were.

Such being the disposition of the natural head of this family it was evident enough also why his house stood on the edge of a marsh and not elsewhere: he had found it there.

That is not a very startling conclusion; but it was interesting to me at the time because it instructed me that, so far as Jonathan was concerned, I might stay over-night.

Yet it seemed to depend upon Israel and Israel's decision.

ISRAEL

EROES find safety in their very fearlessness. Their reckless disregard of caution carries all before them with a rush, and the blow which was intended for their heads falls upon some sluggish follower. So, at least, those gentlemen, who from the security of their studies send forth descriptions of heroic lives, have repeatedly assured us.

But as for me, whose ambition it has been to lead a happy life and not necessarily an heroic one, I do not scruple to acknowledge my obligation to the spirit of caution which has constantly animated me, as in the moment preceding the appearance of Israel.

After satisfying myself that no opposition was to be feared from the easy-going Jonathan or the bright-eyed Mrs. Sarah, I glanced again towards the young women seated at the windows, to see if they looked hospitably inclined and to secure their good-will, perhaps, through some little courtesy. They were looking up, their eyes fixed upon some object at the opposite side of the room. I had barely time to notice that they were decidedly pretty and dressed exactly alike before a ringing voice cried "Hello!" at the back door. The brisk little mother sprung from her chair and threw the door wide open.

There stood a young man, bearing three or four large white birch logs upon his shoulder.

Going quickly to the hearth, he laid down the heavy logs easily as though they had been so many twigs, threw back his shoulders and said: "That will do for to-night." Then, looking me full in the face with a smile of perfect good-will, he offered his hand, saying, "I am glad to see you, sir."

I was a little staggered by the confidence and ease of the boy's bearing. This did not prevent my seizing the offered hand, however,—the first hand which had been offered me in this house in which I desired to be received as guest. I seized the hand, which was no larger than my own, and tried to squeeze it.

Think of trying to squeeze Charles

XII's hand, or the Russian Peter's—hands that crushed horseshoes! The man who offers such a hand to the world, the world may hate, perhaps, but will surely respect.

Fortunately the younger man did not return the pressure and crush me. So then, I did not hate him, but respected his physical superiority.

"Israel," began the mother, "this gentleman wants us to keep him ——"

"Over-night?"

"Yes, my son, if you ——"

"Of course," said Israel, with ready decision, turning to the guest again. "You are welcome. You shall have my own room."

"Oh, no, no, brother Israel! We think that he had better have ours, don't we, sister Grace?" said one of the young women.

"Yes, we think brother Israel must not be disturbed in the evening, don't we, sister Gertrude?" assented the other.

"Pshaw!" said Israel, "I'll camp-out here before the fire, as you know I like to do. Grace and Gertrude, you may do your part by bringing me a bolster and blanket when the time comes. I shall have the best of you all, here before the fire, for it is going to storm like parson

Dewback denouncing slavery." Putting an arm about each sister, he drew them toward the window; then catching sight of my horse, he said: " Come with me, sir, and we will put him up."

Without waiting for me he went quickly down to the gate and led the tired animal in between two leafless lilac trees which did sentinel duty at each post, between the stumps of coarse flowers which skirted the walk, to the front door. There I joined him and together we led my horse to a wood-shed (there being no better accommodation) at the rear of the house.

When we returned, after performing this duty, preparation for supper was being made: a generous supper, never to be forgotten! After all these years I could tell you what we had, even to the several varieties of pie, dressed with frills of paste and ornamental patches upon their round, upturned, homely faces. These are not slight matters if one holds, with the Germans, that one is what one eats, or with the French that he works well who eats well. I remember also how the father took his place behind his chair while the others ranged themselves according to dignity; and how all stood while a formal grace-before-meat was pronounced; and how Samuel entered without greeting me and sat through the meal without uttering one word.

Samuel was but a year or two younger than Israel, and yet the brothers were in appearance so unlike that at first I thought it scarcely possible that they could be children of the same parents. Both were rather above middle size; but while this fact was noticeable in the case of Samuel, whose narrow, sloping shoulders suggested that he had grown beyond his strength, Israel's figure was so perfectly proportioned that an observer would need to compare it with other objects in order to determine whether it was tall or short.

There is a period of overflowing physical strength which visits some favored persons before maturity sets in. Then the great muscles, swelling beneath the skin still soft and smooth as a woman's, seem marvelous. Israel was one of these favored persons, and his strength made him noble in every movement.

As for Samuel, he neither had nor desired great muscles. To have had them would have meant just so much more farm work.

The most striking difference was in the coloring of the two young men. Samuel had light, reddish hair and a sallow complexion. Israel's hair was black and crisp, his eyes well set, almost black and sparkling with vivacity, his cheek smooth, with a ruddy-brown tint. On his right cheek was a small mark of singular appearance. Although too small to be disfiguring, it had a clear outline suggesting some familiar object—I could not at first think what.

While we were still at table the door was opened and a woman entered.

"Here comes Lilly," said the mother, quickest to speak and quickest to act.

"Miss Lilly Lincoln," Israel explained, as she came forward rather bashfully, not having expected to find a stranger.

Well do I remember how poor Lilly Lincoln looked as I saw her for the first time, with her delicate, earnest, wistful face and interesting eyes. How can a climate, which produces no more generous beverage than cider, produce the intense, passionate nature which looks out from such eyes as Lilly Lincoln's? With all our long winters and long sermons inculcating hatred of the flesh, there are hearts beating as wildly, as quick to take fire, as impetuous in their demand for love, here in New England as any in Andalusia. We cannot boast of wine, women and song; but at least we have cider, women and sermons. "Who does not love wine, women and song, remains a fool his whole life long," said Dr. Martin Luther.

The two sisters encircled their friend with their arms and drew her towards the fire. All arose from the table, as our repast was already finished. A glance full of meaning was exchanged by Israel and Lilly, while the parents accepted her presence without comment, as that of a familiar guest. Miss Gertrude introduced me to the new comer. Miss Gertrude, it is to be observed, because this slight circumstance bore precious fruit long afterward, had been my neighbor at table and therefore felt better acquainted with me than did her sister.

"Don't you think brother Israel looks as though he would like her?" asked Miss Grace.

"We do," murmured Miss Gertrude.

"Why, yes—yes indeed; in fact anyone must," I said, wishing that someone would interrupt and so save me from the necessity of concluding.

"We do," echoed Miss Grace; "and we think he is a sweet fellow. He will be twenty-one day after to-morrow," she added.

During this naïve conversation, which somehow had the effect of making me feel wonderfully at home, I was standing opposite Mrs. Slyme, who had resumed her favorite corner by the fire-side. I noticed in her bright, intelligent little face a new expression—an expression of thoughtful curiosity. "But, dear me," I said to myself, "she is looking at the buttons on my coat: they cannot be the occasion of that expression."

While we were thus grouped about the fire, the storm commenced to rage outside with such violence that Lilly was not permitted to return to her home. The sisters amiably disputed as to which should enjoy the pleasure of sacrificing her wish to have Lilly for bed-fellow, and Israel suggested that they should solve the difficulty by putting a bed for her in the little room at the head of the stairs. All this was discussed so affectionately! I wish that I could do justice to the fine spirit which animated this group of four young country people. I soon took occasion to ask that I might be shown my room, and was accordingly conducted by Israel up a narrow, creaking staircase.

Israel's room was extremely simple, its only ornaments being a bouquet of pressed autumn leaves and dried grasses and one picture. This last was the portrait of a young man; an oil painting, showing honest work without much technical skill on the part of the artist. At that time I prided myself upon being a tolerably good judge of painting, and examined it closely.

"Why, it must be a hundred years old!" I said.

"It is almost that," said Israel.

"But, if it were not for the evident age of the painting, I would take oath that you are the subject."

"It is my great-grandfather," he replied. "Here—when I hold the light to it, you see the dress, almost faded out of sight. Can you make out an old-fashioned lace collar and embroidery there? If he had more than one coat like this, he must have been a swell. It is clearly not myself, although the resemblance of the face is striking, even to this mark"—and he pointed out a spot on the right cheek of his ancestor.

As he spoke, the right side of his own face was turned to me, and I glanced again at the curious mark which I had before noticed. It seemed that at the mention of the ancestor's blemish (for it amounted to that in the portrait) this spot on Israel's cheek became instantly more distinct, and I was on the point of recognizing the outlines of a minute spade, when Israel turned to a substantial though rude table on which lay a score or so of books.

"I am ashamed to speak of anything so pitiful," said he, "but such as it is, my little library is at your service. I have bought only such books as I could not borrow from Mr. Dewback, our parson, who is a college graduate and who fitted me for college."

Now my admiration of this youth for his beauty and strength had been at least doubled, it must be confessed, through the discovery that his great-grandfather had worn linen and an embroidered coat. The additional credit which was conferred by this subsequent discovery, that he possessed the elements of a solid education, was much less considerable. Therefore, in expressing my thanks for the polite offer, I turned over the leaves of one or two volumes with only an assumed interest, and soon resumed my scrutiny of the portrait.

"Your ancestor had less breadth of forehead," I commented, "his upper lip is slightly longer and his chin less strong and firm"; but, reflecting that my comparisons might seem too familiar, instead of continuing, I asked Israel about this ancestor.

"Sit down, then," he suggested, "for it is quite a long story; or, better, stretch yourself out on the bed, Mr. Penman."

I complied, and lying across the foot of the bed and looking up at the portrait—glancing now at it and again at the narrator—heard the following account.

THE ANCESTOR

"THIS portrait which has excited your interest," began Israel, "I found five years ago in the garret, in a corner, just above my head as I stand now. The fall before I had strung across some ears of sweet-corn to dry for seed. When planting time came, I went up to fetch that and some other little things stowed away in the same place. They were too many for me to carry in my hands, so I picked up this picture out of a heap of rubbish, not noticing or caring what it was, to put the seeds on. So I carried them down and out into the long field."

Here Israel paused; then walking up and down the room and stopping each time he passed the bed to see how I was taking what he said, he continued:

"It was a bright, warm spring day and I was fifteen; so there were a good many thoughts in my head besides about planting corn. But I need not remind you, sir, that a boy of fifteen thinks all sorts of things on a bright, warm spring morning. He is just beginning to realize how much larger the world is than his own home, how many opinions there are different from those in which he has been brought up, and more than all he is just beginning to feel a restlessness which he can't explain even to himself: strange desires for freedom, for knowledge, for pleasures, for possessions, and stranger, more tormenting desires which he cannot understand because they are entirely unlike those he has felt before."

"In a word, the boy of fifteen doesn't understand himself and is most curious about himself," I ventured.

"Exactly that. So then, you know what sort of questions I was asking myself and you can understand my interest when I had removed enough of the corn to see myself."

"How is that?" I asked, rather sleepily. "Removed the corn to see yourself?"

"When I had uncovered the picture, that is. I saw before me my own face, line for line; only the lines were deeper, stronger, and the face was my own face matured. I saw myself matured. That was an answer to my questions because it was a prophecy of my future."

"Your questions answered? That is better luck than most of us ever have. You understood yourself after that?"

"Yes," he answered very positively. "But I beg your pardon for the reference to my own feelings. I need to explain why this portrait seemed to me from the first so valuable,—why I did not throw it aside as others had done and stick to the occupation of planting corn.

"It is the only object we have left in the family to connect us with the past, and the wonder is that its frame had not been split up for kindlings long before."

I shuddered at the mere suggestion of such violence being offered to a sacred relic. A horse-shoe which my own great-grandfather had forged, had been gilded and was prominently displayed in the Penman drawing-room in Oldhaven.

"I took it," Israel continued, "to parson Dewback, who is a mild, timid little man, and in some respects is certainly a fool. But he is, after all, very well-read and a good deal of an antiquarian. He was delighted beyond measure, of course, and promised to find out all about the painting and its original if I would leave the old thing with him for a month. This I consented to most unwillingly, for I could not bear to let the prophetic mirror in which I seemed to see my own future go out of my possession even for so short a time.

"One month later, at the very hour, I presented myself before parson Dewback and demanded my treasure together with the promised history of my ancestor.

"'Dear me! Well, well!' the old gentlemen exclaimed in confusion; and I feared he had forgotten his engagement. But no: he went to his desk and fumbled among a heap of papers, as ill-assorted and disorderly as his own thoughts on immortality. 'Well, well, well! Now where can it be? Dear, dear, dear! I do not find it, my dear young friend. Perhaps it is just as well.'

"'Oh, no, sir, please don't give it up. Is *this* it?' I asked, putting my hand on what he had been writing when I entered.

"'To be sure! I had only just begun to write it down; but' (with a bland smile) 'I will *tell* the story to you. I will tell to you the story of your—let me see, your great-grandfather, who bore the extraordinary name of Israel-for-Israel Slyme.

Sit down, my dear young friend, sit down and listen.'

"There was not another chair in the room; but I stood and listened none the worse for that.

"The old parson's story was full of windings and indirections. He began with the statement that the name 'Israel-for-Israel' did not signify that my ancestor was a selfish man, seeking his own interest at whatever cost to others. A deeper and scriptural interpretation was to be preferred, he said—this, namely: 'Israel-for-Israel' is as much as to say, The Lord's people are sufficient unto themselves, and should not covet the possessions neither take on the manners and customs of the children of this world.

"Oh! oh!" I deprecated, sitting bolt upright.

Israel laughed so heartily that I felt the bed vibrate and exclaimed:

"You do not approve parson Dewback's interpretation of 'Israel-for-Israel.' Well, I shall never say you are wrong.

"It seems probable that at the opening of the Revolutionary War, Israel-for-Israel Slyme was an adventurer, not attached to the American cause by any sentiment of patriotism, for he apparently held no property in any one of the States. Moreover his conduct and traits of character of which we have certain knowledge accord with this supposition.

"He was neither religious nor industrious; so, in spite of his puritan name, he was not a Puritan at heart. Quite the contrary, in fact. He was a dandy in dress, he was imperious and haughty in manner.

"One of the traditions which parson Dewback unearthed is therefore possibly not without foundation. It is to the following effect:

"My ancestor was the second son of an English bishop. He had led a wild life at the University of Oxford, and so thoroughly disgraced himself afterwards that with the full permission of his respectable parent he fled the country and changed his name.

"Think of his coolly deciding, after he had made up his mind to seek his fortune in the rebellious colonies, to assume a name suited to his new surroundings. The son of an English bishop expressed the opinion of the class he was quitting—their opinion of dissenters generally, and most of all the American dissenters, with whom he was to identify himself—in the name of Slyme. That must have been his first thought.

"Then for a prænomen he chose what expressed to himself yet concealed from others his real intention in taking sides with the colonists against those principles which he had revered, if indeed he ever genuinely revered anything—against allegiance to Church and King. 'Israel-for-Israel' meant to him, 'Myself for myself, and the devil take these whining fanatics after I get through using them for my own purpose.'"

"My dear sir," I interposed, now standing and quite forgetful of my fatigue. "My dear sir! This about your own great-grandfather!"

"I mean," said Israel, "that he was an adventurer like many others whose selfish ambition was very serviceable to the just and righteous cause of independence. That is all I mean."

Perhaps Israel knew that the moral character of his remote ancestor made no difference to me,—who am, nevertheless, personally an honest and honorable man, I hope, and who love honesty and honor in my contemporaries. To how many of us would it have made a difference? Of those who sincerely revere the memory of Oliver Cromwell and in argument re-condemn Charles Stuart to death as a just punishment visited upon a tyrant, how many would prefer to derive their descent from the Protector rather than from the first Charles, King of England? Our sentiment of aristocracy is in this plainly distinct from our sense of morality. The man of the world says to himself, The world may be moved by either sentiment —either superiority or goodness: I take my choice.

Israel continued: " When, after Gates's terrible defeat at Camden, Greene was appointed to the command of our forces in the South, my ancestor served under him.

" This appointment of General Greene seems to me to have been the turning point in the war. From the moment when those scattered forces, which without a common plan of action had nevertheless held their own against the British, were placed in the hands of one resolute soldier, as Greene certainly was, the issue could no longer be doubtful. That Israel-for-Israel realized this fully at the time, I do not assert. I simply mention the circumstance that he cast in his lot with the Americans at this juncture.

"In the memorable retreat through the Carolinas, he bore a part. In the battle of Guilford, 15th March, 1781, he charged with Washington's cavalry; and an incident of that charge brings him forward in a creditable manner.

"The brunt of this engagement was borne, on the American side, by a regiment of Marylanders. It was to support this regiment that the charge was commanded.

"The detachment of the British, thus assailed, wavered; but Stuart, who lead them, succeeded in rallying his men and himself sprang upon Captain Smith of the Marylanders. 'The latter, parrying Stuart's small-sword with his left hand, brought down his heavy sabre on his head with such force that he cleaved him to the spine. The next moment, wounded by a musket-ball, he fell upon his antagonist. Scarcely had he touched the body when the soldier who had fired the shot also fell across him,' struck down by the sabre of Israel-for-Israel, who spurred all alone among the guards. In an instant the rest of the cavalry followed and the battle would have been won, had it not been for the artillery of Cornwallis, which now opened upon friend and foe alike.

"The field remained with the British commander, and it was supposed that the young cavalryman who had come to the front at a critical moment had fallen in the subsequent indiscriminate slaughter, for he did not rejoin his company.

"But what seemed for the moment to be a British victory, turned out to be in effect defeat. Cornwallis had lost one-fourth of his army and began a precipitate retreat.

"Cornwallis retreating into South Carolina, Greene followed him.

"After suffering another defeat at the hands of Rawdon, Greene joined General Marion, who had been pressing the siege of Fort Motte. Here Israel-for-Israel, who had joined Marion's command shortly before, reappeared.

"Fort Motte fell. Israel-for-Israel again served in Greene's command, was present at the storming of Ninety-Six, at the disgraceful battle of Eutaw Springs and the capture of Charleston, where he took the fever and retired to the bracing air of New England to regain his health.

"The convalescent had been faithfully nursed by a certain Prudence Johnson,— my great-grandmother. He married her and through her secured this sterile farm at Oskawask.

"During a relapse, Prudence Johnson heard the sick man raving about hidden treasures and Indians and a guardian of the hoard — never once about the war scenes in which he had been an actor. After his recovery he still brooded, and in answer to his wife's repeated inquiries finally told her that when the battle of Guilford turned unfavorably to the Americans, he formed a sudden resolution to join the band of partisans who supported the invincible Marion.

"The last reports received from Marion indicated that he was about to raid in the vicinity of Augusta. Taking this as his objective point, my ancestor from the very field of battle, alone and without a guide and with little knowledge of the country, struck off to the westward.

"Becoming involved in the spurs of the Blue Ridge mountains, he lost himself completely in their defiles.

"Judging that it would be hopeless to seek for a pass and fatal to abandon the direct south-westerly course which he had hitherto followed, he sacrificed his horse and on foot undertook to climb the mountains which rose before him.

"After a week of incredible hardship he reached the southern boundary of this rocky wall. There a landscape of perfect beauty was unfolded before him.

"I ought to have said that his greatest inconvenience was due to the fear of hostile Indians, into whose hands he barely escaped falling time and again. This being the favorite hunting-ground of the red men, it seems miraculous that he could have passed through it unharmed. Strangely enough, this last southern eminence was entirely free from the red tormentors. There was no game there, either.

"Amazed by this circumstance, he ascended the highest point of the mountain and looked about him.

"The mountain stood alone, separated by a narrow valley from the general range, which here trends north-east and south-west. For five miles on either hand, like a great wall, it stretched away with an almost even elevation.

"A mountain ten or twelve miles long, three or four miles in width: he the only human being there.

"The point where he stood dominated the whole mountain, even as the mountain itself, standing alone and as it were in advance of the great army of peaks to the northward, seemed to dominate them all.

"Enjoying the security of this point and impressed by the mystery of the great silence, my ancestor rested here and strengthened himself for the journey still before him. Evidently the most difficult portion of his journey was past; for far as the eye could see to the southward, there stretched out a great plain, across which he could make his way with comparative ease.

"In the mystery of this great silence he passed the night. Stretched upon the bare rock he heard, or fancied he heard, as the night fell and the sounds of the woods ceased with the breeze which had blown warm from the southern plain,—in that more perfect stillness, with his face pressed against the rock, he seemed to hear in it, within it, beneath it, a faint groaning and sighing, as though from a spirit imprisoned within the heart of the mountain.

"By the first light of the following morning he descended the mountain and came upon a torrent which, issuing from a cavern only a thousand feet or so below the summit, fell in a slender column of spray so far down in sheer descent that the noise of its fall scarcely ascended to its source. There even the voice of the waters was hushed in the universal silence."

"Is this a fairy-tale, my dear sir?" I exclaimed. "There is no sufficient explanation, following your description, at least, of a considerable supply of water at so great an altitude."

"I don't answer for a word of the whole legend," Israel said, with a laugh. "My authority is parson Dewback, and I am using his own words, pretty nearly."

"Go on, go on," I said; "I accept it, then, as you tell it."

Israel continued to walk up and down the room with a certain leonine impatience. As he passed before me, he looked at me with a peculiar expression, half searching, half mocking, and proceeded:

"The first thing that struck my ancestor was that this stream must be the issue of an underground current which had groaned and sighed to him through the rock above.

"The next thing was, that the cavern was much higher and broader than so small a stream required for its passage, and that he might as well ascertain how far it extended.

"He went in and up until he made sure that it was growing larger instead of contracting. . . . . I say, think of looking from this dark cave, from its utter darkness, where the splashing and roaring waters sounded like the voices of a thousand devils after the stillness outside,—looking through a circular opening below one, seeing through this opening, thousands of feet below, the giant pines of the plain, in size like blades of grass, standing on their tops or seeming rather to be suspended from a solid heaven! There is nothing about that in the story, but it occurs to me.

"Well, he noticed that the floor of the cavern spread out to a considerable size, that it was fairly even and covered with gravel and small stones.

"Having no light, he contented himself

with this for the time, filled his pockets with loose bits from the floor and retraced his steps.

"Arrived at the entrance, he emptied his pockets. They contained ——"

Israel paused an instant before me, looking down at me with a smile.

"They contained fragments of rich gold-ore and the head of a stone implement, like a rude hammer-head. That is all.

"When he thought to go back into the cavern, he saw, seated within in the shadow of the entrance, a gigantic figure, apparently sleeping with head bowed upon his knees. He might have passed this sleeping guardian without perceiving him, for the motionless gray figure was like a great fragment of granite. He might have stolen in a second time without being perceived; but he did not attempt it. He said: 'That thing was not there when I went in or when I came out;' and he confessed to his wife, Prudence, that he was greatly terrified, because he had believed himself to be alone upon the mountain.

"That is about all of the story as parson Dewback unearthed it.

"My great-grandfather served under

Marion and Greene until the termination of the war in the South, as already related; but that he understood the art of peace as well as war is shown in this, that he yielded to the curiosity of the wife of his bosom, my great-grandmother. This complaisance can, however, hardly be regarded as a mark of attachment; for he soon left her. He never ceased, so the legend runs, after the subject had been once broached, to refer to this treasure in the Carolinas. He was discontented at home, and it was possibly a relief to my great-grandmother when, after a few years, he went away. He was never heard of afterwards.

"That is the end of Israel-for-Israel Slyme. All that is left of him you have seen, Mr. Penman: his descendants, who have forgotten him and his portrait, rescued from the garret."

The story had been told half earnestly, half flippantly. I knew that Israel must be genuinely interested, from the importance which he attached to the portrait; but he made no apparent effort to interest. He seemed to be telling the story with a view to finding out how it would impress the listener.

The result was that this absence of effort made the narrative all the more impressive. I was affected in a manner which will be described in the next chapter.

THE STORM

HEN Israel bade me good-night and descended to his place by the fire, I was not by any means in the mood for sleep.

The storm, which had been holding some of its forces in reserve for a final, decisive attack, now advanced with a mighty purpose to establish King Winter in the bleak New England territory and drive out or imprison every remaining adherent of Summer. On it came with a resistless charge, while the tall trees bent before it, the free waters shivered beneath it and the submissive earth shrivelled and chapped and hardened in roughness.

Every form of life which the kindlier season calls into being submitted. Only man, who constructs and maintains about himself a feeble imitation of the kindly season, opposed resistance to the invader. So then the great wind fell upon the dwellings of men, tugged away at their eaves to unroof them, battered against their sides to level them with the ground, and, with cunning not inferior to its strength, insinuated itself between the window-sashes, crept in through every crevice, to steal away the very spirit of resistance from the garrison within, while the ice-crowned emperor of half the world from without commanded, Surrender!

At least once a year, even the staunchest son of New England is tempted to yield. Why not surrender to this bitter, tireless antagonist, and, withdrawing to the generous southern country, live at peace with the climate—not, as here, barely exist in spite of the climate?

Traitorous thought! When once this suggestion has spoken distinctly within the breast, our defenses are down. How the icy wind then bites and rasps and embitters! How we hate everything and everybody; and especially, how the trembling and creaking and groaning of an old house, beset by the first terrible storm of winter, is to us the language of our own mutinous spirit.

S-s-vish!—bang! commanded the wind, laying hold on both gables at once and tugging away.

Oo-oo-woe! roared the old house through its chimney.

"Br-r-r-r," I chattered beneath several blankets. "I wonder if that questionable ancient Slyme, whom the yellow fever sent from the Carolinas to New England, and the gold-fever took away from New England to the Carolinas, ever slept in this house. It looks old enough. It can never outlast this generation, if indeed it withstands this storm. One comfort is, it's too late in the year for a cyclone or a tornado."

Ziz-z-z-z—rei! shrieked the storm wind, tearing a shutter from its fastenings and with it belaboring the wall near my head; then wrenching it entirely free and whirling it away like a leaf.

At the same instant there was a dull rumbling sound of bricks falling within the chimney.

This was too much for me. I went across the bare floor to the mantel-piece and lighted the tallow-dip; then took a long pull at a pocket flask, containing spirits of matured virtue, and speedily tumbled back into bed.

The candle illuminated with a flickering light the portrait of Israel-for-Israel.

I was stouter-hearted now, owing to the warmth which radiated, as it were, from the stomach.

"I have never met a more interesting person than this young fellow," I reflected. "Such courtesy, such superiority, such open-heartedness, such a pair of shoulders—all these united in one person and that one person a country lad on a puckertown farm! It is as incredible as a newspaper.

"What impresses me most is his open-heartedness. He speaks to me, an entire stranger, with a freedom I could not use until I had known a person intimately for years. I suppose he does not know fear in any of its forms. He barely glances at me once and then welcomes me, gives up his own room to me, with the air of an hospitable lord.

"I express a little interest in a picture: that is enough for him. He tells me the whole story to the end with artistic simplicity.

"But this complaisance is so far removed from servility that somehow every service he renders increases my respect for him.

"His open countenance discloses his inmost thought."

Here I looked up at the portrait to confirm my judgment.

Strange! There was no such genial look in the face before me. On the contrary, the resemblance of this old portrait to the young man had disappeared. The face upon the wall had lengthened, changing the whole expression and even the shape of the features. There were still the dark, crisp hair and vivacious eyes, but the forehead stood out prominently and was scarred by a deep, perpendicular line. The eyes had retired cavernously and the light in them was not dancing, but a steady gleam. The nose was thinner and slightly aquiline. The lips wore a sinister, cruel expression.

"The lips!" I exclaimed. "I must have been dreaming! This ancient Slyme wears heavy mustaches hiding his mouth and a beard which covers the mark on his cheek. I don't wonder he wants to hide such an evil expression and such an awful mark: a blood-red spade, that seems a sore ready to burst. See! It throbs like a pulse, showing that it reaches to the heart. . . . . Fudge and nonsense! I am, with due respect to myself, either a fool or an idiot. The old fellow hasn't a bit more beard than the back of my hand. It is a young, smooth, extremely handsome face — the face of a fine gentleman. I might as well put out the light and go to sleep; much better than making a fool of myself over this preposterous Winter's Tale."

The wind was wrestling with a second window-blind as I, in consequence of this resolution, slipped out of bed and was about to extinguish the candle.

"Good night," said I, holding the light before the dark canvass and scrutinizing the features more closely than ever before.

There it was, starting out from the darkness, — the youthful, strong, aristocratic face, with a minute mark upon the right cheek.

"Good night, ancient vagabond!" I said.

Either a disdainful expression passed over the face and curled the lips of Israel-for-Israel, or my flickering candle was at fault. It can never be known which; for when I attempted to discover the source and origin of such suggestions by a still more searching examination, — this time without all nonsense,—

Bang, bang! the shutter thrashed against the clapboards.

Ou-oo-ouf! groaned the chimney.

And one sharp-shooting blast sped right to the mark; so that while the general volley discharged by the storm passed by harmlessly, this particular gust put out my light and made the frame just before my face rattle against the wall with the hollow sound of old dead things. It passed beneath my one garment and ran like a cold hand over my body.

I shivered, whether with cold or fear, threw my top-coat over my shoulders, made a vain effort to pull the right boot on the left foot and, failing in that, crept in my stocking-feet down the stairs.

Reaching the foot of the staircase, I noticed that a flood of light poured through a wide crack in the warped door out into the passage. Here I hesitated for an instant.

Some random idea entering my head, or perhaps only my habitual caution prompting me thereto, I did not either open the door or knock at it without first reconnoitering by means of this aperture, which rendered a portion of the interior visible—that is, by bending or stooping somewhat.

In this way I informed myself as to the condition of things within.

Several fresh logs had been added to the fire and the flame was devouring these in the fierce draft with its eager tongue.

Seated before this and looking fixedly into it sat Israel upon the floor—or rather on a spread of some kind laid down upon the floor.

He was fairly transfigured in this great light, which made a glory around about him.

Lying with her head pillowed upon his knees, her face upturned towards his, her almost girlish figure stretched out so that the warmth poured over and covered her, slept Lilly.

She was motionless in the deep sleep of perfect contentment.

While I, spell-bound by the vision of beautiful creatures—beautiful as gods in this perfect naturalness—still bent over and devoured with my eyes now his perfection, now hers, Israel turned his head and looked down into the face of his companion.

Was it possible? That very expression of disdain which I had fancied that I had caught upon the face of the portrait! To see it upon the face of a lover whose mistress was sleeping within his embrace!

An exclamation escaped me. It was only half uttered, half suppressed; yet like a flash the eyes of Israel were fastened upon the door. I thought that such a glance must discover me in my concealment. It seemed to pierce the very boards of the partition.

But as a flash, so this glance ended, fell upon the happy, upturned face of the sleeper, then changed into a smile. He muttered something—perhaps, 'It was only the wind'; at least he looked again into the fire and the glory of the fire was again about his head and Lilly's form.

I stole noiselessly away.

Through half that night the storm raged until the whole land submitted to fierce King Winter. Within the old house, which held its own against the invader, save for the loss of several shutters and of a brick or two from the chimney-top, some of us rested sluggishly, one tossed about, getting little rest, one saw his own thoughts glowing in the wood coals, one tender little lady slept in the security and perfect peace of love.

Before dawn all was still, both within and without the old walls. The sun rose in a cloudless sky, and the morning smiled —coldly, it is true, but yet it smiled.

It smiled upon me through the curtainless and shutterless window while I was making a hasty toilet. It lighted up every nook and corner of the stairway and passage, which had seemed so mysterious the night before; and as I descended I thought how pitiful and plain and commonplace every object there was, after all.

Mrs. Slyme and her two daughters were bustling about in the kitchen.

"And where is Israel?" I asked, after the greetings had been interchanged.

"Israel is gone with Lilly to 'tend her home," said the mother.

"Yes, he does everything for her, doesn't he sister?" said Grace. "And father's down at the falls."

"Yes, father loves to go to the falls whenever he can, doesn't he, sister?" said Gertrude.

"Is it far to the falls?" I inquired.

"Oh, no; just at the bottom of the garden."

"Just at the foot of the hill," chimed in Grace.

"Would it be asking too much of you to show me the way?" I asked, addressing myself to the last speaker.

Grace looked at Gertrude and Gertrude looked at Grace. They were not to be separated.

"Perhaps you will both honor me——" I began.

"Run along, girls, and tell father to come in to breakfast," cried Mrs. Slyme.

The young girls drew their shawls over their heads and shoulders and started out, their arms around each other.

I confessed to myself that they were charming. Together they made one charming person, with one will and one heart, but four red cheeks and two pairs of crimson lips.

Ah, but a young girl, dancing along a path across the fields in the open air of a bright November morning, who is not pretty then! Who ever heard of such a thing? Especially after my restless, lonely night, I will surely not be blamed for thinking them so.

The sisters leading, we followed the course of the weedy stream, which itself followed the windings of the sandy hill until, suddenly turning away from this, it made a dash towards the south, with a display of spirit which surprised the observer coming upon it from above. Freeing itself by a single leap, it sped along merrily, in active independence, as far as one could see from this point.

At this point stood Jonathan Slyme. It was too cold for him to be whittling; but with hands plunged into his deep pockets, he was fumbling the wooden model that we know, his horn-handled knife, and whatever else those pockets contained.

He was looking first up and then down the stream as the party of three approached—an occupation which he intermitted for an instant in order to nod to the stranger, without, however, addressing a single word to him.

The girls took possession of their father, one holding each arm, and led him back towards the house.

"That there is the best place and the easiest to make a mill-dam in this county," drawled the man, speaking to anybody or nobody, when about to pass through the door.

*　　*　　*　　*　　*　　*

After a substantial breakfast, the entire

family followed their departing guest down the front walk to the lilac trees.

Before mounting I put my hand into my pocket, asking Jonathan Slyme: "How much do I owe for the lodging, my friend?"

"Nawthing, sir."

But Mrs. Slyme came forward.

"If you will kindly give me one of the buttons from your coat, sir——" she suggested.

I took out my pen-knife, thinking that she had asked a very small return for the service rendered me, and was deciding which button I should sacrifice, when she said:

"I have the scissors right here, sir."

1864.

IN the year 1864 I escaped from a Southern prison.

In company with old sergeant Ezekiel Perkins, without whose aid I could not have either effected my escape or survived the hardships of the subsequent flight, I made my way through the mountains of North Carolina towards the Northern lines.

Pressing forward by night and lying hidden during the day, we found ourselves one morning just before daybreak in the neighborhood of what appeared to be a deserted and ruinous town. One ugly brick edifice, with iron bars at the the windows, was frightfully suggestive of that abode of misery from which we had escaped; besides this there were half-a-dozen shanties or hovels and the decaying walls of what had once been a planter's homestead.

This wretched, dreary place accorded well with the condition of ragged, half-starved fugitives; and our hunger gave us boldness to remain near the edge of the clearing about the town in the hope of finding some opportunity to obtain food.

There was no sign of life anywhere, even after the sun rose, until finally from one of the hovels crept forth a negro man, almost destitute of clothing, who seated himself at the threshold in the sunlight, shutting himself up like a jack-knife. We had recently learned only too well what that position meant: it meant that the black man was starving.

Without further hesitation we went forward and questioned this representative of the race in whose behalf a great war was being waged.

He said that he had been a slave of Colonel Owner, whose plantation lay a few miles to the westward; and then he told about his master's death and about Squire Lynch who had lived "over yonder", pointing to the ruinous mansion, where no person had dared to dwell since the blood-marks had been tracked up the stairs. This he explained as well as he could and said the place was called Americus City, although it was a cursed spot, and lately all the inhabitants, even the prisoners who had been released from the jail for that purpose, had gone away to fight.

And the women?

He did not know what had become of them.

Again and again he besought the two soldiers to give him bread, and he refused to be persuaded that white men also could be without food.

This inborn and ineradicable belief in the superiority of white men moved the good Perkins so that he forgot his own condition and swore " by the Etarnal " to give that negro one good meal, if it took a week.

It did take all of that day.

"Who is the nearest neighbor?" we asked.

The negro pointed to a mountain which rose just above the town.

"Come along!" cried Perkins, and seized the negro by the arm. "Come along and we'll git ye somethin' ter eat!"

But the negro expressed all the terror of which a human being is capable. His eyes rolled until only the whites were visible; his teeth chattered; he shook all over as with a violent chill. Neither persuasion nor threats took any effect upon him. He said that the Devil lived upon that mountain; he had rather die than go there.

We left him in the power of that fear and struck right through the woods, in the direction indicated by "Caesar" (so the negro gave his name). If a planter lives here, we will soon come upon a road leading to his house, we reasoned. But no. On and on we went, the forest becoming only more wild, the trees larger and the silence more oppressive.

We had begun to ascend the mountain.

"We may as well go high enough to get a view. Then we can surely see the house," I suggested.

But higher and still higher upwards we climbed without being able to look off through the luxuriant foliage and rank growth.

"I guess I might shin up this here and take a look for that gol' durned house", said Perkins, laying his hand upon the trunk of an enormous magnolia tree.

"I think I would not try", I answered, pointing to a piece of rope, dangling from the lowest limb and a small heap of bones below it. "That has a disagreeable look."

Presently we were guided by the sound of rushing waters and came upon a beautiful wild stream, tumbling down the mountain side. The course of this we followed upwards until finally we were repaid with an extended prospect.

The whole country was spread out at our feet. There was Americus City itself, "like a scurf-spot," said Perkins; but no plantation or planter's house.

"*Good* day, gentle-*men*", spoke a smooth, velvety voice almost in our ears.

We turned quickly and filled with sudden fear, as you may imagine; but only to find that the voice proceeded from an inoffensive looking, tall, thin man, very plainly but most neatly dressed in a gray suit, wide-brimmed hat and stout walking-shoes. He was very thin, that was the only peculiar thing in his appearance—except, of course, that he had appeared at all. He was leaning against a tree-trunk and when he saw that he had secured the attention of the two soldiers he lifted his hat politely and deferentially.

"Excuse the interruption, gentle-*men*," he continued, after the long pause in which the startled fugitives had stared at him in stupid amazement: "I supposed you might be looking for my master's house."

Receiving no immediate answer,—for this remark only added to the surprise which he had already excited—he indicated, by waving his hand, what he had called his master's house.

There it was, surely enough, not far off; and yet it is scarcely surprising that we, weary soldiers, whose eyes had either been fastened upon the ground before us, as we climbed the steep and difficult way, or turned from the mountain, seeking the plantation upon the plain below,—it is not surprising that we had not noticed this house, still somewhat above us.

Such a house! If the largest forest trees had fallen together in regular order, their great trunks crossing and forming a hollow square, upon which some skillful workman had then fitted a sloping roof with wide eaves, the result would have been such a house.

Such a house! It was in the forest and of the forest. Externally the gigantic logs were untrimmed, untouched, save for being fitted together at the extremities. The thing had been done with such care that it seemed the work of chance. Surely the storm wind made this house and man only put the finishing touches.

Such a palace! From without it appeared rude; not a bit of cultivation about it; unbroken forest to its very eaves. But within!—smooth and polished and shining floor and walls and vaulted ceiling of the natural wood. Even here art seemed to be held in check.

One enormous chamber, one vast fireplace, one great window, filled with lozenge-shaped panes of glass, commanding the southern view, the western end of the chamber curtained off, as though for a sleeping apartment, an assortment of firearms,—bird-guns, rifles and revolvers—in a case near the door, a generous table: think what such a sight must have been to two famished wanderers, who had tasted nothing better than prison fare for months and not a morsel, good or bad, for twenty-four hours!

That table was a sight never to be forgotten.

There were mountain trout, brown and crisp; there was a juicy leg of mutton, smoking hot; there was the incomparable ham, the sweet, mast-fed ham of the Carolinas; there was a small mountain of snowy bread and a dish of golden butter next a pot of golden honey; there were fruits, especially grapes, in a kind of woven basket and there were crystal pitchers filled with richly-colored wines.

These things—which seem plain and simple enough, being written down here and read of us who have just risen from or are just going to seat ourselves at a similar table,—think how these viands, placed upon a great round slab of polished oak, must have charmed the eyes of starving men!

"My master's breakfast is prepared, as you see, gentle-*men*. I expect him every moment."

"Who *is* your master?" I asked.

"Captain Johnson. Hark! there he comes with the hounds, gentle-*men!*" said the thin man in gray.

The two soldiers exchanged glances full of meaning.

"'Captain,'" I said.

"Confed. captain," echoed Sergeant Perkins, in the same tone in which he might have said, Confounded captain. "*And* hounds," he added.

"Captain Johnson will be delighted to see you, gentlemen. He never allows strangers to come here; but friends, gentlemen he knows,—it never happened before, because his hounds are very fierce, splendid animals, gentle*men!* *You* will appreciate them, gentle*men*. As I was about to take the liberty to say, it never happened before that friends of my master came here; but he will be delighted, no doubt, none at all."

As the polite man in gray uttered this in a bland, drawling tone, rubbing his hands together and bowing repeatedly, first to me and then to Sergeant Perkins, there came into his lean and strongly-marked face a certain sly and evil expression, not at all reassuring.

Companions in arms and in misfortune, sergeant and lieutenant acted upon a common impulse in hastening from the house. Then we heard, borne upon a gentle breeze and mellowed by the distance, the cry of a pack of hounds. We did not cease to hasten, in fact we ran at full speed, with many falls by the way but fortunately without serious injury, down the mountain side until we hoped we were out of reach and knew we were out of breath. Then we fell upon the earth and rested.

I had never aspired to the distinction of being a very brave man (thus I reasoned, within myself, while gasping for breath); but Ezekiel Perkins was brave, as everybody admitted. If anybody ever made fun of me, Lieutenant Penman, for running away from the captain of ever so many blood hounds, for vindication I should simply refer the scoffer to Sergeant Perkins.

Having settled this point satisfactorily, my hollow stomach prompted the next thought, which found utterance:

"Think of that ham, Perkins!"

"What can we do for pore Caesar?" the other said, showing that his thoughts had taken a very different turn, much to his credit.

"We might go back to the road and follow it until we come to a house."

"Ef they don't keep blood-hounds, all right," he assented.

So we trudged along and did finally get what we wanted. A large, squarely-built man, who looked somewhat like a parson and rather more like an hotel keeper, who lived in a large square house, not only gave to us but gave the best he had; and when we had eaten he added for our journey a large loaf and a jar of jelly.

He was disposed to enter into conversation, telling us that his name was Oldboy and that if any person molested us were to say that we knew him, when it would immediately "be all right." But Ezekiel Perkins was impatient, finished his meal hastily and, seizing the loaf and the jelly, started up.

"Yes, we must be going, and we thank you, sir, more than ——" I began.

"Oh, that will be all right, I reckon! Remember, Oldboy is the name!" he interrupted; and he waved his hand to us with quite a grand gesture as we turned down the red-clay road.

We returned with all speed and with lighter hearts to "Americus City;" but when, late in the afternoon, we reached that ill-fated town, its last inhabitant, "pore feller Caesar," as Ezekiel Perkins said, with trouble and complaint and lament in his rough voice,—"pore Caesar" was dead.

1882

R. and Mrs. Crosstrees occupy the largest house fronting the Oldhaven green. True, their house can not be called a strictly handsome one; for in spite of its six or seven stories piled one upon the other, and in spite of its imposing ground-plan, which gives the structure a solid and substantial appearance, showing clearly that it was built before the day of elevators or lifts; in spite of its thousands of panes of shining window glass, a red and white barber's pole protruding from one corner and a black and gilt sign, bearing the inscription "T. R. Houser, Tailor," mar the architectural effect.

Mr. and Mrs. Crosstrees are always "at home." No matter at what hour you may see fit to call upon them—early morning, noon, midnight—always they are prepared to receive you and indeed overjoyed to entertain you. The longer you stay, the better are they pleased. Coming with or without introduction to them, it makes no difference. Coming singly or with all the good friends you have in the world, one and all will be given the freedom of the house and the table. Such hospitality seems truly princely; yet Mr. and Mrs. Crosstrees are not even aristocrats.

Hospitality has been the mark and the distinction of the upper classes throughout the history of our race. Even in the earliest times we find Hrothgar, the treasure-giver, most praised as he dispenses hospitality in the high hall, Heorot, while queen Waeltheow bears about cups of mead to the guests. And yet Mr. and Mrs. Crosstrees, the proprietors of so large a hall, the tireless host and hostess of the Elm House, are not even aristocrats.

"Perhaps that fact may be explained by the manner in which they dispense hospitality," someone suggests.

Dear sir, nothing could exceed their fitness for this occupation. Their manner is perfection itself. Even in person they seem to have been designed by nature to complement each other and together to discharge every duty of the complete host. Mr. Crosstrees is very large and very stout—too large and too stout for the smaller rooms of this great house; but in the vast dining hall, or in the hallway, or expanding upon the broad sidewalk before his hospitably wide front door, he truly leaves nothing to be desired. He occupies his house. No one could do it better. But of course it is imperatively necessary that such a house as this, in order to be truly hospitable, should be occupied by its host; and accordingly Mr. Crosstrees is proud and happy in the thought that he does his duty and can not help doing his duty, when he stands with one puffy hand fumbling his heavy watch-chain, which is drawn through the lowest button-hole in that mountainous region of his waistcoat, while with the other puffy hand he draws out to their greatest length his bushy side-whiskers in order to increase by their addition his lateral extent, bowing and smiling to every person who comes in or passes out and equally ready to exclaim genially that it is a fine day to a guest who looks ruddy, or with a shudder to protest to a guest who looks pinched that it is "bitter cold indeed, sir!"

Mrs. Crosstrees does not occupy the

house, nor is it even an easy matter to find her in any one smallest corner of it at a given time. She is a short, thin, midge of a woman, who darts from garret to cellar, from front to rear, always choosing narrow doors for her sudden and noiseless exits and entrances, narrow and dark passages for her going and coming; always pouncing upon some idling servant girl and stinging her into a sense of duty, doing wonders in wardrobes and pantries and such small nooks, always active, everywhere useful, seldom seen. Mrs. Crosstrees keeps the "Elm House." Surely no guest has just cause to complain of an hotel thus occupied and kept by Mr. and Mrs. Crosstrees.

One day, a few years ago, these good people were in a most unusual situation,— that is, in the same room, although it was high noon.

This is a circumstance so exceptional that it is to be observed at only one period in the entire year. Merely to mention it brings to our minds the conviction that the dull season had settled heavily down upon Oldhaven. The Elm House, sensible of this condition of the town generally, required so little occupying on the part of its landlord, and so little keeping on the part of its landlady, that both of these efficient persons found their occupations gone during a portion of the day, and improved the opportunity for seeing something of each other in a new light —namely, the daylight.

It was, in fact, the middle of August. The air was heavy and motionless. It seemed to be laid upon the city and to press down upon the spirits of men with an intolerable weight. People had gone away to the mountains, to the sea-shore, to Europe. The Elm House guests were to be found wherever the winds blow.

Although long experience had taught them not to expect any person at this season, and especially at this hour of the day, yet Mr. and Mrs. Crosstrees were occupying and keeping a room which commanded a view of the approaches to the front door of the Elm House from all directions. From force of habit, it would seem, Mrs. Crosstrees had out her pocket-handkerchief and was flicking imaginary particles of dust from the cover of a small table which stood in the window; while Mr. Crosstrees stood upon the central rose of the flowery carpet, bowing and smiling at his helpmeet and observing frequently that it *was* a very warm day.

"It might be worse," spoke up the little woman, when he had given utterance to this sentiment for the seventh time.

"Very true, *very* true, my dear," he rejoined with a beaming and responsive expression; continuing then, as though she had said something further of a cheerful nature, "Yes, indeed: I hope so, indeed!"

"Crosstrees!" she cried in her biting way. "You are a—— Why! there's someone knocking!" and she darted to the door.

It was the hall-boy. "Gelm'n down stairs," he muttered.

"A gentleman down stairs!" repeated Mr. Crosstrees. "And how did the gentleman arrive, Sidney? I have not seen any gentleman drive up, or walk up, or come up, I think." Nevertheless he did follow the nimble hall-boy, bowing as he went.

A very thin man, in rough traveling suit and tall hat, stood at the office, entering his name in the register. Crosstrees advanced to within a few feet of the stranger, and then, striking his inevitable attitude, said in his blandest tones:

"Ah! A very warm day, sir!"

The stranger completed the entry, blotted it carefully, and laid down the pen before answering. Then, without turning his head, he replied: "Rather. Can you give me rooms, Mr. Crosstrees?"

"Certainly, certainly, sir! When will the other gentlemen arrive, sir?—or perhaps Madame—(here he read the name over the stranger's shoulder)—perhaps Madame Gray?"

"There are no other gentlemen; but I want two or three large rooms adjoining —opening into one another, Mr. Crosstrees, if you please."

"Certainly, Mr. Gray. Undoubtedly, sir!" cried the delighted landlord, before whose mental vision a vista of unexpected profits began to disclose itself. "You can be accommodated, sir, I should hope!" Here he glanced again at the entry in the register. "From Oldhaven, sir! You are of our town? Now I flattered myself that I had some acquaintance among the leading families, in the way of my business, sir, but your name and your face are— until this moment have been——"

"I have not lived here before, Mr. Crosstrees, my good sir," interrupted the stranger in a very polite and insinuating manner; "but at present here I am and here I mean to remain. That will not be unpleasant to the good people of your lovely city, I sincerely trust."

"Quite the contrary, quite the contrary: most agreeable and flattering, Mr. Gray. And permit me to say that you could not have chosen a more favorable point to alight and begin your acquaintance with our town—our lovely city, as you say,— than the Elm House. Here you will find all the comforts—I think I may say it, sir, for I ought to know—all the comforts of home; and among the guests of the Elm House you will meet many of our best people, belonging to the most exclusive circles. To be sure," he added with some misgiving, "this is not exactly the most favorable season. You happen in upon us during the quiet season, Mr. Gray." This was said in an indefinitely generous fashion, as though to intimate that at other times great crowds surged along the pavements and a press of vehicles blocked the way before the Elm House.

"Never mind that," said the agreeable

Mr. Gray. "This quiet season is most suitable for my purpose, about which, by the way, I should like to have a few words with you, my good sir; for I see that you are a man of the world who understands that it is for the advantage of his city to encourage strangers to settle—strangers who have a little money to invest, you know. Eh? Mr. Crosstrees, that helps things along, I reckon, eh?"

Thereupon Mr. Gray and Mr. Crosstrees adjourned to the reading-room and entered into a conversation in which the latter became so absorbed that he was only recalled to a realization of his other duties by the entrance of the hall-boy, summoning him to superintend the final preparations for dinner. This conversation we shall not report in full; for anyone who desires may hear it word for word from the worthy landlord's own lips.

It is not too much to say that it made a tremendous impression upon Mr. Crosstrees. This affable Mr. Gray! How modestly and genially he at first proceeded to interest the listener in vivid descriptions of travel and adventure, touching upon the wonderful and beautiful cities and palaces and hotels which he had seen in all parts of the world, with such power of word-painting that even the heavy-witted Crosstrees seemed to see the glories of Europe and Asia and Chicago and California pass in review before his fascinated gaze! How deftly then he changed the theme from himself, who had enjoyed all these advantages, who knew all languages and had conversed with all the magnates and celebrities of the earth in their respective native tongues,—from himself, who lived like a prince, requiring the best *suite* of apartments and the best "turn out" to be held for his exclusive use, to his master!

His master! The attentive auditor could not trust his ears. Surely he had mistaken the word. But no: Mr. Gray repeated the startling expression; and if he had shown himself an interesting talker when the subject had been his own experiences, how eloquent did he become in praise of this master! Surely, surely, nothing in real-life had ever approached the magnificence of this being whose forerunner and herald and humble servitor Mr. Gray himself was. If Mr. Gray, secretary to Donald Livingstone, Esquire, can be satisfied with nothing less than the best rooms in the Elm House, what must Donald Livingstone, Esquire, be, and wherewith can he be satisfied? That was indeed a question enticing Mr. Crosstrees' imagination into unknown regions where he felt unsafe and nothing seemed real.

One thing, however, was clear: Donald Livingstone in his own good time was coming to Oldhaven, and Oldhaveners would some day awaken to the fact that there was a great and good man in the country whose existence they had hitherto ignored. He was not merely a millionaire. (Mr. Gray darkly hinted that perhaps the most colossal fortunes were those of which the existence was not even suspected by the public. A careful financier, he suggested, might distribute his securities so widely that only a few millions would be found in any one market.) Oh, no; he was not merely such a millionaire, but a person of magnificent abilities, a clean record (Mr. Gray did not intimate that "clean record" and obscure past were equipollent terms), and of a charming and commanding presence.

Donald Livingstone was about to return to America after a prolonged absence and much travel in foreign countries, where he had devoted himself with all his vast intellectual resources to the study of various forms of society and government. He was now intending to enter public life in his native land, and had chosen Oldhaven for his residence because the reputation which that town bears for learning and solid merit assured him that he would find congenial spirits there. This preference he accorded to Oldhaven rather than to another American city, it was most significantly added, notwithstanding the fact that he had already an enviable reputation as well as great social and political influence elsewhere. His business connections extended like a network throughout the West, while in the South he had enormous estates.

We can hardly censure our fleshy and commonplace host for the simple delight he took in this wondrous tale. As a substantial citizen he was, with good right, concerned for the prosperity of his city, which the coming of such a grand personage would greatly promote. He wanted to believe that Donald Livingstone, Esquire, was the wealthiest and most excellent of living men; and which one of us can afford to cast the first stone at a decent fellow who believes what he wants to believe?

If Secretary Gray had in view certain ends of his own when he thus favored his host with a friendly exhibition of his conversational powers, he probably was gratified with the result. The immediate consequences were twofold: Mr. Crosstrees trumpeted it with full cheeks. No person in Oldhaven occupied a better position for publishing a bit of interesting news far and wide. As proprietor of the most popular hotel, and as habitually stationing himself in its hallway or doorway in the manner which has been noticed, the whole population was, so to speak, within reach of his voice. If we had a civic Fame, that divinity smiled, and bowed, and fumbled its watch-chain hospitably and expansively in the Elm House. So, then, every person who had remained in Oldhaven through the dull month of August knew that a great and good man intended to honor the town. If our publican Fame uttered extravagances in this connection, those of a skeptical turn ascribed so much as they could not believe to Crosstrees' human side and believed the rest. We also wanted to believe the report, and did.

The second consequence referred to was that Crosstrees sought to show himself worthy of the affability and condescension of his guest by communicating to him every bit of gossip, every morsel of local and private history which his memory supplied. Perhaps these disclosures formed a portion of the contents of Secretary Gray's daily letter to Donald Livingstone, Esquire.

But it will be readily assumed that Secretary Gray's circle of acquaintances rapidly increased, first of all, naturally, among the boarders at the Elm House. Crosstrees—or rather Mrs. Crosstrees—furnished an excellent table, and even in summer the large dining hall was quite well filled with guests. It was a cool and airy room furthermore. The gentlemen had the habit of resting there after dinner, and Crosstrees being always present and addressing everybody in turn, serving as a kind of introducer or chamberlain, the conversation was apt to become quite general. Under these circumstances, the natural center of interest and attention was the secretary of that semi-fabulous personage who was to come.

I had been passing a few days in Oskawask, whither I had escorted my mother, but returned to Oldhaven soon after Gray's arrival. Several important cases of which I had charge were set down for the next term of court; so I had no choice about returning. But I found the house very desolate (my dear father having died three years before), and decided to shut it up and live at the hotel during my mother's absence. Accordingly, one morning I entered the Elm House, and, finding that breakfast was not yet served, turned into the reading-room to have a look at the "Chronicle."

The various papers were laid in order upon a large table in the center of the room, but the "Chronicle" was not among the number. Almost any other might have answered the purpose as well, no doubt; but it had been my habit for many years to read that particular newspaper before breakfast or at breakfast, and it seemed a rather irritating circumstance that the "Chronicle" should have been selected from among so many by the only other person in the reading-room.

For it was the "Chronicle"—I recognized it beyond a doubt—being held up before the face of a man who sat in the corner farthest from the window.

"Is the fellow very short-sighted? Is he asleep?" I muttered, walking up and down the length of the reading-room and treading rather more heavily than was my custom, for the purpose of rousing the sleeper, or perhaps only because very small things irritate one before breakfast.

"Will he never finish?"

At this instant the reader laid the paper across his knees and looked at me. It was a very mild and inoffensive glance; yet I was quite startled by the sudden answer to my unspoken thought and by the face itself.

Where had I seen that face before?—When?—An unpleasant suggestion in it? Yes.—Long while ago? Yes.—Oskawask? Yes. First visit there? The old portrait? Yes.—No, it couldn't be that: that was like Israel. What then? A *most* unpleasant suggestion. Dogs! Is it like a dog's face? Not that, exactly. Dogs, though, that was certain. Hounds—blood-hounds! The southern mountain! The too polite servant in gray. That is the very face!

If I stared rudely, as I fear, at the gentleman who sat in the corner most distant from the window, at least that person did not resent or appear conscious of such rudeness. He again held the paper before his face and continued to read for a moment; then arose and advancing towards me, offered me the "Chronicle" in a very civil manner, saying, "Perhaps you would like to look at this paper, sir."

"Perhaps I would," in my surprise I repeated,—surprised and startled even more than I had been a moment before; for when he came forward and spoke, this man seemed to be a total stranger, quite unlike that drawling, servile man-in-gray in several particulars. There were, to be sure, the same sharp features and cavernous eyes: the general outline of the face also was the same: but these features were less strongly marked than those indelibly impressed upon my memory by the terror and the humiliating flight down the mountain side. This man was also not older—perhaps even younger—than that one had made the impression of being.

"Confound that rascal," I said to myself. "He has at any rate been punished by growing into an old rascal by this time!"

Of course I sought to atone for my rudeness, in staring at this stranger and repeating his words, by showing him some attention when we met in the dining-hall.

Among other things I took pleasure in speaking at some length about John Eaton and his adopted son Winthrop, when Gray intimated that he knew somewhat, and desired to learn more, of the young man's strange history.

However, I saw this Gray only three or four times at the Elm House table; for on the second day my mother returned quite unexpectedly, and I of course resumed my home life.

Less than a week after his arrival in Oldhaven, Gray had purchased "the palatial Hopkins residence"—so the local papers informed us. Then, the lot upon which this elegant house stood not being large enough to accord with his notion of his master's importance, he purchased also the adjoining places, to the number of eight, caused all buildings to be removed therefrom—excepting one which he reserved for a porter's lodge—and by means of grading and turfing and adding serpentine walks and other novelties, created quite a little park in the center of the town.

Next he fell to work upon the house itself, and, without attempting, as a less considerate person might have done, to transform it into a German Schloss or a French château—anything in fact which was foreign to its original design—, he evidently realized that he had in hand one of the best houses in the city, and succeeded so well in perfecting all its appointments that it became distinctly and indisputably the very best house in the city.

All this work was done with such admirable rapidity, by means of a lavish expenditure of money and the employment of a host of laborers, that admiration for Gray infected all classes of Oldhaven's citizens. He was looked upon as the real millionaire, the real owner of this splendid new place, the real friend of the laboring men and the shop-keepers. Say what he could, the good people who received so large an amount of good money from Gray would not believe, could not conceive, that another stood above him and commanded him. "The man who pays is master": such was the lesson of their daily lives.

When all preparations had been completed, Donald Livingstone arrived.

The sensation produced by this event answered Gray's expectations and fully rewarded his exertions. On the day following his arrival several important particulars were announced by everyone to everybody: Mr. Livingstone was unmarried; he was apparently about fifty years old; he was a remarkably handsome man with a full black beard. In the natural course of events I saw this hero of the hour: in fact he presented to me a letter of introduction from a person of distinction. The interview, being brief and formal, may be dismissed with few words. Whereas I had anticipated little pleasure from meeting this person, whom I had feared I should find a showy and pretentious upstart fellow, I was on the contrary charmed and delighted.

OSKAWASK IN THE YEAR 1883

"OUR village street is beautifully shaded : suppose we walk down to the library,—unless you prefer riding, Mr. Livingstone; in which case you have only to speak the word, sir. Let me ring this bell, and the carriage will be around in less than five miutes, I can promise you. Everything goes by the sound of a bell here, sir, in Oskawask. A manufacturing village, Mr. Livingstone: everything done to the sound of a bell!"

"Thank you, Mr. Slyme. If my friend Mr. Penman is willing, we will walk down."

"Let's walk, by all means, Samuel," said the gentleman last named.

"Just as you say; entirely at your service, Mr. Livingstone. It is such a pleasant morning—such a fine air stirring this morning — it might be pleasant, as you say. My habit is, as my brother-in-law that is to be, Mr. Penman here, will tell you, to ride to my office and from my office. A plain manufacturing town, sir, but we have our comforts."

"You are too modest by half, my dear sir, permit me to say. Your own house and grounds are charming, Mr. Slyme,— charming. I enjoyed a little stroll about the grounds before breakfast and looked into the conservatories. This should be called elegance and luxury: it is more than comfort."

"Such commendation from you, Mr. Livingstone, is gratifying, highly gratifying."

"I can't thank you enough, Mr. Penman, for having introduced me here. You should know, Mr. Slyme, that my interest had been aroused by what I had heard said about Oskawask; and when I learned that Mr. Penman had the pleasantest relations with the leading family here, I took the liberty of requesting him to introduce me to you, sir."

"All the more flattering on that account, I am sure," said Samuel Slyme, trying to appear less flattered than he really was.

During the foregoing interchange of compliments (I thought them very tiresome and was ashamed of Samuel's company manners) the three gentlemen had sauntered away from the door of the new and imposing, if somewhat too ornate, Slyme mansion and now caught step as they passed through the gate and turned down Main-street.

"How old is your village?" asked Livingstone.

"That depends," replied Samuel with more assurance, although still nervously conscious of the impression he was making and desired to make. "In the sixteenth century, its dwellings were circular in form, about ten or twelve paces in circumference, made of logs split in half, without any regularity of architecture and covered with roofs of straw nicely put on,—so at least an Italian—a Florentine—what's his name?"

"Verrazzano," I suggested, although knowing that this hesitation was for effect.

"Verrazzano—that is it. Verrazzano, writing in 1524, so described them."

"That is, the dwellings in your town were not so fine then as now, while the trees, I presume, were even finer and much more numerous," said Livingstone, smiling.

"Exactly so, Mr. Livingstone. Capital, sir!" assented Samuel, and then pursued his theme: "Nothing remains of that ancient village except its name and an abundance of arrow-heads and rude stone implements, buried in the earth and brought to light by subsoil plowing.

"It was the capital of a tribe of Indians.

"Now the Indians and our ancestors were too entirely different in very many respects to live side by side."

"Ah, I see," said Livingstone. "It is true that in our own day the African savage has been domesticated, so to speak, and while still but half domesticated, has been made our political equal: but the African was imported, and that makes the difference."

Samuel Slyme rarely looked one full in the face; and after the last remark he merely glanced at his distinguished guest to see if he could be chaffing. Livingstone however was apparently all earnestness and attention. The manufacturer continued:

"I know almost nothing about the history of that older village. There is no record except a very meager one. A hundred years later than the Florentine's visit, our ancestors surrounded the Indian village and, after a fervent prayer offered by their leader, the pious Straitcut, attacked it with fire and sword. If any of the inhabitants escaped, the historian is in error; for he says all perished."

"Eloquently simple," observed Livingstone blandly. "Quite like that famous record in the Anglo-Saxon chronicle: 'An. 491. In this year Ælle and Cissa besieged Andredesceaster, and slew all that dwelt therein; not even one Briton was there left.'"

Samuel again raised his eyes to meet the attentive gaze of the great man at his side, but faltered and proceeded in some confusion:

"As for the spirit in which this was done, we have the evidence of our village name. Our ancestors had determined to call the new settlement, on the site of the Indian fort, Mercytown, in recognition of God's goodness in delivering the stronghold of the heathen into their hands; when their leader, who was as learned as pious, explained that the Indian name, Oskawaska, signified 'The town of the children of the Great Spirit.' Wherefore it seemed good to our ancestors to retain the Indian designation.

"That is all we know of the history of the older village; so I can't tell you how old it is, if you mean including that.

"If you mean from the white-man's taking possession, I can't be much more explicit. It didn't deserve the name of 'town' till long afterwards. The first settlers must have been unprosperous, for the new 'Town of the children of the Great Spirit' did not grow. Probably only two or three houses, or rude huts, and a few acres, half cleared and unthrifty, were to be found. It is mentioned but once in the records of the Colonies, and that at a time when every place, by the irresistible force of circumstances, offered some gift to the new-born nation, if any good thing it possessed. During the Revolution, one volunteer from Oskawask distinguished himself in the battle of Guilford Court House. His name was Slyme, sir.

"That is all I know about the history of our village for two hundred years.

"Even its name was almost lost; for, at the beginning of the present century, the citizens of Northbrook, ten miles from here, called the wretched, decayed, tumble-down place 'Puckertown,' in derision."

"Is it possible that the prosperity of Oskawask is so recent, Mr. Slyme?"

"Nothing is impossible in America, Mr. Livingstone, as you and I know, sir. When this century was half used up, my father's life had been more than half used up in the hopeless struggle to win a livelihood from this leachy soil. He was gray and worn before his time and lived with my mother and his grown-up sons in a wretched little cottage which I shall take pride in pointing out to you. But he was a descendant of the Revolutionary soldier. He would sit and brood through the long evenings, trying to contrive some betterment for his large family.

"One evening a stranger applied to him to be taken in for the night. One more in the crowded little hut ——"

"Oh! Oh!" I objected; but no matter; "hut" sounded more story-like.

"One more or less—it made no difference. He was received.

"As this impoverished family sat about the wood fire, the old lady—(I beg pardon, sir; but the story has been told so often that I fall into the habit of speaking as others do)—my good mother raised her eyes from her sewing and looked intently at the elegant coat worn by our guest.

"The next morning our guest went on his way early. I remember it perfectly,—how he stood at the gate ready to mount his horse, and put his hand into his pocket.

"'How much do I owe you for the lodging, my friend?' he asked.

"'Nothing, sir,' said my father proudly.

"Then my mother stepped up, and said she:

"'Will you kindly give me one of the buttons off of your coat?'

"My father didn't like that.

"'Oh, certainly!' said the stranger, and took out his scissors——"

"Knife," I suggested.

"Of course! took out his knife.

"'I have scissors right here, sir,' spoke up my mother; and before you could say Jack Robinson she cut off a pocket button, where it didn't matter much, did it, Horace?"

"Not at all, thank you," I absent-mindedly replied. My thoughts had begun to wander from this familiar tale.

"Ah, Mr. Penman, you were the stranger, then?" Livingstone courteously inquired; and, receiving an affirmative answer, continued: "I congratulate you upon your good fortune. It is your fortune, is it not, to be present when interesting things happen? And you certainly have the happy faculty of enjoying and appreciating them. But forgive me, Mr. Slyme, and please continue the story."

"Mr. Horace Penman mounted his horse and rode away——"

Livingstone interrupted with, "What became of that horse, Mr. Penman?"

It was a rather odd question, but the answer was given in good faith: "The brute became so vicious from that day that I had to sell him."

But Samuel Slyme was not the man to be cheated out of a privilege. His story "had an end as well as a beginning," he said, with an effort to appear sprightly; and then continued:—

"My father began to expostulate: 'Why, really, Saray!' said he. But my mother cut him short.

"'Jonathan,' she said, 'see here. This button that looks so fine is nothing but wood covered with cloth. Dear me, I can do that, and Grace and Gertrude can help.'

"Pretty soon my mother had the neighbors in, to help cover buttons, and my father, who was a natural born mechanic, like all New Englanders, sold his farm and put up a little mill to do the same thing by water-power.

"The business was profitable, sir,—enormously profitable. The whole neighborhood engaged in it, but my father had the best patent, and they all had to fall in line behind him.

"Then the war broke out. Half a million of men to be furnished with uniforms. My father got the contract for cloth-covered buttons."

"I never did quite understand that, Samuel," I observed. "I was under the impression that our soldiers were supplied with metal buttons. Certainly all I ever saw were metal."

"Horace," said the manufacturer, laying his hand on my arm, his manner suddenly becoming almost unpleasantly familiar and insinuating, "Horace, if our gallant army did not use those buttons,—I say, if those buttons were never used, or, for that matter, never wanted—that did not concern Slyme & Son, and it did not concern the congressman from our district, I guess. Those buttons were made and sold at a rattling good figure and paid for in mighty good money. That's all it concerned us to know, wasn't it? What is the consequence, sir?" (Here the speaker became eloquent without affectation, and pointed to the evidences of prosperity which surrounded him.) "The consequence is a magnificent home industry; two thousand laboring men and women furnished with employment at a spot where two dozen couldn't have got a living before! That's what I call out-and-out, uncompromising and beneficent protection of American industries!

"Yes, sir! With that start the thing went on growing. Mill hands flocked in from all quarters. We began to make our own cloth, and then we went on to make almost everything.

"Look up and down this street, Mr. Livingstone, sir! The owners of these comfortable houses owe their fortunes to cloth-covered buttons!

"This town is the creation of my father. Even his critics acknowledge as much. Such as it is, he made it and impressed his character upon it, and fixed that character forever by his will. All the principal public institutions here—the library, the academy, the—Oh, everything,—he created by the provisions of his will, and by the same will he regulates them to-day. So the critics call it 'Willtown,' and say:

> There was a man who owned a mill;
> And when he died he left a will.
> The mill, I hear, is working still;
> The will, I fear, is working ill.

"Foolish critics, Mr. Livingstone! Sentimental vermin, sir, who pretend they don't like to do everything factory-shape, to the sound of a bell!"

"They might run away from your protected industry, and protect their idleness in some more congenial clime," Livingstone suggested.

"'Protect their idleness!' Ha! Ha! Well put, Mr. Livingstone, sir!" said Slyme, falling again into his nervously polite manner. "But I promised that my story should have an end, sir. Here it is. 'How old is our village?'—In one sense, as old as the discovery of America; in another, as old as the Revolution; in another, as old as the cloth-covered button industry. But here we are at the library. My father endowed that, sir."

After early supper that evening the same trio were smiling oftener and using shorter sentences, for the sake of the ladies, in the elegant new drawing-room of the elegant new Slyme mansion.

The ladies, Misses Grace and Gertrude Slyme, we need no introduction to, for we have met them before, and in appearance they have changed very little in the last twenty-eight years. Twenty years before they had been young ladies; in 1883 they were still young ladies. They had been too happy, in their own gentle way, to grow old. They had not feared the work of Time, nor peered into their mirrors to discover signs of that destroyer's yearly and daily and hourly visits; so that Time, finding them always "cheerful without mirth," and quite unspoiled by "mighty passions and so forth," had really not harmed them, but only added a trifle of roundness to their figures and a grain of confidence to the modest expression of their faces.

So at least I thought, and had been thinking year after year. Is it not true that the longer one is able to entertain a conviction, the more likely that is to be well grounded?

Withdrawn somewhat from the blaze of light which was emitted from the many burners of the sparkling glass chandelier, these young ladies and I were conversing with that freedom and good understanding which is the privilege of accepted, requited, acknowledged and then thoroughly tested affection.

For twenty years these young ladies had continued to share and to reciprocate, equally and impartially, the sentiments and attentions of their lover. It would be impossible to say whether they or I cared less to know with certainty which one would become Mrs. Penman when the time came.

These three lovers (one has to use this word to convey the proper idea, although it is a shade too warm to convey the exact idea in this case), now exchanging confidences in an undertone, now listening to or joining in the conversation which was being kept up between the master of the house and Mr. Livingstone, were seated under the full-length portrait of the deceased Jonathan Slyme. Samuel stood with his back turned to the white marble fireplace; for, although there had not been a fire in that particular grate for a month, it struck him as a genial-looking position for the host to take up. Livingstone sat in an easy-chair, facing him and evidently much interested in what he was saying.

"Your father left a large amount to the school—or college, is it?—I understood you to say this morning."

"A cool three hundred thousand, Mr. Livingstone. Just so much taken out of legitimate business. On educational topics I entertain positive ideas, sir. I value book-learning and appreciate the advantage that an educated man has in many of the walks of life over one who is uneducated. Still, I believe that any successful business man is an educated man. He may know nothing about Greek; nevertheless he is a professor of his business. I think a man who understands his trade, is as much entitled to the title of professor as a teacher in a college. The college professor could not build a sloop, a house, or a steam engine if his life depended on it. The great practical problem of life is, how to get on. Any man who has solved that problem is a professor. If I want to consult anyone about financial matters, I go to Professor Sharper, of the Mechanic's bank; if I want to learn anything about chemistry, I go to Professor Litmus, of the Slyme Seminary; but when I want a house built I talk it over with Professor Sim Ferris, a negro, who can neither read nor write, but understands his own business thoroughly."

Grace leaned forward and in an undertone said to me: "Tell us about our sweet nephew."

"Yes, brother Horace, tell us about that dear Winthrop Eaton," echoed Gertrude.

"Just think, brother Horace, he has not been to see us for three months; and he knows we think he is a sweet fellow ——"

"A sweet fellow," said Gertrude at the same instant. Both speaking at once, in this manner, the sweetness seemed very sweet indeed.

It will be noticed that each of the ladies addressed me as "brother." That was as much as to say, When the time comes, marry my sister Gertrude—or Grace, as the case happened to be. Could anything more considerate be imagined?

"We fear Winthrop's wife is a great care to him," said Grace.

"Yes, we fear he married too young," said Gertrude, with a sigh.

Grace sighed also, and repeated, "too young;" and I added with conviction that it was a shame, and that the reckless young pair were being punished for their improvident haste.

After uttering this rather harsh sentiment I paused, for my attention was drawn to what the other two gentlemen were saying.

"Yes, I can readily understand that," Livingstone observed. "Your position here is very exceptional. Oskawask is, in effect, what the English call a 'pocket Borough,'—that is, you might use your overwhelming influence here for political purposes, if you saw fit.".

"Precisely, sir! That is the case more —er—more truly and really than I should care to have everybody know. Between you and me, Mr. Livingstone, I can defeat or elect any man who is running for office in this part of the State. The political parties are pretty evenly balanced and the vote is manageable. How much do you suppose these naturalized factory-hands— these thousands of Irish and Germans and French and Italians—and what not—care for party principles? I needn't go into the subject, sir, but I guess it's pretty plain that if I get my back up and say—in one way or another—using arguments that they understand, sir, and the only kind they *do* understand, because these arguments touch their own pockets and their own wages and they can buy meat and beer with these arguments :—if I say, Elect this man and bounce that man, I guess the result will be according!—— Not that I have cared any to do it and not that I do care; but if I did ——." He left the sentence unfinished so that his guest might fill in the blank with a series of pleasing mental pictures: Samuel Slyme, Esq., as Governor; the same, as Senator; the same, as President.

"Now that we are speaking so frankly, as one man-of-the-world to another", responded Livingstone, "it simmers down to this: that the man who controls the manufacturing interests here, controls the vote."

"Exactly so, exactly so, Mr. Livingstone. That's the fact nobody can get around. I have worked hard in my life, sir, and this is my reward. 'The laborer is worthy of his hire,' I take it. I don't know, I don't know," he continued, as though a question not in the manufacturing line was full of difficulty, "I don't know but I'll come forward myself one of these days. I've been thinking it over lately, and it seems high time I made myself felt for all I'm worth—politically, I mean. Who knows what may happen if I wait too long? I never had any fears until I began to think of coming forward myself. Who knows but these sneaking politicians might contrive to steal my rights! One can never tell what they'll be up to next. Why, lately there's been a fellow here—a smooth-spoken fellow, who went around among the workmen, but wore good clothes and lived in style himself—what was his name? Brown? Gray? Gray, that's it. I have my own sources of information, Mr. Livingstone, and I'd be willing to swear that that man meant mischief. He was up to something, or why did he take so much interest in my affairs and the way I stood with the people here? Besides, the man looked like a snake."

"Gray?" I called across the room. There was something in this description which struck me. "Did you say his name was Gray, Samuel?"

"Yes, we saw him," murmured Grace

at my side, "and we thought he must have cold hands, didn't we, sister?"

"By the way, Mr. Livingstone, where is your Gray now?" I inquired. "I have not seen him in Oldhaven lately."

"I am sure I don't know," replied Livingstone indifferently. "He asked for a little vacation; and he has been doing so much for me—getting my house ready and all that, you know—that I let him off willingly for a fortnight."

"If he is connected with you in any way, Mr. Livingstone, sir," said Samuel hurriedly, "I beg your pardon and take it all back, sir, I am sure."

"No harm done," said Livingstone rather coldly; and then rising and standing before Samuel Slyme, who looked a very poor figure in comparison, he continued: "If this person was my Gray, I should not take anything said against him as applying to myself in the remotest degree."

Livingstone evidently understood the man he had to deal with. If he had expressed the least regret for the annoyance which his agent had caused the owner of Oskawask, that local grandee would have felt himself wronged. As it was, Samuel

Slyme again apologized for a fault he had not committed, and, bringing the conversation once more to the subject of his own political aspirations, grew surprisingly confidential in the course of the evening. It was not an edifying conversation, but for all that it seemed to interest Mr. Livingstone, who consented, after much urging, to remain for a day or two in order to examine the field thoroughly, and so to advise more intelligently.

1885.

IN the spring of 1885 Samuel Slyme failed.

Oskawask was shaken as by an earthquake; all western Massachusetts sensibly trembled; the country at large and manufacturing circles abroad were promptly informed of it. If the love of notoriety is the passion of our age, as very respectable observers gravely assure us, then this was the hour of Samuel's triumph.

Poor fellow! he did not see it in that light. To him it did not seem a brilliant and sensational event: it was not to him sufficiently sudden and unexpected for that. Losses, losses, one after the other during the two years since we last saw him,—the sum of these losses seemed the sum total of the event to him.

Such losses,—such besetting evil fortune,—surely no experienced and, if anything, over-cautious manufacturer ever before had to contend against. Industries the most meritorious, investments the most approved, securities the most secure, dissolved and became thin air the moment he touched them. Banks failed, correspondents forged and ran away, real-estate depreciated, whichever way he turned.

"I never had a bit of luck," said Samuel, "since I took to politics and since that Gray set the 'hands' against me."

"That was the time I brought Livingstone here and introduced him to you," I said, with vague misgiving.

"Oh, Mr. Livingstone is another matter! He has stood behind me all this time and helped me. Why, do you know, Horace, he must have almost ruined himself for me. He has bought all the claims against me and holds them to-day. They are not worth fifty cents on the dollar, and he knows it; but instead of selling out while my credit was good and he could have got what he paid, he holds them, sir, and never presses me!"

I did not dispute any part of this statement nor attempt to warn the victim when it was already too late. Before ever a suggestion of these facts had come to me, the thing had been done and the fact become unalterable. It remained only to make the most of the alleged good disposition of Samuel's principal creditor in order to save something from the wreck. To this end I strove, and my attempt was so far successful that Samuel was appointed, by the directors of a new company which was formed to carry on the business of Slyme & Son, general manager. President of the new company, was Donald Livingstone, Esquire; his associates being various little great men of the neighborhood whose connection with the business was scarcely more than nominal.

In the matter of this appointment, as in all his public acts after the great failure became known, Livingstone showed a magnanimous spirit which won him praise from all sides. The extent of the pecuniary sacrifice which he made in accepting this arrangement was not concealed. That brought him nothing but credit. The readiness with which he came forward to secure to thousands of operatives continued employment, won the hearts of the poor and the hearts of the friends of the poor,—that is to say, of everybody. His was the reward of the man who is generous *and* prosperous.

As for certain rumors, doubtless invented by malicious persons, about an appearance of system and method in the successive blows which had overturned the house of Slyme & Son, as though they could not have been the work of chance but must have been planned by some selfish and diabolical agency, these quickly fell to the ground. Who could have found his own advantage in such an attack? That was a question nobody could answer; and so rumor subsided.

In fact rumor had other material to feed upon. It began to be whispered that, far from there being less work done at the mills under the new company, there was to be more. The buildings were to be enlarged; new machinery had been ordered; an era of greater prosperity was to begin in Oskawask.

Would Donald Livingstone consent to exchange the "Esquire" at the end of his name for a "Senator" to be written before it? He had only to say the word.

But while it seemed well enough for Samuel Slyme, the fallen duke of Oskawask, to accept service under the usurper, I would not consent to see the sisters dependent upon a dependent. Hence a momentous decision.

After twenty years of more or less active courtship, I resolved to marry the sisters immediately.

Promptly, yet without unbecoming haste, a month being allowed to elapse between the announcement and the ceremony, this resolution was carried into effect.

On the morning of a warm summer's day, the front room on the second floor of a small, aristocratic boarding house not far from the Oldhaven green, was the scene of confusion,—that is, so much confusion as could be found in the apartments of two quiet ladies. The ladies were arraying themselves for their wedding, which was to take place before noon. The process of decoration advanced impartially. It is true that Gertrude's hair was done a moment before Grace's; but seeing this, Gertrude would not allow her maid to proceed to other matters before Grace's maid had caught up. Then there was an intermission of five minutes for the sisters to intertwine arms and kiss each other upon the cheek and throat and wherever that could be done without disarranging things. And so on until all was finished.

Full half an hour before the appointed time, these two sisters were waiting in the parlor, caressing one another as well as that can be done in tight new sleeves, and patiently expecting the few invited guests. These arrived duly and all drove together to the pretty Episcopal church. That was surely a friendly way to do such a thing.

All entering the church together, we proceeded at once to the altar. Mr. Winthrop Eaton, Mr. Samuel Slyme and I were the only gentlemen present. The ladies were, Mrs. Eaton and the heroines of the occasion. During the service the two sisters, dressed in gowns which were exactly alike, stood so near together that one could not tell which was the bride.

When I repeated: "I, Horace, take thee, Gertrude," Mrs. Eaton added in a loud whisper: "And Grace"— whereat we all laughed.

After the ceremony all repaired to Mrs. Eaton's house to breakfast.

"Where are you going?" asked Winthrop.

"Nowhere!"

But Mrs. Eaton insisted that the happy

pair should go away for at least twenty-four hours; and after much persuasion we consented.

On the following day we returned, and then started off on a sensible wedding-trip, taking Grace with us. After a very pleasant journey we returned and settled down. How cheerful my old home became! Both Grace and Gertrude continued, and to this day continue (the heavens be praised!) to call me "brother."

Through this marriage I came to be very intimately connected with Winthrop Eaton, whose name has been several times mentioned in the foregoing pages. He is the son of Israel Slyme and Lilly Lincoln, and was adopted and brought up by John Eaton. John Eaton was, until his death in 1873, my dear friend. Now family ties were added to the bond of old acquaintance, Winthrop being Gertrude's nephew. His father, Israel, had deserted his family immediately after my first visit at Oskawask, and his fate has remained a mystery to this day.

I say that his fate remains a mystery; but Mrs. Winthrop Eaton has maintained the contrary, as the reader will presently see.

The foregoing chapters were originally written at Mrs. Eaton's request. She assured me that it had become of vital importance to her and to her husband that the mystery above referred to should be cleared up, laid great stress upon the undeniable resemblance between Donald Livingstone and her husband, and urged me, as the oldest family friend, to set down what I knew from my own experience about Israel and Mr. Livingstone. That I accordingly did, without addition or diminution.

Mrs. Eaton, I should observe here, is a woman of singular beauty and unnatural intellectual brilliancy. Her father was the Rev. James Addison, an Episcopal minister, settled in a small town near Oldhaven. Winthrop met her at an age when he should have had no thought of marriage, was completely fascinated, and with improvident haste took her to live with him at "Westwood."

Of all the pretty places in the neighborhood of Oldhaven, "Westwood" is, in my opinion, the most charming. Be pleased to imagine the gently sloping hill-side, from all points of which the view ranges over a cultivated plain, in the foreground broken here and there by comfortable little houses and by the course of a small river with wooded banks; while far away the towers and steeples and loftier buildings of the city display their summits above the leafy covering of elm trees, like an architectural crop just beginning to spring up and promising to grow into a town in the course of a summer.

This hill-side Winthrop Eaton called his "farm;" and one of the chief allurements of the place was that he did treat it as a farm. Not fine and pretentious and meant for show, like a villa, it was generous and homelike and meant for use and comfortable living. Yet with exquisite taste Winthrop had known how to add touches of art, where these would serve to heighten the charm of naturalness. The house itself, built of warm-colored, brown stones which had been selected from that abundant supply which the fields of "Westwood" afforded, vine-covered and surrounded by wide verandas, was not the least agreeable feature in the landscape.

But, in spite of its southern exposure, there was always a shadow covering every foot of the territory of "Westwood." Winthrop had inherited it from the good-natured John Eaton with that encumbrance which good-nature is so prone to inflict—debt.

Another shadow was there also, for which John Eaton was in no way responsible. The old portrait of Israel-for-Israel hung in the library. It was the visible reminder of a family disgrace; none the less Winthrop valued it, because it was said to resemble his father, Israel, whom he had never seen.

Such was the home from which young Winthrop Eaton was striving to lift the double shadow of debt and of disgrace when he married Miss Addison. Since that event the husband has been a plodding worker and the wife one of the leaders of Oldhaven society, famous for her eccentricity.

Mrs. Eaton's request was for facts concerning Israel and Livingstone which had fallen within my own experience and observation. Having stated these, my task is ended.

PART II.—BY MRS. WINTHROP EATON

CHAPTER I

AT my urgent request Mr. Horace Penman consented to write down his personal recollections of my husband's father, Israel Slyme, as he used to be called, or Donald Livingstone, as he is to-day called. I have just read those recollections and I am greatly disappointed.

Horace Penman is a dear, good old gentleman, and I have as much respect for him as for anyone; but he has a foolish dislike for putting two and two together. He has restricted himself to the bare facts, and declined to draw the obvious conclusions. He has even refused to avail himself of information derived from trustworthy persons—from his wife, from Winthrop's foster-father, John Eaton, and others—as though fearing to trust anything except his own immediate observation. It might almost seem that he has it in mind to shake my belief in the identity of Israel and Livingstone. But if I had not one atom of proof, I should know what this monster of selfishness really is. Can I not read his story in his face?

As for its being wiser not to stir up the past, as Mr. Penman suggested when I first consulted him, that is a good rule for those who are happy in the present; but how can I, with this burning sense of wrong, remain silent?

The whole course of his wickedness is wonderfully clear to me. I can hardly explain to myself this distinctness; and yet I could as easily doubt what I know of my own life as doubt any portion or particular of Israel's life, written by revelation upon my brain.

My poor husband! Proud, sensitive, noble Winthrop! He has pledged his life to redeem the faults of others, while I—I myself am a chief cause of his suffering. I added the burden of my ungoverned ambition and of my exactions to the load which he was staggering under. That I cannot change. My impulses I cannot control; but I shall compel Donald Livingstone to be just to his own flesh and blood.

* * * * * *

In the year 1855, an hour or so before Mr. Penman rode away from Oskawask, Lilly Lincoln and Israel were walking across the fields toward the home of the former. Both were in the highest spirits: Lilly, as she herself said, in a perfect gale, Israel singing with a great, booming voice.

So they went, hand in hand, until they could no longer be seen from the house. Then Lilly's gayety passed all bounds. She danced in little circles about Israel, seizing him every now and then by the hand, and kissing it a thousand times; then, throwing this away and hanging about his neck, she kissed his cheeks and eyes—too light-hearted to touch his lips with her own.

As for this favored young man, he felt through and through him those thrills of love consummated, intoxicating every sense; that devouring passion of the heart after every sense has been gratified; the glory and happiness of possession—not the hunger of a lover, but the far more perfect and universal passion of the acknowledged master and lord.

Gloria! sang the young man's heart, while he drank of the being of this woman transfigured by love; while he drank in the delicious after-storm air as in great draughts of sparkling wine; while he felt tingling at his finger-tips and racing through his arteries the abundant streams of a strong young life, now perfect, now blessed and complete.

They were at the brow of a hill, or rather the side of a vale, which was still dark and cold, being unvisited by the sun as yet: still dark and cold below, where a very tiny tributary of the weedy stream trickled in crystal purity beneath leafless laurel bushes.

The path was narrow and steep and rough, but Lilly danced down it, whirling around recklessly, her little hands lifted above his head, her eyes flashing, her cheeks flushed with exquisite pink, and one splendid lock of golden hair, escaped from confinement, falling like a serpent across her shoulder and into her bosom.

With all this wild motion, she yet kept very close to Israel. Her warm breath was on his cheek and her clasped hands were ready to descend about his neck when her foot dashed against a projecting point of stone and she fell backwards. But, quick as thought Israel had seized her, terrified but unhurt, and catching her up to him and so holding her, the poor little throbbing heart pressed against his own, bearing her easily, he rushed onward down the path.

It seemed to her that they were falling down, down, locked in each other's embrace; and she closed her eyes and her heart suddenly ceased beating as she awaited the end of their descent—the terrible instant when they should lie crushed and mangled in the bed of the little stream.

The swift motion ceased, and yet she felt no pain. Timidly she opened her eyes and saw that she was still in her lover's arms, and that he was looking down into her face with a smile.

"Why, you are pale, my child!" he exclaimed. "Did it hurt your foot?"

She looked with a shudder from him to the steep path along which they had flown. Then her eyes fell upon the unpolluted waters within reach of her hand.

"Will you have some water?" he asked.

Lilly only shook her head for reply, pressing close to him with all her strength. Then she said:

"Take me to live with you. Do not

take me home. Away from you I am dead. O, take me, take me!"

"Are you not happy, dearest Lilly? Are you not happy as it is?"

She put her hands upon his mouth and pushed his head back until she could look into his face. Then, with her whole soul shining through her entreating eyes, and her voice vibrating strangely, she cried:

"Take me! Take me! Take me! Are you not my husband?"

"Yes; in the matter of love for you, I am certainly your husband. What do you mean by this? A moment ago you were as happy as you should always be. What has changed you, little one?"

"You love me?"

"Yes: have I not told you so many times?"

"Then that is enough. Then am I not your wife?"—putting her cheek against his. "Call me wife!"

"Darling little lady, am I not kind to you? Do *you* not love *me*?"

"Oh!"—so reproachfully, yet so tenderly spoken. No one who conceives how that was uttered will judge harshly poor little Lilly's self-sacrifice. "You do love me, Israel. I have never doubted it.

It would be wicked—it would be a sin to doubt that. You did not mean to ask me—what I thought you asked. You know—you must know. Oh, my husband, think—or, rather, do not think—what a creature I should be if I had not done all because I worshipped you—because I adore you. You are my god. I have no will but your will. What you say has taken the place of God's word to me, because I have no life apart from you. Forgive me if I have loved you too much!"

Lilly's eyes were streaming and her speech, low and rapid, poured out as naturally as her tears.

This incense of her blind adoration ascended to the nostrils of her god, and must have been grateful to his sense; for Israel held her so strictly bound in his arms that this tender worshiper gasped for breath.

For a moment both were happy, yet not in the same way.

Then Lilly made a great effort and cheered her heart, and smiled at him through her tears. Her happiness came over her as a flood of light and warmth.

"My Superbness!—Oh, I must take

satisfaction, gorgeous being,—my saint!" And she seized his face almost fiercely and bit his cheek just above the peculiar little mark. "There!—Poor face, did it hurt you?" Then she covered every feature with quick, burning kisses, returning with preference to the birth-mark.

But, Lilly, do you notice that this mark almost vanishes now? It is so faint that one could scarcely see it. There must be magic in your kisses.

Thus Lilly appealed to Israel's love, not without effect; yet he did not answer according to her wish.

Then she called up past scenes of pleasure, into which we dare not intrude,—in which, as Israel recalled them also, she seemed to him a flower quite unlike the lily, yet more than ever desirable.

Thus she appealed to his selfishness, without realizing that for this the opportunity had passed and her advantage had been sacrificed.

The birthmark showed very distinctly again, but this she could not notice, for as a last appeal she hid her face in his bosom and whispered something—a secret fearfully kept even from him until that moment.

No man born of woman but has at least an impulse of pity for that condition. Israel kissed her tenderly and promised: "I shall openly acknowledge our marriage to-morrow, Lilly, so surely as I am here to do it."

Thereupon she became radiantly happy. "'So surely as you are here!' Why, nothing can happen to you, my magnificence. To-morrow! I—Oh, I shall be so proud! .... Oh, my husband, is it possible? Tell me I am not dreaming. Tell me I shall always be close, next to you—always. .... What will you call me? Say it! Call me—— How thoughtful and sad you are, sweet face! .... Israel! Are you angry with me, darling? Are you angry with me for being so happy?"

But she could not conquer his dark humor, and they finished the way in silence.

Returning alone, Israel paused in the glen where they had rested together, realizing how free he was without her.

"Why, I could as easily run up that path alone as down it with her," he muttered. "If she were only a different nature, the question might change. If she were helpful, or even independent.—But how can I carry her with me in my race against the world for the first place in the world? Perhaps I might do that and yet win. I will not acknowledge that there is anything I can not do. But after I had won, she—— Oh, she would not be a companion for me. When I am all that I feel myself able to become, she will remain little Lilly Lincoln. I can make myself what I please; but she would not, could not, change. The more perfect and complete my success, the wider would grow the breach between us. She would be only more and more, as time went on, an incumbrance. No! The woman fit to share my whole life does not exist. For this part of it, Lilly : and it is true, as she said, that she has added to my happiness in this part. For the next ten, twenty years, no person, woman or man, can share my life or know my thoughts. As for Lilly—why, she would be unhappy if I kept from her my secret thoughts, and if she knew my secrets they would kill her. No, I say, no! After these ten or twenty years of struggle——? Why, then, a woman born to the station to which I shall have fought my way. Then some princess who is now unborn, who shall be then fresh and exquisite as Lilly is now—from whom I may draw a new life: for I shall be world-worn and tired then. Why then I shall begin to live! Everything near me then shall be, must be, sparkling and young, to warm me again. Lilly at that time? Lilly would be forty—faded—a poor, faded lily—a stranger to my heart, yet holding by right the first place in my life. Lilly would point backwards with constant reminder to my needy, hateful past. She would remind me of how much more? Of what I had done? No one shall know that! But then I shall need to forget. Then I shall begin to become what I should be now, if I had not been born in a hovel. I curse it, and it shall be cursed. Curse these fools—these country simpletons! Here is a great big world with men in it, and sparrows, and toads. And I have a few years of life, and my whole nature cries out for all the good things that the earth has, and that is the first law of my nature. And these fools would hold me to them—to a rocky farm—to a living death. My few years of life given to this groveling misery! That would be disobedience to the first law of my being: so great a sin that no other—that all others together could not equal it.

"They want me, because they love me. I do not love them. That is the plain truth told to myself.

"They love me because I am nobler than they. I can not stay with them for the same reason.

"They have done all they could for me. I must leave them now."

And then his thoughts came back to Lilly and he started up.

"I must be away before to-morrow," he concluded; and he ran up the steep path, for the pleasure which the exertion gave him.

CHAPTER II

EFORE twelve o'clock that night, Israel was on his way. After a few minutes of rapid walking he passed the Lincoln house. He had neither thought of avoiding this nor preferred the road which led past the home of Lilly. Simply, he was on his way.

As for Lilly at this hour, we can be sure of only one or two things. She was not asleep, she was very happy, and in the silence she kept whispering to herself, "To-morrow, to-morrow," until with a joyful throb she began to say, and never tired of saying, "To-day, to-day he will take me to live with him."

So then Israel Slyme came of age in the grand air, on the highway, marching swiftly through the night towards the south.

*   *   *   *   *   *

Twelve hours later, when the sun stood directly above his head, and he had begun to reflect that there were some warm noons in November, Israel arrived at the foot of a long hill. Here the road branched, one way leading over the hill and another, equally traveled, skirting its base. A sign-post stood at the crossways, but its inscription was quite obliterated.

He was about to take the upper road when a farmer, driving a team of spirited young horses harnessed to an open wagon, overtook him. This farmer turned off into the lower road.

"Helloa! Is that the way to Oldhaven?" cried Israel.

"Yaas, I'm going ter Oldhaven. Air ye bound in that direction?"

"Yes."

"Whoa, Nelly! whoa, Bob! Git in an' I guess I'll give ye a lift ez fur ez ye go."

The offer was gladly accepted.

"Come fur to-day?"

"Fifty miles."

"Whew! And whar' from?"

"From jail," said Israel.

"Why, ye don't look ter me like that sort of feller. Ye would kiver up that spot onter your cheek, ef ye was 'fraid of bein' recognized. Whar did ye say yer was goin' ter?"

"Into the ground."

"I guess you're kinder facetious, aint ye? An' what might yer name be?"

"James Johnson."

"Thunder! Ye don't say, now. Why, my wife's folks' name's Johnson, from up Massachusetts way. Oskawask is the name of the place. Ye don't happen ter have heard of that, perhaps."

"Yes, I have been through the town."

"Dew tell! An' whar did ye say ye was goin'?"

"I told you I came from jail and that I was going into the ground; but I did not know that your wife's name was Johnson, or I'd have been more explicit. Now then —but first let me ask if I shall have a chance to get dinner anywhere on the road."

"Air ye hungry?"

"As a wolf."

"It dews seem as though my woman put up something for me."

"Oh, I don't want to take your dinner."

"Whoa, Bob! who-up, Nelly there!" cried the farmer. When the wagon was brought to a stand-still, he said angrily: "Ef I aint good enough fer ye to eat with me, James Johnson, and fer me ter eat with you, why, good-bye to ye."

Israel burst into a laugh. "In that case," he said, "you'd lose the story that I am about to tell, and I'd lose my dinner. Drive on, man; and if I eat more than my share, remember I've had fifty miles for appetizer."

"You air a likely hand to do a day's work," said the farmer, measuring Israel with his eyes, "but I guess there's enough for both on us"—and he started up his team again.

"Well then, Mr. Perkins—"

"That beats all! I disremember that I told you my name is Perkins!"

"Ezekiel Perkins, isn't it?"

"Ezekiel H. Perkins, that's my name. I don't know ez I've any call ter be ashamed on it. But how on airth did ye come ter know?"

It was quite natural that Israel, who had passed his life among the few families of Oskawask, should know whom Kate Johnson had married and should have heard from the old parents at home all about their prosperous son-in-law in Connecticut; but Israel had in mind a little experiment to test the intelligence of the man beside him. To carry out this experiment he deviated from the plain truth.

"I was asking the way a piece back—a couple of miles or so, I guess," he replied, falling into the dialect of his companion, "and an old woman with one eye told me as Ezekiel Perkins drove down to Oldhaven carrying chickens and eggs to the market, every Saturday, behind the best team of horses in the county; and if I would wait for him, he'd give me a lift and never leave the straight road. So when I saw your horses, I made sure it was you, Mr. Perkins."

"That was like enough old Betsey Turnbull," said the farmer. "Waal, they air a likely team enough. I raised 'em myself from colts. Nellie is eight and Bob he is nigh onter seven year old. Git up, there. Steady, old gal"—putting the team on their mettle.

So Israel had uttered a lie, seasoned with a little flattery, and was believed without further question.

Pursuing his experiment he continued:

"Now for the story:—There has been a gold mine in the possession of my family for three generations "——

"A gold mine! Why ye don't look ter me like that kind of a dandy."

"Just so. I have been kept out of my

rights: kept in bondage, out of my lawful inheritance. That's what I meant by saying I came from jail."

"Whar might this gold mine lie?"

"South of Washington."

"That might be the Gulf of Mexico or South Ameriky."

"Exactly what I have always said myself. I agree with you entirely." This answer staggered the good farmer, who did not quite catch the drift. Then Israel continued:

"That's where I am going. My great-grandfather is there and I expect to find him. Didn't I say I was going into the ground? That is what I meant. I am going into a gold mine and when I come out I shall be rich enough to buy the whole State of Connecticut."

"See here, young James Johnson, I like funnin' and I like fooling, but you suit me too gol durned well."

So Israel told the truth, as well as he understood it, and was not believed.

But inasmuch as the results of the experiment were not at variance with his previous experience, he did not reflect upon the false judgment of the world, but plied his new acquaintance with mingled falsehood and truth, according to the caprice of his overflowing humor. The fact is, Israel was fairly intoxicated by the freedom of his situation and the infinite prospect of adventure which stretched out before his mental vision.

It is to be observed, however, that even this which seemed reckless humor proved serviceable to his interests; for Ezekiel Perkins not only shared a substantial lunch with our young adventurer, but felt himself greatly honored by the other's condescension in praising the cold meats. So far indeed did this manner of Israel's accomplished the purpose for which it had been assumed, or rather permitted to show itself, that before sunset Ezekiel Perkins pronounced his companion to be an amazingly entertaining young fellow who knew a thing or two if only he could stop joking long enough to show it.

The sun was setting when they drew up on the brow of a hill from which the waters of Long Island Sound were visible.

"Thar is Oldhaven," said the farmer, "and a right pretty town it is, an' no mistake."

There indeed lay the town at their feet, spreading out as it chose, like a great village rather than a city,—not crowding its inhabitants in upper stories for lack of ground-room, but occupying only a small portion of the generous plain which lay between the encircling hills and the sea.

Israel sprung from the wagon.

"Good-bye!"

"Ain't ye goin' inter the town?"

"Rather walk, thank you."

"Er—how long ye say ye stop here?"

"Long enough to get money to continue my journey."

"And whar then?"

"To my gold mine, I told you."

"Did ye say yer grandfather stopped down thar in the ground?"

"Great-grandfather, to be exact."

"Waal, take care on yerself. Don't ye stop down thar in the same way. Say," (with hesitation), "I know yer foolin' about gold mines, but I guess I'd kinder like ter hear from ye sometimes, that yer all right."

"You'll hear from me again, don't you be afraid."

"Waal," said the farmer, with a kindly light in his grey eyes, and leaning out to shake Israel by the hand, "waal, I guess it'll be a right smart while before I furgit ye. Git along, Nellie, ol' gal!"—and he drove off, leaving Israel standing beside the road.

Perkins did not forget this encounter, for he told Horace Penman of it when they were serving together in the war. It was after their adventure on the inhospitable mountain, from which they were driven by blood-hounds; and Perkins began by saying that the name of Captain Johnson reminded him of a young fellow whom he had met nine or ten years before.

CHAPTER III

FROM the point where Israel stood, the view is beautiful. That faint, irregular line on the southern horizon is Long Island, thirty miles away. Nearer is a splendid sea,—its waters crisping and curling beneath the November breeze; then a harbor with its fleet of white-winged oyster-boats; then the wide salt meadows, dotted over with hayricks, following the course of two small rivers far inland; then the generous plain for shaded streets to lead across, for pleasure-gardens and for market-gardens—a comfortable dwelling-place for men; then the rampart of hills, enclosing and protecting the territory of Oldhaven and marking it off as a thing apart, peculiar and superior.

Standing out prominently from this wall of hills, two cliffs guard the town from the east and from the west. Not high enough to be grand, these "Rocks," as they are called, are nevertheless suggestive and interesting. They are the final effort of the Green Mountain range, and descendants of Mansfield and Camel's Hump in remote Vermont. They are not mere upstarts from the vulgar plain, therefore. They point with pride to their noble kindred.

Why had Israel chosen to alight from the wagon and to enter the town alone? For a very simple reason. He did not know where he should apply for work, and was unwilling that anyone, even a chance acquaintance, should be witness of his indecision. It was his way to act with decision, as though there could be no doubt or question about what he did. He knew that this confidence was contagious, communicating itself to others, leading them to repose unbounded confidence in his powers. He was quite logical, therefore, in affecting more than usual assurance of manner when really inwardly perplexed.

Observe him closely now, while he is off his guard, alone in a country road. We may now catch a glimpse of the natural man. What do we see?

We see a fine-looking young fellow walking slowly along beside a stone wall. Every few minutes he takes a large stone from the wall and casts it across the road—a great distance to put so heavy a stone. He seems to have nothing to do and much strength to spare.

That is a distinct and simple picture; but no more distinct to me than is every scene which I shall describe. What do I care for evidence to prove these things?

Israel must have assisted in the construction of many such barriers on the farm in Oskawask; for it required skill as well as strength to cast the heavy stones to the very place designed. One heavier piece, however, fell short by several feet. Thereat Israel was provoked, and selecting a smooth boulder twice the size of its predecessor, raised this to his shoulder and cast it so fairly that it alighted upon the very top of the opposite wall, carrying away several large pieces from that and making a breach.

"Bravo! Well put, sir!" cried a friendly voice. "Well put, indeed!"—and John Eaton, his face beaming with delight, hastened up to Israel. "I have been watching you for some time. I suppose I ought to apologize for that. Taking my afternoon walk across the fields, you know. It so happened that I could hardly help seeing you. That was a magnificent effort, that last!"

"Is this your fence, sir, that I have been pulling to pieces?" asked Israel, bluntly.

"Oh, no harm done! Magnificently put! Let me see, fifty, sixty feet at the very least; and a stone I should not care to lift!" He looked up into Israel's face with childlike admiration.

Israel pointed across the road to the breach in the wall. "The more power one puts into that sort of work, the worse for everybody," he said.

"But if you had the humor for constructing instead of destroying, what an amount of fencing you could do in a day!"

"You have stone-fencing to be done?" asked the young fellow, quickly.

"A mile or more. This is my place, which I am trying to get into good shape. See—" John Eaton put his hand on Israel's arm and pointed. "I own from where we stand to the top of that farther hill. Millions of rocks! The place has never been properly improved."

"How much will you pay by the yard for fencing?"

A shilling, and furnish the team," replied

Mr. Eaton, trying to make this sound business-like.

"I will do some of it for you."

"You!" cried John Eaton in amazement. "Well, well, I am in luck. The unexpected happens. Come, come with me before you change your mind." So he led Israel across the fields to his home, chatting gayly all the way.

Did he charm Israel by the refinement and gentleness of his manner?

I know what kind of a man John Eaton was. I know this from what my husband, who was his ward, and Horace Penman, who was his bosom friend, have told me. Winthrop loved him more than he loves me, and Mr. Penman says that in the course of his long life he has never met another character so noble. In Oldhaven he was little known; for although his name stood in the catalogue of the university as "Professor of Anglo-Saxon", his duties in that connection were slight, and he was rarely seen in the town, except as driving to or from the library in an old-fashioned carriage with shining brass trimmings. On such occasions the multitude of books to be returned or to be taken away, almost filling the interior of this stately vehicle, might well have raised a doubt in the minds of onlookers as to whether the center of learning was the college or "Westwood."

As for his manners, John Eaton was one of those Americans who imagine the manner of cultivated foreigners to be perfection itself, and who place this ideal before them as a model. They are therefore striving, not to be English or French or Italian, but to be perfect. Amiable illusion!

Did he charm Israel by the refinement and gentleness of his manner? I shall answer that question presently.

CHAPTER IV

SO then, Israel fell to hauling and piling stones—an occupation into which he put all his heart and all his strength, knowing that every rod of fence constructed meant so many miles of his southward journey made easy and swift.

As for John Eaton, he took his morning cigar in the fresh air, watching Israel's progress with silent delight; and in the afternoon left his books—even the translation of Beówulf which he was making—to study the great muscles of this young giant's bared forearm and throat.

"There!" he would say to himself. "There is the explanation of those incredible feats recorded of the northern hero. Beówulf swims five days through the icy sea, tracks foul spirits to their den beneath the water. Impossible? Why no. Here am I now, shivering under my warm overcoat while that young fellow welcomes the keen air to his bared breast. He is a step backwards toward the noble past.

He is a connecting link between ourselves and the heroes. I am giving my life to the study of heroic lives—to the depiction of inspiring careers in quaint language. Alas! I have given it away. It is too late now for me to change. But I was not made of heroic stuff. I may at least try to be great enough to admire that which I am myself not able to become, and to admire without envy. God help me! . . . . I could love a man with such a chest as that."

Then the good gentleman would perhaps speak a few kind, modest words to Israel, (calling him James Johnson, for Israel had retained this *alias*,) or forget himself completely in the absorbing interest of a great question which had occupied his mind for a year.

"A long period of gestation," he would admit. " I must soon be delivered of this happy thought which I know is somewhere in my brain, and which, when it issues, will reconcile the harsh expressions of the ancient original with the refinements of modern taste."

He was in search of a measure which would suit the great Old English poem, and yet be musical.

One afternoon when this whimsical question was fairly burning within him, he came up and stood by his hired man. Strangely enough, it seemed to him that if Israel should open his mouth to speak, his first words would contain the answer. He looked long and earnestly at the youth, so that Israel smiled, but said nothing and continued his work without a pause. Then John Eaton walked aside, and the solution which had seemed ready to come to him became again only a faint possibility. Then he turned back and passed by Israel: again the answer almost attained,—a throbbing at his ears which, if he could quite catch it, would be the accents of the long-sought rhythm,—a wavering line before his eyes, that was almost a perfect verse. Then, when he had passed the silent workman, the old vacancy and impossibility.

"Why this," said he to himself, "this is the children's game of 'Hot and Cold'. I am nearer the idea when I am near Johnson." And he returned to him, saying: "My dear man, would it be asking too much of you to come to me when you are rested this evening,—to come to me in my study? I have something to read to you."

Of course Israel assented.

The same evening Israel entered the study,—a large room almost destitute of furniture; red curtains drawn close; not a picture upon the walls, or other decorative object to be seen save, above the simple fire-place, a bronze statuette of the Venus of Melos. The entire center of the room was filled by a table, so large that one could scarcely reach objects placed farthest from its circumference. There was a litter of papers and books upon this table.

John Eaton asked Israel to sit before the fire and, in order to make him feel at home, spoke first about the study.

"This room," he said, "is for earnest thought; and I, who am by nature prone to rambling fancies, have removed from it every object the sight of which might tempt my mind to wander away from the subject I have placed before me. Concentration: that is the watchword of my sanctum. To encourage myself in concentration, I banish whatever suggests the outside world or its inhabitants. Even books I am not using I will not have here.

"When I first took up my quarters here, I was less strict. Then I allowed myself one picture at a time,—as the Japanese do, who you know, however many works of pictorial art they may possess, enjoy these one at a time, keeping the others rolled up and put away. But soon I found that in this way I was destroying my relish for my entire collection. I noticed that after a week or so each picture in turn began to seem inferior."

"Did you try landscapes?" asked Israel.

"No: my windows are my landscapes. The prospect from these being so fine, I have never felt a need for landscape painting. The lack in my household is the lack of society, of friendly men and women and children. So I have peopled it with creatures of art,—representations of human beings who become familiar and endeared to me little by little and do very well in the place of real people.

"But as I was saying, the pictures which pleased me most in other rooms of the house for some mysterious reason lost their charm quickly when exhibited here."

"Was this copy of the Venus standing here at that time?" Israel asked.

"Yes. I never will be separated from that. I bought it years ago in Rome; and how many of my better impulses have been inspired by its perfections I hardly dare assert. My opinion would sound extravagant."

Israel suggested that the contrast with this Venus spoiled modern pictures.

John was thoughtful for a moment and then beamed upon him, saying, "You are right."

Then the simple-minded John Eaton exclaimed: "Now we are students together, you and I; for we have considered a nice question in criticism and you have helped me out of the difficulty. You have the master-key, taste,—an inborn love of the best. I thought I could not be mistaken. Do you know, now I feel that you have a perfect right, even in my study. I feel that you are at home here. The same quality, I trust, will make you feel at ease with me."

This was said in an appealing, modest way, which won a polite response from the younger man.

"I am quite at ease with you, sir; but I attributed that to your cordiality rather than to any merit in myself."

"Now let me tell you why I asked you to come to me this evening,—that is, if you are not tired."

"Not a bit, sir. On the contrary, I am eager to hear."

Thereupon John Eaton took up from the table a small volume neatly bound in black. It was the copy of Beówulf which Winthrop still treasures for his foster-father's sake, and from which I have gained some knowledge of the poem.

"I have had my translation bound in with the text, page for page, line for line, as you see it," said Eaton. "But, dear me! I have not told you what it is."

He handed the book to Israel and leaned back in his chair, crossing his knees with the evident intention of beginning deliberately.

"It is a story, a very old story,—yet you may find in it if you choose the story of yourself."

"Of my future, perhaps," said Israel. "There is nothing interesting or worth telling in what I have done up to this time."

"May-be, may-be. I do not read the stars or the lines of the hand; but I love to forecast the future of young people. If you had lived in the time long gone by, when Beówulf lived, you would have been like him; and if Beówulf were alive to-day, I think he would look like you, my dear Johnson."

"So this is the Anglo-Saxon poem of Beówulf?" said Israel, opening the volume.

"You know it? You have read it?"

"No. But in the history of English literature I studied, there was an account which interested me of the single manuscript—of the ninth century, was it not?—in which the poem exists."

John Eaton leaned forward and spoke eagerly: "Yes, a single manuscript, in part illegible, contains this precious relic of antiquity. I studied that long and zealously in the British Museum, making my text from it. The time seemed to fly in this congenial occupation, which transported my spirit to remotest ages when the figures of men were godlike and the ambitions of the greatest were noble and simple. Those were happy days. It seemed to me then that the words of the original yielded their meaning so easily that it would have been profanation to tamper with them, to put our flimsy modern forms of speech in their place, to translate. But I have changed my mind in that respect. If only the antique thought could be interpreted to our understanding in the right way; if the most noble of our modern words could be cast into a form of verse preserving the movement of the original, yet musical according to our taste, that would be grand! Why, even for educational purposes, there is more of real value to be learned from this poem than from a dozen dry-as-dust histories of Old Germany and Old England!

"I have for the last ten or twelve months been trying to hit upon just the right metrical form in which to cast my translation. As you see it there, in the book you hold, it is literal,—line for line, word for word, so far as possible.

"I want to read you a few of the best passages, and I will sketch the story up to the point where they begin.

"Hrothgar was king of the Danes, and his kinsmen gladly obeyed him inasmuch as he had fortune in war, honor in battle.

"It came into his mind that he would command his subjects to construct a great mead-hall, in which he might feast and distribute treasures to young and to old and dispense hospitality.

"In time all was ready. The hall towered aloft, high and long, the greatest and most splendid building of those days. Hrothgar called its name Heorot.

"Together with his thegns he feasted within, distributed gifts and listened to the sound of the harp and the clear song of the gleeman.

"But a mighty demon who abode in darkness began to devise treacherous assaults. This grim stranger was called Grendel, who ruled the moors, the fen and the fastness.

"After the night had come, Grendel went out to attack the high house; found therein a company of nobles sleeping after the banquet. He took thirty of these and with this feast of corpses fared home.

"The next night he inflicted a yet greater death-woe. So did he war against right until the best of houses stood empty and deserted.

"Twelve winters' tide the Danes endured his violence; therefore it became widely known that Grendel warred against Hrothgar.

"This report was carried by traveling gleeman across the strait to the Swedish Goths. Among these Goths lived the strongest of mankind, Beówulf.

"Beówulf ordered that a ship should be made ready, chose fourteen companions and set sail. He offered his service to Hrothgar.

"The distressed king gladly accepted this offer and departed out of the hall with his company of Danes. He stationed a guard against Grendel; but Beówulf would trust neither to these nor to his own followers, but to his own proud might. Then he doffed his iron corselet, the helm from his head, and gave his sword to a serving man, bidding him guard the war-trappings.

"Spoke then the hero certain bold words before he ascended the bed: 'I do not count myself weaker in battle or warlike deeds than does Grendel count himself. Therefore I wish not to slay him with the sword. He has no advantage of weapons. If he dare seek me, then the wise God shall award glory even as to him it seems meet.

"Bowed himself then the valorous: the pillow received his face. Round about him many a keen sea-fighter bent to his rest within the hall. Not one of them thought that he should thence seek his beloved land again.

"The shade-wanderer came, advancing in murky night. The spear-men who should have defended the antler-crowned house slept,—all save one.

"From the moor came Grendel advancing under misty cliffs: God's ire he bore. The wicked enemy of the human race meant to seize upon some one in the high hall; strode under the clouds until he full well perceived the guest-house, the gold hall, variegated with golden plates. That was not the first time that he had sought Hrothgar's home; but in the days of his life he never found a sturdier man. To the building came then the joyless creature. The door soon gave way, although fastened with forged bands, so soon as he touched it with his hand. The plotter of evil dashed open the building's entrance, for he was enraged.

"Quickly after that the fiend trod on the checkered floor, moving in wrathful mood. From his eye shot a hateful gleam, likest a flame. He saw in the building many men, a band of friends sleeping together, a number of kinsmen-warriors: then his heart laughed. The accursed being thought that ere the day came he would sever each one's life from the body; for in him was aroused the hope of a full feast.

"The wretch thought not to delay, but quickly seized the nearest, a sleeping warrior, tore him at unawares, devoured his flesh, drank his streaming blood, greedily swallowed bite after bite. Soon had he feasted upon every morsel of the lifeless one.

"Forth he stepped nearer; laid hands upon the stout-hearted Beówulf as he lay upon his bed. The enemy reached out against him with his hands. But Beówulf quickly seized the menacing one and leaned upon his arm.

"The author of evils soon discovered that he had not met upon this mid-earth in another man stronger handgrip. He became fearful in mind and soul: none the more could he escape.

"He fain would have fled to his lurking place and haunt of devils. The good hero bethought him then of his promise, stood upright and grappled him fast. The giant's fingers burst as he strove outwards. The earl stepped in front of him.

"That was an evil excursion, when this mischievous spirit went to Heorot, dinned the lordly hall: All the Danes who dwelt in the city had their ale spilled.

"Wrathful were both the struggling mighty chiefs. The building resounded. Then was it great wonder that the guest-hall withstood the war-beasts: but it was fast within and without with iron bands, forged with workmanlike care.

"Then from its prop was wrenched many a gold-adorned mead bench, where the enemies fought. Little had the wise men of the Danes thought that ever any man could by force break it asunder, the goodly and horn-decked hall,—unless arms of flame should swallow it in smoke.

"Strange clamor arose. Direful fear seized upon the Danes, every man of them,—of those who from the wall hearkened to the outcry: the enemy of God singing his frightful lay, his cry of defeat,—the thrall of hell bewailing his wound.

"He who was strongest of men in that day of this life held him too fast. The protector of earls would not for anything leave the murderous guest alive, nor did he deem his life useful to any people.

"Then many of Beówulf's earls brandished their swords and would have shielded the life of their lord and renowned chief, if so they might. The brave sons of strife, when they attacked Grendel and thought to hew him and seek his soul, knew not that the choicest blade in the world could take no effect upon the mighty plague: for he had spelled him against victorious weapons.

"Yet his life-parting must be wretched and the lone spirit journey afar into the power of fiends; for he who had been mirthful only as he framed many treacheries against mankind discovered now that his body would not follow him, but the bold Goth held him by the hand. Each was loathed by the other.

"Bodily pain awaited the grisly wretch; on his shoulder appeared a mortal wound; his sinews sprang apart, the bone-casings burst. To Beówulf was allotted the honor of the conflict.

"Sick unto death fled Grendel under the moor-cliffs, to seek his joyless dwelling. He knew only too well that his life's end was come, the measure of his days.

"After the deadly struggle, the wish of all the Danes had been accomplished. He who came from afar, wise and stout-hearted, had cleansed Hrothgar's hall,—had freed it from assault. Heorot was filled with friends."

Here John Eaton paused; for he suddenly bethought himself that, carried away by his enthusiasm for the poem, he was giving more than a mere sketch of its plot. His voice had grown sonorous, and his face expressed the force of his subject while he recited the story. The gentle scholar was fairly transformed. Then with a sudden change of tone he added:

"And so forth and so on, my dear Johnson. It is a tale of the glory of conflict, leadership. Beówulf is grand because he is the strongest and leads."

"What was the fate of the hero?" asked Israel.

"After other noble exploits," said Eaton, "Beówulf was made king of the Goths. He ruled the people well for fifty years. Then a fire dragon began to lay waste the land. Beówulf slays the dragon, but is himself mortally wounded. That is perfect art, because it is necessary. No other termination of such a career would be artistic. What would we have? The hero struggles nobly throughout his life and perishes in the arms of victory. A hero is not a god, to conquer always."

"Then a hero's character is imperfect, and his end is tragical?"

"Yes: in the very nature of things."

"But the hero is supposed to be the highest type of manhood."

"Yes: I love to read about them, and so to pass in their companionship, as it were, the hours which other men employ in social pleasure, because they are so much nobler than the men of to-day."

"There are no heroes then to-day?"

"That I am not willing to say; but I know none."

"I know none of the kind you describe. But is there not a higher type possible to-day? Are there to-day no Beówulfs without the tragical chapter,—who triumph from first to last,—who overcome the fire-dragon without being scathed? That would be still more admirable, would it not?"

"Ye-es," replied John Eaton, doubtfully. "That might be more admirable. But then there would be no sacrifice; and the element of self-sacrifice is necessary to the conception of a hero. Why, a man always successful would be selfish. Take away the element of self-sacrifice from your hero and there remains——a devil!"

"Then it follows," said Israel very quietly, "that there is a more admirable type than hero,—namely, devil: not an inferior devil, like Grendel, but a clever devil, superior to the hero and unscathed by the dragon. Let us give the new type a name: The Devil of Selfishness."

"But," said John Eaton, much perplexed, "but that is an ideal unattainable by mortals; for mortal man cannot always succeed, always combat for his own selfish cause and be always victorious and saved harmless."

"Cannot!" cried Israel scornfully. "Cannot? Until his powers fail and together with his powers desire ceases, and so the whole story is perfectly rounded off,—no tragedy, no defeat? A man can assert himself so long as he desires that and then cease to exist! From what you yourself say, Mr. Eaton, this seems a more perfect ideal than that of the hero. For instance, this would be the tone of such a life: Success, gladness, assurance of superiority—everywhere and at all times, as in this passage":—

(He opened the volume of Beówulf and read, wilfully misreading John Eaton's translation.)

"Then from the moor came, under the mist-cliffs,
  Grendel striding, scorning the wrath of God——"

"Stop! stop!" cried Eaton, springing from his chair and evincing the wildest excitement. "Read those lines again! Wait one moment, till I get paper"; and with a trembling hand he seized a pen, dipped the wrong end into the ink bottle, flung it away and snatched up another. "Now, now, read those lines again, please. Forgive me, but read quickly! Oh, no! never mind. I can remember them. How could I ever forget?

> Then from the moor came, under the mist-cliffs,
> Grendel striding, scorning—no, *bearing*—the wrath of God."

John Eaton wrote down the words in sprawling, irregular characters; then, with the energy of delight, seized Israel's hands and wrung them, beaming the while into his face through tears of joy.

"That is it,—the lost metre! A happy inspiration has revealed the secret. You have given me what I have sought so long and vainly!"

Israel was one of those players who know when to stop. He had won largely in two casts,—in the suggestion about the Venus and in discovering the metre—so he pocketed his winnings, as it were, and while admiration was still lighting the eyes of his master, took his leave and retired to his room.

These were Israel's thoughts, and this is the answer to the question at the end of the preceding chapter:

"This man John Eaton is more of a fool than I am. His ambition is more extravagant than my own, because, as anyone ought to see at a glance, that old fossil of a poem has no music in it. It is his mine; and there is no gold in his mine but what he takes in himself.

"Even if he should succeed, what good would it do him? His world is the past; and dead men cannot return to praise him. He does not care for the praise, as he could not support the criticism, of these degenerate times, as he calls our own times. He is pure, unselfish, enthusiastic, elevated, trustful: that is to say, he is an old fool."

CHAPTER V

N the second Sunday of his stay at "Westwood," Israel became restless. The almost feverish work of the week being followed by a day of complete rest, the change was too sudden. Accordingly he strolled out, intending to see something of the town.

He walked across-country towards East Rock, meaning to return from that point through the streets. Coming to the ridge along which ran Tutor's Lane, he turned to follow this wood-road.

There are not even now any dwelling-houses at this point; but thirty years ago the road was much more wild and much less frequented.

Israel was walking along rapidly, saying to himself: "My service is ended. I have enough now, putting what I have earned with what I brought with me, to take me to the end of my journey. Yes, to-morrow I shall go, without warning that simpleton, John Eaton.

"At last I am free! I am perfectly free now for the first time in my life; for I have the means to do what I will, and there is nobody hanging about my neck."

A piercing shriek, a cry of mingled joy and terror, seemed to proceed from the earth itself just behind him. Israel turned sharply about. There, a few feet from the edge of the road, a woman was crouched upon the ground.

Lilly!

The woman was trembling so that she could not rise or speak. Her face was deadly pale, her eyes like those of a wounded animal.

Israel stood looking down at her,—at her stained dress and disordered hair, at the dark lines under her eyes, at her white, quivering lips. Then he said:

"Lilly, what are you doing here?"

"Oh, come to me!" she moaned. "Don't you see me?"

*   *   *   *   *   *

At first Lilly was too overjoyed to think of anything except the recovered lover.

At length Israel compelled her to explain. Then she told of the sorrowful birthday in Oskawask: how she had waited for his coming, and finally the sisters, dear Grace and Gertrude, had come, thinking Lilly might know where he was; how she had then gone back with them to Israel's home.

"And, oh, my darling husband! there we sat, four helpless women (for even your mother seemed helpless) and waited. Worthless, weak women, who must wait and suffer! How I wished I could be a man then!"

"You had father and Samuel," interposed Israel.

"Yes, but your father went down to the falls, and back and forth between the falls and the house: that was all. Samuel went about his work as usual: he has no heart! Oh, I mean a *man*, like you, my superbness! . . . We waited all through the day until evening; then your mother rose and with a little sob which broke my heart, she is so cheerful and brave usually, she put away the"—(Lilly herself sobbed) "the presents for your birthday. . . . Is this you? Really, truly you?"

Words failed her, and she clung to him in order to assure herself of this possession, this precious fact. Her face was hidden, pressed against his breast. As for his face, which she could not see, can you conceive the expression of disgust rendering a beautiful face perfectly ugly?

As though she had drawn force and confidence from him, Lilly continued:

"Then the others went about their work again; but I waited and waited, day after day, until all hope was gone. No, not that; for when I began to despair I began to hope again. I saw that it would kill me to give up hope. . . . I resolved to find you, and set out alone. I took the southern road because your thoughts always took that direction. I inquired as I went. The first day there was no trace."

It will be remembered that Israel made this portion of the way by night.

"The next day I was about to give up and try another direction, when?"—— here Lilly began to laugh and grow radiantly happy as she recalled the first encouragement—"I met a milkman, who said that on the very day, you know, Friday, he had been stopped in the early morning by a young fellow who asked for a drink of milk and offered to pay for it. And he said he had—I mean, you had—a mark on your cheek. Do you see! Even he knew you were magnificent!

"So I went forward until I came to the foot of a long hill, where I took the wrong road."

"Was there a sign-post at the cross-roads?" Israel asked.

"Yes, with nothing on it but names of people and hearts and darts carved in it," laughed Lilly.

It was there that Israel had been overtaken by the farmer. Lilly had had no such good fortune, but had toiled up over the hill only to find that she had come miles out of the way and in consequence must take a road which enters Oldhaven from the north-east.

She had met expenses on the road with the little money saved up for her wedding. Her last stopping place was a few miles from town. "On the other side of that hill," she said, pointing to Mill Rock. She had been so weak and ill in the morning that she could not stir; but in the afternoon had mustered strength enough to come so far. Here she had been resting when she had seen Israel pass, and cried out.

"My darling little lady, you have done all this for me!" exclaimed Israel; and by that one sentence Lilly felt more than rewarded for all.

Then he soothed her, telling her that he had been earning money for her; that this was necessary in order that they might be married; that he had not told her his intention lest she should have refused her consent.

Then he persuaded her to return to the house, on the farther side of the Rock, from which she had just come.

"Of course I can let you stay there until to-morrow only,—no longer than that,—my dear little wife," he said, gayly. "Meantime I look up a nice place for you near where I am working. . . . Listen: I have enough now to provide a little cottage, with only two or three rooms to be sure, but all the better. You cannot be out of my sight when I come home from work in the evening. It will be some distance from town, for I have not much, you know,—but all the better: we shall have no neighbors to interrupt us, and if you feel lonely, you can just put on your things and run over to watch me at work. That will be good for your cheeks, my dear, which are rather pale to-day; and after a little while you will not be lonely even when I am gone ——."

See that red brand on his face!

It was such a lonely road that Israel did not hesitate to carry her in his arms part of the way; and when he left her near the house on Second Lake, she was entirely trustful.

*   *   *   *   *   *

The next day, Monday, Lilly waited vainly until late in the afternoon. Then an idea occurred to her which made her hurriedly don her wraps and start out into the cold air.

"He must have meant that I was to meet him there, where we met yesterday," she said to herself.

In her eagerness, she almost flew along the road.

"He will be waiting: he may be angry," she thought.

Poor Lilly! She stood alone, waiting by the stone at the roadside until it grew dark.

Then she returned alone, with a woeful heaviness at her heart.

CHAPTER VI

ILLY LINCOLN was by no means a helpless person, without energy or resources in herself. The blind passion and complete self-surrender with which she had attached herself to Israel are not to be mistaken for evidences of weakness; for indeed, in this matter of loving, it is oftener the small and weak natures which hesitate, deliberate and are wise in their own interests.

After the first shock of her disappointment, she began to realize that there might be some simple and natural explanation of Israel's not appearing at the appointed spot in Tutor's Lane. It had occurred to her immediately, as already suggested, that her lover might even have waited for her there until his patience was exhausted, while she, through a misunderstanding, had been expecting him at the farm-house on Second Lake. This explanation she clung to, because it seemed to make all the fault her own.

"Or, if that is not it," she reasoned, "he may have met with some accident. Handling those heavy stones I have always heard is very dangerous. Oh, if he should be suffering away from me!"

She recalled also that charming picture of domestic happiness which Israel had painted in words that seemed to her more glowing than the brightest colors of a New England sunset.

So then, after a little, she had conquered whatever bitterness or misery at first entered her breast; and if any doubt or mistrust of Israel applied at the door of her heart, she would not admit it or even listen to it. She was a proud little woman in her own way. Love and doubt could not dwell together in her nature.

Israel was either justly angry with her or he was in need of her. That he had deserted her was quite unthinkable. Of course she must search for him and find him.

But he had not told her for whom he was working: how should she set about finding him?

This is what she did: she went right into the center of the town to inquire for Mr. Penman. He had been in Oskawask the night before Israel's first disappearance: there might be some connection between the two occurrences. He might even have persuaded Israel to seek his fortune in Oldhaven.

This thought made her pause. How she would hate him if that were true!

But after all, he was the sole person whom she knew in all this strange town, even by name. And then, too, he had looked and spoken kindly that evening. Surely he could not have been so wicked. No, she would not believe it.

On little Lilly went, trying hard to look very courageously, and painfully conscious of the rustic and unfashionable dress she wore as she passed in front of those substantial residences—which seemed to her palaces—in the better part of the city.

"Will Israel be ashamed of me here among all these fine people?" she asked herself.

On she went beneath that beautiful Gothic arch of elms on Temple-street until she came to the green.

She had a vague notion that upon arriving at the very center of the city she would find one house much larger and more splendid than all the rest, and there

Mr. Penman would live. He had seemed to her so much finer than the neighbors in Oskawask, when he was riding through on his way to Boston and when Israel had given up his own room to this stranger, that Lilly naturally thought he would be finer and grander than all the inhabitants here also.

At the green, however, the largest buildings were evidently not dwelling-houses. On one side were chiefly shops and hotels; on another a row of brick factories or jails, she thought; then many churches and residences, among which she could not decide upon the probable home of Mr. Penman.

Wandering about with indecision for a time, she finally mustered courage to address a workman—one of many who, as the custom then was, were idling upon the corner of Church and Chapel streets, waiting to be employed. Their rough dress was more familiar to Lilly, who feared to stop any of the fine gentlemen who passed and, with a woman's instinct in such matters, never dreamed of appealing to one of her own sex.

"Can you tell me where Mr. Penman lives?" she inquired.

The man thus addressed was a brutal, stupid German, who stared at her pretty face upturned towards his and made a motion to put his grimy hand on her shoulder.

She was about to turn and fly when a middle-aged gentleman walked up to the crowd of workmen and said:

"I want to hire two men by the week to work for me on my place. They must be strong fellows, for the work is heavy; but I am ready to pay you well and feed you well. Which of you understands fence-building?"

Something in this gentleman's voice or manner informed Lilly that she could speak to him without fear, so she turned to him repeating her question:

"Can you tell me where Mr. Penman lives, sir?"

The German crowded her aside and took off his cap deferentially before the gentleman.

"Mein Herr—" he began.

"What do you want?" the gentleman demanded.

"To work, gnäd'ger Herr."

"Don't you see the young lady has spoken to me? Stand aside!"

The churl slunk away, casting an angry look upon Lilly, to whom the gentleman then spoke in the most kindly, amiable way.

"Did you ask for Mr. Penman—Horace Penman—child? Why yes, he lives but a few steps from here. I will accompany you."

"Oh, no, sir! Don't take that trouble," said Lilly, secretly hoping that he would, however, for she felt wonderfully well with this stranger.

"In one instant," he continued; "as soon as I have arranged with these men,"—and he chose two from among the applicants, directing these to come to Westwood; then joined Lilly and walked with her, smiling and chatting, along one of the diagonal paths of the green.

Horace Penman and he were old friends, he explained. He never came into town without visiting him and had been on the point of going there when she spoke. Mr. Penman had been away for a fortnight and had just returned. They would surely find him at the house with his parents this first morning.

A sense of security, of peace and quiet happiness seemed to proceed from this man and entered gratefully into the overtaxed spirit of his companion.

When they reached Mr. Penman's house on Temple street, Lilly found that it was one she had passed without suspicion. It was a plain, humble, wooden structure, in general appearance much like the New England farm-house,—one of many such scattered throughout this city and, together with the abundance of trees, giving to the whole the appearance of a large village. There was a narrow strip of lawn between the house and the street. In the rear was a deep, old-fashioned garden.

There were two sufficient reasons why Mr. Penman, with his aged parents, lived in so modest a mansion.

First, this house, standing upon this very spot, had been inhabited by three generations of Penmen, Horace A., Horace B., and now plain Horace. It would have been unbecoming in the present representative if he had let the property pass into strange hands.

The second reason, which may appear sufficient in itself, was this: The third Horace was, at that time, not independent in money matters. A rising young lawyer of good reputation, his clientage was still somewhat restricted; and there being several persons whose claims upon his extremely moderate income seemed to him equal or superior to his own claim, he was only too happy to be able to keep up the old family home, to offer its shelter, as had been the custom of his father and grandfather, to relatives visiting the city, and in a word to maintain that unambitious style of living, neither shrinking from accustomed expenses nor inviting new ones, which prevailed among the older families.

They found Mr. Penman at home, being treated for a severe cold contracted during his horse-back excursion to Boston. Lilly's kind guide was most solicitous about his friend's health. Mr. Penman reassured him and promised to be out in a day or two at farthest.

"Then you must come to see me, my dear Horace!" cried the other. "Come the very first day you feel up to it. I have something important in a literary way to communicate. I have found, or rather a happy chance has revealed to me, the proper metre of Beówulf. It is grand; and the manner in which it was discovered is most singular and interesting. I owe it all to a young man named Johnson —— but I must not keep you now. Come as soon as you can!"

He took leave of Lilly with especial courtesy and, as he passed down the street, turned to wave his hand to Mr. Penman, who stood at the window watching him.

Lilly had begun to fear that she was forgotten when Mr. Penman crossed the room to where she was sitting and placed himself in front of her.

"Well, Miss Lincoln," he said, "what can I do for you?"

This had an unfriendly sound to Lilly; but she answered with praiseworthy firmness:

"I came to ask your assistance, sir; but I fear I intrude, and ——"

"Pray don't be offended, Miss Lincoln," Mr. Penman hastened to interpose. "I did not speak your name just now because a lawyer can never know why people come to him, and it occurred to me that perhaps you might not care to have it mentioned before a stranger. How are they all at Oskawask, and especially, how is the son, Israel?"

Lilly told her story very simply and

concluded by asking Mr. Penman's aid to find Israel.

At a loss for something better to say or to do, Mr. Penman rubbed his hands together and repeated that well-worn formula, " We will see what can be done; we will see what is to be done." Then he tried to imagine what John Eaton would do under like circumstances; for the case seemed one of peculiar delicacy. Perhaps in this way he came upon a suggestion which seemed at least a good beginning.

" You can be of great service to me, Miss Lincoln," he said, "if you will take my place with my parents while I go out in this matter."

" Oh, do you think they would like it?"

" I am sure they will,"—and he went out of the room, presently returning with a tall lady of slight, erect figure, whose sweet face was framed by snow-white curls.

" Mother," said he, " this is Miss Lincoln, —one of those who were so kind to me in Oskawask, you know. I wrote you about it, don't you remember?"

Mrs. Penman blushed as she took Lilly's hand, thanking her for the imputed hospitality. Her son thought there was nothing so lovely in the world as these girlish blushes upon his aged mother's cheeks: but then, Mr. Penman had not up to this time ever had any other sweetheart than his mother.

Then Lilly was taken to see the old father, whose infirmities seldom allowed him to quit the sitting room on the second floor. Both these parents were delighted with the pretty young country maiden, who was accordingly left in their care—or they in her's, as you choose to look at it.

Mr. Penman was so extremely interested in the matter that he could not remain indoors, but, regardless of his doctor's injunction, wrapped and bundled himself warmly and went out to search for Israel, wondering at the same time what he should do with such a young Hercules even if he succeeded in finding him. Towards night he returned without having accomplished anything further than the restoration of his own health, for the hard exercise in heavy clothing cured his cold.

The following day he went to see John Eaton and told him Lilly's story.

" Now I thought the moment she spoke

to me that there was something most interesting in her sad young face!" cried John Eaton. "But, dear me, I am always imagining a romance for each new person I meet. For instance that James Johnson, who was working for me but a few days ago: my dear Penman, nothing, positively nothing, is impossible in connection with that young man. How I wish he had remained so that you might see him!"

"The most hopeless feature of this case," Mr. Penman continued, giving no heed to what his friend had said, "is that the man who has betrayed and deserted this poor girl cannot be frightened or coerced into doing his duty by her. If we succeed in laying hands upon him, he will resist and make a bad matter worse." And then he confessed how deep an impression the young Israel had made upon him, that evening in Oskawask, concluding with a description of the beautiful, proud face.

John Eaton had become very thoughtful. "I promised to tell you about the wonderful discovery of a new metre for Beówulf," he said, "and this is the right time." He spoke of the superhuman strength and noble bearing which had distinguished the adventurer and made him seem a person peculiarly fitted to enter into the spirit of daring adventure so powerfully expressed in the old poem.

"Well, then," he added gravely, "your description of his appearance leaves no room for doubt. Your Israel and my Johnson are one and the same person."

CHAPTER VII

FATIGUE, exposure and excitement had their natural effect upon Lilly: she fell sick.

At one time she thought herself dying, and evidently had a great weight upon her mind. Mr. Penman strove to comfort her, and offered to renew his efforts to find Israel; but she smiled at this and said:

"He will come. If only I could go out to meet him in Tutor's Lane!"

Mr. Penman notified the family at Oskawask of Lilly's sickness. They wished her to return to them; but she would not consent to leave Oldhaven, where, as she persisted in believing, she was to meet Israel.

These formal letters were the beginning of an interesting correspondence, of occasional visits and many passages of friendship, in the course of which Mr. Penman began to have a tender feeling for one or both of the sisters, Grace and Gertrude.

It is to be noted that a great change was

coming over the Slyme family. Fortune, which had averted its face throughout several generations, began now to smile upon them. The explanation of this change has been given by Mr. Penman. They were beginning to feel quite prosperous and in the spring there was talk of damming the weedy stream and putting up a small mill immediately. These were happy days for Jonathan Slyme, days of plodding industry for Samuel, days of subdued grief for the sisters, who mourned their brother and their friend. As for Mrs. Sarah, she directed everything and inspirited everybody as usual.

So winter and spring passed and summer arrived.

One day towards the end of June, Mr. Penman heard that John Eaton's only son had died in Havana. He took occasion soon afterwards to drive out to "Westwood," in order to express to that dear friend his heartfelt sympathy.

John Eaton gave to the conversation which ensued a somewhat unforeseen turn.

"How soon is the child expected?" he asked.

"Very soon."

"Would Madame Lilly consent to my adopting it, think you?"

"Yes: but under the circumstances she is hardly to be consulted." Mr. Penman told of her strange fancy about meeting Israel at a certain spot in Tutor's Lane, and of her earnest desire and futile efforts to go thither each afternoon—a thing quite impossible now, of course. Her mind was undoubtedly affected, he said, although her disposition remained wonderfully sweet.

John Eaton discussed the probable character of the expected. "If he should combine the father's strength and brilliant mind with the mother's heart and disposition, what a noble fellow that would make!" he cried.

There remained one doubt to vitiate the whole assumption. "How do you know," Mr. Penman asked, "how do you know that it will be a boy?"

John Eaton's countenance fell. "It must be," he said; and Horace Penman saw that his friend was thinking of the lost son, who had never been much comfort to his parents nor had ever returned his father's deep love.

Therefore Mr. Penman suggested no further difficulties or doubts when his friend proceeded to sketch the possibility of training such a rich nature and bringing forth excellent fruit.

Shortly after this conversation a male child was born.

The young mother's love for this child was something wonderful to behold. It was an eager, fierce love. She could not endure any other person's touching the little stranger in pink or taking him from her even for a moment. The dear old Mrs. Penman shook her grey head over such conduct. " It is not natural," she said.

Mr. Penman, for his part, saw with grief that the good result he had hoped from Lilly's confinement had not been realized. On the contrary, symptoms which alarmed him became daily more apparent. Lilly would hold the child pressed close against her face and speak to it by the hour, quite forgetful of any other presence. At such times she would utter thoughts which a woman hides at the bottom of her heart, speaking as though to her lover. Whoever chanced to be near then would tiptoe away, leaving her alone with sacred joys.

Often she would look up if one spoke to her and explain mildly : " It is not mine but for a little while. I must give it back to its father, you see. So I am loving it and telling it all I can while it is here."

No one guessed the real state of poor Lilly's mind but Mr. Penman, who could not bear to add this anxiety to his mother's cares; for which reason Mr. Penman undertook himself to watch her and save her from harm when his other occupations left him free,—that is, of course, after doctor and nurse had taken their departure.

It was with this thought uppermost in his mind that he hurried home one evening in July. The mother met him in the hallway, looking pale and agitated.

"Mrs. Lilly has gone out," she said. "I do not know where. I went upstairs to your father and when I came down again—about an hour ago—she was missing. I did not know whether to send for you. Oh, I fear it will do her much harm to go out now!"

"And the boy?" Mr. Penman asked quickly.

"She must have taken it with her."

"Tell David to follow me in the buggy, dear mother, right out Tutor's Lane."

It was plain enough. Mr. Penman felt almost relieved that what he knew must come sometime had occurred when the air was so mild that Lilly and her child would probably take no harm from exposure to it. Without hesitation he bent his steps towards Tutor's Lane, confidently expecting to find her waiting for Israel at the appointed place.

Quite far out on the road he met her returning alone, her arms hanging free at her side, a divine resignation glorifying her pale, pure face. She smiled at Mr. Penman, saying:

"He will be happy now! He will take baby first and after a while, when he has money enough, you know, he will come to meet me there. Oh, it is not far! I can easily walk out each evening until he comes. And then I shall have them both together. I pray God it may not be long, sir, before he comes."

Mr. Penman told her to walk on slowly until she should meet the carriage and then drive home. He himself pressed forward and found the child asleep, nicely wrapped in the shawl which Lilly had worn when she came to Oldhaven, by the well-known rock near the roadway. He took up this pitiful little bundle and carried it by the nearest way to John Eaton at

"Westwood,"—retracing thus the course which Israel had taken on that memorable Sunday afternoon in November.

It was his intention to leave the child with this kind friend only upon condition that Lilly's delusion should continue and she should be happy in the sacrifice. That proved to be the case. Lilly continued until her death to be an inmate of the Penman home. She was very pale and quiet and always wore a mysterious smile, as though she knew her thoughts were strange and that something wonderful beyond belief was in store for her, which no one else should hear about until the time came.

CHAPTER VIII

> When the south wind, in May days,
> With a net of shining haze
> Silvers the horizon wall,
> And, with softness touching all,
> Tints the human countenance
> With a color of romance—*Emerson.*

HOW gloriously Spring comes to the southern mountains!

How lofty are these mountains; yet timbered to their very summits, rich in the flora of every clime, rich in clear waters, in mineral springs,— the source of noble rivers which run from them into the Atlantic and the Gulf of Mexico.

This was the delectable land of the Indian tribes, their terrestrial paradise, their happy hunting ground.

Those living here before the arrival of the white adventurers had mastered a certain science of government, together with some of the arts of civilization. They were the proud masters of all the neighboring tribes.

But they were driven out by the white man and their lands thrown open to settlers, who poured in from the adjoining States.

These whites were vagabond fellows, welcoming an opportunity to live without tilling the soil, coming with long, heavy rifles and without hoes or plows.

The game which the Indians had preserved was exterminated by these ruthless, improvident scamps.

Now the old haunts of the deer are invaded by half wild swine and lean kine giving watery milk; and the white men eat dirt.

See these cabins of unhewn logs, partly chinked with red clay. One room serves for the entire family and oftentimes for three generations, — tenants enough to clear a few acres of land (leaving large stumps), to scratch the surface and plant it.

They are not exactly a rough set, but in their own phraseology a "low-down" set; not actively vicious, but they lack little of being nasty. They have parsons: scamps, except the man J——, who goes dirty and hunts down converts as the local curs hunt woodchucks. They have doctors of medicine: these accuse each other of malpractice and themselves stand convicted of ignorance. Illicit stills are everywhere. They hardly recognize such a thing as virtue in women.——Faugh!

A few of the aboriginal lords are left, and these live where the waters divide,— where the streams flow, some to the east and some to the west.

Living together in a little village, these have degenerated and become much like the " white trash;" yet they still keep a few of the old customs,—enough to make them superior to their destroyers: they are frugal, temperate and silent.

Here is the source of one of the rivers emptying into the Atlantic Ocean: a single shaft of spray, falling at once two hundred feet over a brown cliff, softened with tufts of grasses and flowers. Wooded walls of a narrow valley enclose this perfect picture. A pair of hawks circling above cast twin shadows which course in swift silence over sunny bank and silvery waters.

Here is the Indian village. Enter it. It seems deserted, for the inhabitants are all assembled in one central building to witness a wedding.

The spectators are ranged in a circle about a young man and maiden. All stand, except the venerable chief, who is seated near the bride and groom.

All are silent. The chief makes a gesture, full of dignity; and then the young man speaks:

"I promise to supply our household with game."

The young woman rejoins:

"I promise to supply our household with bread."

This traditional formula, uttered in the native language, defines the duties of man and wife.

A murmur of assent comes from the spectators.

Then the chief arises, takes from the shoulders of the bride the blanket of many colors which she wears, while the bridegroom lays off his own, equally gay.

For a moment they stand thus, unclothed but unabashed, because they are without blemish.

Again the murmur of assent from the spectators.

Then the chief places the maiden's blanket upon the shoulders of the man and the man's upon the maiden.

In this manner the contract of marriage is symbolized and evidenced.

Then the chief, with a gesture of dismissal, seats himself again. The ceremony is complete and the assembly dissolved.

One of the spectators and the chieftain remain.

The latter deserves a few words description. He is an enormous man,—almost a giant—still erect and powerful, although evidently very old.

His feature are massive, ugly and yet fascinating; his eyes small, deeply set and lustreless; nose broad; mouth firm, with thin lips; chin and jaw square, strong and too prominent; complexion colored and marked like alligator-skin. Such features in a white man would indicate brutality; but this Indian is wise and just.

The other man, who, riding-whip in hand, now advances to interrogate the taciturn chief, needs no further description. It is Israel.

"Is there gold in these mountains?"

"Yes."

"Where?"

"Everywhere."

"But not these wretched washings, that pay no better than hoeing corn. A gold mine?"

"What is *mine*?"

"Much gold together in one place."

A long pause before the answer comes: "Only in one place much gold—cursed!"

"Cursed?"

No answer.

Israel produces a tobacco-pouch and offers it to the chief, who gravely accepts it and gives his own in return. The pipe of peace has not yet burned out.

They sit opposite one another and smoke in silence. At length Israel begins again:

"More about this gold."

The chief tells of a mighty prince, lord of the Blue Mountain, who had once ruled all the world. He was grand and wise and rich—richer than all other men north or south.

"What was his wealth?"

The Indian, being at a loss for the English word, thrust his hand into his pocket and took out a magnificent specimen of mica, saying:

"This, one; gold, two."

"Ah! he was rich in both mica and gold, but thought most of the mica," Israel explained.

The report was brought to this prince

by young men of a subject tribe dwelling to the southward, that pale-faced strangers had come to them in ships, which they at first supposed to be sea-monsters. Moved by curiosity, the Indians had flocked in great numbers to the shore.

Then the white-faced stranger had taken two, a man and a woman, to the ships, dressed them and let them go free.

The king of the country, learning how generously the man and woman had been dealt with, sent fifty of his people, bearing gifts. Then the white strangers visited him and he received them hospitably.

But these treacherous strangers invited the Indians to visit their ships. When the vessels were crowded with these innocent people, they sailed away and never returned, taking children from parents and husbands from wives.

Then the lord of the Blue Mountain, when he had heard these tidings, declared that the prophecy had been accomplished; that a curse had fallen upon himself, his home and his treasure; that this pale-faced stranger was the great enemy whose coming had been foretold by their wise men.

'The white men,' he said, 'are greedy for the yellow metal, which we hold inferior to mica, but which is their god.

'Upon us the curse will fall most heavily because our mountain is the great source of gold for all this region. The enemy will be drawn hither, lusting after this, and we must finally yield: so runs the prophecy.

'Cursed is this spot, formerly so blest. Its blessing has become its curse. Go, my children, leave me alone to guard our riches, to drink alone the curse of the place, to become like the poisonous weed that grows upon the grave of the murderer. Our treasure is our murderer and this spot is cursed by the overthrow of a mighty people.'

So he sat there and would speak no more nor raise his eyes from the ground. And the people were afraid and left him desolate.

A few were faithful and would not go; but these he did not greet neither answer their greeting. These sat also in silence, gazing off towards the great waters, where their foe was, until they saw their prince arise and lift his eyes to the sky and speak with the Great Spirit. Then he looked for the last time upon his servants and went into the cavern.

"What cavern?" cried Israel.

His treasure-house upon the Blue Mountain.

Those waiting without presently heard a sound as of moaning within the bosom of the mountain, and this grew into a mighty noise and a torrent burst forth, rushing out from the cavern and leaping down the mountain-side. But the cave had always been dry, save for a little spring of sweet waters.

They who saw this miracle cried: 'The curse has indeed fallen upon us;' and they ran fearfully away.

One, who was the prince's son, ventured to return; but the cavern was no more to be found. Only a great and angry torrent burst continually from the mountain-side.

"What has become of the descendants?"

The old chief pointed westward.

"What became of the prince?"

"He is there."

"Where?"

"In the cave, seated, looking down."

"Where is the Blue Mountain?"

The chief pointed to the south-east.

"Where the high peaks sink into the

bosom of the plain, the last, alone. No man lives there. No man knows."

*   *   .*   *   *   *

When Israel is about to ride out of the village, a young Indian maiden who had been present at the wedding, springs from the bushes near where he has tied his horse, looks upon him with the expression of a wild animal in love, tears off a piece of shining mica from a string of such rude ornaments worn around her neck and falling down to her dark breasts, hands this to him and, when he tries to seize her, slips away with the nimbleness of a squirrel, and he hears her laugh coming back through the thicket.

CHAPTER IX

UST beyond the northern boundary of South Carolina, the Blue Ridge Mountains rise quite abruptly to an imposing height. Far as the eye can see to the southward, a vast pine forest covers the undulating country, traversed by streams flowing to the south-east: a land of foxes and snakes —few men.

Yet here and there human habitations are to be seen. The visitor wonders why they are located in such a desert; but the natives do not wonder or even think,— they only " 'low."

Offering a striking contrast to such unprofitable acres, the bottom-lands along the river-courses are extremely fertile. Unfortunately these bottoms are narrow and the market for their produce very distant; nevertheless planting on a considerable scale has been done there by men of wealth and a certain kind of energy. These planters formed a small class, distinctly superior to the " white trash " described in the foregoing chapter and referred to in the last paragraph.

Five of these planters met one afternoon in July, at the house of one of their number. Inasmuch as they had the intention of founding a city, it is but right that their names and honors should be recorded without delay.

Dr. Curesome was a very thin man, smoking his pipe and drinking incessantly and referring to his wife as authority for every statement.

Dr. Oldboy was a theorist. He had a theory for everything in heaven and upon the earth. Furthermore, he was a fighting, gaming parson. He was public-spirited and he did what he pleased. It is told of him that when he thought the neighborhood needed a Sunday-school, he put up a notice in the local post-office to the follow-effect: Sunday-school at Dr. Oldboy's house next Sunday morning. Every person attending will receive five cents. C. D. Oldboy.

Col. Owner was a polite, case-loving, generous Southerner, with cordial manners and many noble traits of character.

" Billy " Miller was local politician,

banker, postmaster, surveyor and whisky-dealer.

These gentlemen, all well-dressed, were seated on the veranda of Squire Lynch's house. They were smoking, drinking mint-julep and playing poker.

Squire Lynch was smoking, drinking mint-julep and looking on over Col. Owner's shoulder.

Half-a-dozen negro boys, slaves and body-servants of these gentlemen, were standing within call.

"Gentlemen," said the squire, "it is for you to say, but I reckon we might stop with this deal. You began, Billy,"—addressing the colonel's left-hand neighbor—"so that makes it all square, I expect."

"I reckon I'll go out," said Curesome.

"Five," said Oldboy.

"Raise you twenty," said Owner.

"See your twenty-five," said Miller.

"Not yet," said Oldboy. "There's your twenty-five and twenty more."

"There are your twenty and I raise you the limit," spoke the colonel, betraying some excitement.

"I'm not afraid of you, Owner," said Miller, "but the parson's the devil. I reckon I'll go out too."

"Trust me for the limit. Four fours," said the Rev. Oldboy.

"Take in the pile, my friend," said the colonel. "Cæsar, you dog, another!"

The boy thus addressed was a genuine African with a flat nose and nostrils so distended that they were like a pair of dark eye-glasses perched upon his protruding upper lip. He sprang forward and took away the colonel's tumbler to refill it.

Col. Owner pushed back his chair and cleared his throat. "Now, gentlemen, for larger game," he said. "One win, all win in this enterprise. You are sure there's no doubt about setting off a new county, Bill?"

"Not the least. I have it straight from the Governor's secretary, colonel."

"And the appropriation for the courthouse and jail?"

"All right, colonel."

"And the railroad to run through here?"

Dr. Oldboy's hands were thrust into his well-filled pockets. With great satisfaction he answered:

"The petition and the subscription-list are drawn up in the most satisfactory manner. I did it myself. There can be no question about the result, sir,—none.

Why, sir, there must be a line of railroad connecting the great ports and commercial cities of the South with the grain and cattle markets of the West. Where else can it pass, sir, but by the foot of these mountains? Farther to the north it could not run, sir. There is no pass through these mountains; and as for going farther south, that is sheer folly. But wait"—and he produced a folded paper, tied with red tape and inscribed "Americus City." "I have set forth the reasons and arguments at length, and perspicuously here. This"—laying the paper upon the table—"this is entitled to convince our legislators."

"Regular as pig-tracks," said Miller, approvingly.

"My wife shakes her head over it," put in Dr. Curesome; then, catching a smile on his neighbor's face, he added quickly: "But I reckon I rule the roost."

Col. Owner burst into a hearty laugh. "Eh, Curesome! The best part of the population in our southern country wears petticoats, I reckon, eh? Now then, gentlemen, here is the plan of 'Americus City,'—streets laid out, public squares, rows of trees, building lots numbered. Take a pencil and each put his name on as many lots as he wants. I will take the rest."

"How much shall we say for a town lot?" asked Oldboy, deliberatively.

"Five hundred dollars at the very least."

"Well, the land is only worth two dollars an acre," ventured Curesome.

Everybody looked at him scornfully.

"Five hundred dollars, that's the figure. It sounds handsome," said Miller. "I reckon I'll take this and this and this."

"Suppose we let it go round and take one at a time," put in Oldboy. "I mark this corner lot."

"My wife—I mean, I don't see what good it will do if we don't get anyone else to come in," observed Curesome with diffidence.

"What harm?" asked Miller.

"It will make a grand impression and bring us lots of capitalists," said the fluent Oldboy.

"In fact that's all damned nonsense of yours, Curesome, ——" began Squire Lynch.

"Sir!" cried the little man, starting to his feet, his eyes flashing and all diffidence at an end.

"Come, gentlemen both, let us leave

abusive language to the Yankees, who employ such terms because they are afraid to fight. You didn't mean that, squire, did you now?" The speaker was Col. Owner.

"For a fact I did not and I beg your pardon. Shake my hand and take a drink with me, neighbor," said Lynch.

The fire-eating but henpecked Curesome allowed his ruffled feathers to subside and proposed a toast:

"Well, here's to our city! May her citizens be many and —— her citizens be many. I reckon that's about all there is to be said."

At this moment the attention of all was drawn to an approaching horseman.

"I bet a coon it's Red Jones! No: it's nobody that lives around here," the Squire said, judicially.

A stalwart young man, much sunburned, drew rein at the gate, lifted his hat and asked politely, "Have I the honor to speak to Squire Lynch?"

"Yes, sir, —— that is, my name is Lynch. Won't you alight?"

"I bet five dollars he'll join our scheme," said Oldboy.

"I take that," said Curesome.

The stranger came forward. "Squire

Lynch," said he, "my name is James Johnson."

"Glad to see you, Captain Johnson. This is Col. Owner, Dr. Oldboy, Dr. Curesome and Squire Miller. Have a seat, sir."

"Squire Lynch," began Israel, after saluting the other gentlemen as they were introduced, "I have heard that there was a prospect of building up a town here; and as I was intending to make a small investment in lands somewhere in this neighborhood, I decided to ride over and talk with you about it,—that is, of course, at your leisure. I see you are engaged at present, and ——"

"You have come at the most favorable moment, sir—Capt. Johnson," Dr. Oldboy interrupted, with a greedy look in his face. "You could not have come at a better time, sir! The gentlemen present are all promoters of this grand enterprise which is destined to transform the face of the surrounding country. You see here, sir, in these few gentlemen, the wealth, the aristocracy, the talent and the energy of this entire region represented. What should engage the attention of such gentlemen, I ask? What, but an undertaking which will convert the wilderness into a lovely garden, where thousands of their fellow-beings will live happily and prosperously."

Curesome folded a five-dollar bill and handed it to Oldboy.

"Such was the theme of our conversation at the very moment of your arrival, Captain Johnson; and now let us proceed to unfold the plan in all its details."

The six men drew up around the table, from which cards and poker-chips had been removed and, with the assistance of various papers spread out before them and the untiring imagination of Oldboy, in less than one hour had constructed a thriving city, with busy shops and shaded avenues, elegant residences, palatial hotels — yielding a princely revenue to the originators of all this prosperity. Israel entered into the scheme with evident enthusiasm. He led the van in extravagant proposals, so that even Oldboy found himself outdone in his own specialty.

But the latter was saving himself for one crowning effort.

After he had made sure that "Captain" Johnson was fairly caught and a share of his "small investment" ready to drop into his, Oldboy's, pocket, he pointed to the mountain with the attitude of an orator approaching his climax.

"One thing, gentlemen," he said impressively, "one thing, which I venture to assert will be the grandest and most unique feature of the future Americus City. Look there, sirs! Captain Johnson, look at that, sir!"

It certainly was a beautiful sight, the near mountain-side, covered with enormous forest trees, and it was to Israel a strange sight; for although very near at hand, it was blue, as distant mountains commonly are.

Then also it seemed to stand alone, independently of the general range, and to be more lofty and more regular in outline. This symmetrical appearance was heightened by a white line, as though drawn from a point near the summit perpendicularly to the base. Dr. Oldboy's long forefinger indicated this peculiar white line.

"See that magnificent and unequaled cascade, gentlemen! What does that mean to us? It means, not merely an object which will draw lovers of the beautiful from all quarters of the earth as soon as its existence becomes published abroad, and our railroad is put through, but it means, here, right here, within a rod of where we stand at this instant, if we choose to have it here, a fountain! Such a fountain as the world has never seen—three hundred feet high, sirs! Why not? Nothing to do but to lay pipes from the source of that cascade: that is all. *Three* hundred feet? — *Five* hundred! Three thousand! As much pressure as the pipes will stand—that is the only limit! I have sometimes desired, gentlemen, to go abroad to see the Leaning Tower; but never, if it be possible for us to enjoy such wonders as this fountain at Americus City!"

The orator paused to note the effect of this effort. "Captain" Johnson seemed deeply impressed. His gaze was fixed upon the mountain.

"Is this Blue Mountain?" he asked.

"Yes, captain."

"Then the proposed site of Americus City will be a portion of the Blue Mountain; for this foot-hill must be regarded as part of the mountain."

The five Southerners exchanged significant glances.

"I have heard very unfavorable reports

about the Blue Mountain," Israel continued. " Is the climate bad ? "

" As for climate," cried Oldboy, "did you never hear of the 'thermal belt,' Captain Johnson? No? That is perhaps the most wonderful thing of all. Why, sir, there is a band or strip or belt of this mountain, say one thousand feet in width and six or eight miles long, in which there is never any frost. It is distinctly warmer, sir, perceptibly warmer than the land above or below. So much is this the case, that I have seen, after a snow storm, the ground white above and below and this 'thermal belt' just as dark and warm as ever." Here he appealed to his companions, who all assented and seemed deeply interested.

" Of course I do not mean that it is never cold in this belt; but it is warmer, a great deal warmer, than anywhere else around here, and one thing is certain: there never has been a killing spring-frost in the thermal belt in the forty years that I have lived here. Spring flowers come out there weeks before they do at the foot of the mountain or any place fifty miles south of that.

" Now, my theory is, that some peculiar

quality in the soil itself on that portion of the mountain produces these effects. One thing is sure, and that is that the climate there in the thermal belt is magnificent.

"Think of this, Captain Johnson: peaches! Peaches, sir, the great fruit-crop of the South, yearly suffer untold losses from spring frosts. But there you have, sir, eight miles long and one fifth of a mile wide, the best spot in America, an area which should, and undoubtedly will, be planted thick with the choicest peach trees—a perfectly sure crop, because there is no danger from frosts! So much for the climate, Captain Johnson."

"If the Blue Mountain is so fertile and all that, why is it uninhabited?" asked Israel.

"Exactly what my wife says!" Dr. Curesome involuntarily exclaimed. "Something ails it."

"Fiddle-dee! We will prove the contrary," cried Oldboy. "But since the subject has come up, Captain Johnson, let us grant that there are foolish stories told about this mountain. Let us look the facts in the face, sir, and see what they amount to. Nothing, sir. Mere idle talk!

"The facts are these: At the end of

the last century, one man claimed the whole mountain as his own private property under a grant from the State. Nobody knew anything about him,—who he was or where he came from. He lived all alone and never had dealings with a soul."

"Did anybody ever try to deal with him?" asked Curesome, rather sulkily.

"No, sir; and that was natural enough. There was plenty of land unoccupied; and this old man, besides his claim of right, threatened to protect himself against encroachment."

"Did anybody ever hear of this old man's dying?" continued Curesome.

"I can't say as they did. He attained a great age, Captain Johnson, and that does not look like a bad climate, I should think. No: this old man—a—disappeared, at any rate. Now my theory is that he went away."

Perhaps because there was nothing startling in this theory, Oldboy paused to let it have all the effect it could.

Curesome, Miller, Lynch and Owner shook their heads.

"An old man like that doesn't go away until he goes into the ground," said Lynch.

Curesome asked: "How about Jem Davis, who moved up onto the mountainside after that? He and his whole family died mighty sudden."

"Milk-sick, sir!" replied Oldboy. "Undoubtedly they died from milk-sick, which is common enough among the mountains, but which this man, coming from the low country, did not know how to guard against." And then the unconquerable Oldboy explained for Israel's benefit that "milk-sick" was a disease which cattle contracted if they were not kept-up at the proper times, and which rendered their milk poisonous.

"I don't believe it was milk-sick. I have lived too near this cursed mountain and too long already. I never had any luck sence I came here," objected Squire Lynch.

Oldboy had worked himself up to fever heat in his defense of the scheme. Now he turned threateningly upon Lynch and his voice trembled with excitement as he cried:

"You are a ——"

"Stop, Oldboy! Why, what are you thinking about, Lynch? I propose, gentlemen, that we adjourn for to-day. Oldboy, you ride with me. I want you to try some Madeira wine which I have just received from Charleston." With these words Colonel Owner separated the two angry men and the session of founders stood adjourned.

Israel remained with Squire Lynch, who was hospitality personified.

Israel had seen enough.

It was evident that the scheme would fall through of itself if these five movers in it should come to blows.

Meantime, the doubts which he himself had suggested would retard it.

He decided that the scheme must not only fail, but with such terrible emphasis fail, that no one ever again would attempt to dwell near the Blue Mountain and spy his going out and coming in.

"I don't know what I may have to do; but I certainly do not care to be watched," said Israel.

As for these five planters, he saw evidence enough of their hot temper and lawless spirit. Living in this remote district, they were almost beyond reach of the law, whether to be defended by it or punished by it. As a natural consequence, each strong man took the law into his own hands and not unfrequently made himself judge, jury and executioner in his own cause.

Israel decided, therefore, to make them exterminate themselves, by setting one against another.

CHAPTER X

IN accordance with the hospitable custom of the country, Captain Johnson had received warm and cordial invitations to visit at the houses in the neighborhood. These invitations he promptly availed himself of and entered into the fox-hunting or poker parties with that spirit which always distinguished him.

His companion in all excursions was a son of his host, Dal Lynch,—a young fellow who was looked upon as a scapegrace, even by this graceless community.

Dal Lynch and Israel being thus thrown constantly together, the impulsive young Southerner disclosed his secrets, especially his secret griefs, to Israel as to the only respectable person who showed him kindness. The boy was only wild,—not bad-hearted.

It so happened, about three weeks after the scene last described, that Israel let fall a careless, bantering suggestion. Dal had told him that he was in great need of a considerable sum of money for a particular purpose. (Dal's purposes were not always mentionable.) He must have it, he said, and the old man had refused him.

"You know that all I have with me is promised for this land-speculation," said Israel. "But, cheer up, man! Why don't you gamble for it? That's the way Billy Miller gets his pocket-money."

"I can't take the risk. I have no luck."

"Then take the money without risk," said Israel. "Colonel Owner won almost a thousand dollars to-day at draw-poker. It was the biggest haul of the season and your father lost more than any one else. Take that. What difference it makes whether you take money from another man because you hold a higher card, or because you are stronger or cleverer than he, I can't see for the life of me. But seriously, Dal, you people living out here in the country ought to be more careful about locking up your doors and windows at night. I should be willing to take that purse from Owner's room this very night myself, just for the fun of the thing — and of course laugh with him about it to-morrow." And then he went on speaking about indifferent matters.

A day or two afterwards, Israel and Dal, with rifles and dogs, were tramping over White Oak Hill. They had been shooting squirrels and Israel's game bag was quite well filled; but Dal appeared to take no interest, although he was usually a keen sportsman and a crack shot. He was drinking at short intervals from a large pocket-flask containing the villainous corn-whisky called "Mountain Dew."

"What's up, Dal?" cried Israel. "You're as melancholy as Dr. Curesome at home!"

The young Southerner leaned upon his long rifle and replied with a husky voice:

"I reckon I've drank too much to shoot straight to-day, captain. I—I—sit down: I want to talk to you."

Israel complied and Dal proceeded:

"That money burns my pocket."

"What money, Dal?"

"You said you could take Owner's cash out of his bed-room."

"I was joking, Dal: that you know very well," said Israel, sternly.

"I did it," said Dal Lynch.

"What! you took Owner's money?"

"Yes, I stole it and it burns in my pocket, I tell you!" groaned Dal. "What shall I do?"

"Give it back," said Israel promptly.

"You know I can't do that. I dursn't."

"Then I have nothing more to say."

"But they'll be coming! I believe they'll be there when we get home."

"Who?"

"All the neighbors. Owner will get them all together and come after me!"

"How does he know you did it?"

"He sent word to everybody this morning that he'd been robbed and to come and help him catch the burglar, only not to father. He must suspect me."

"The squire and the colonel had a quarrel yesterday. That's probably the reason why he didn't send to your house," Israel suggested.

"Do you think so?" said Dal, greatly relieved. "What would you do if you was me?"

"I am not you."

"Oh, help a fellow, Captain Johnson! What shall I do?"

"I have told you already. If you can't do that, go straight to Colonel Owner and offer your services."

"What! Run right in his way?"

"That will look as though you were innocent. Then when the affair has blown over, you can give the money back in some other way."

With drunken, foolish gratitude Dal thanked Israel; then made the best of his way to the stable, saddled his horse and rode to Colonel Owner's plantation.

Very naturally the colonel's suspicion was aroused by this unprecedented display of zeal for justice, on the part of a notorious scapegrace. He therefore questioned Dal, and receiving incoherent, evasive answers, ordered a negro to search his person.

Dal resisted, and in the struggle his light jacket was torn from his back; he escaped, rode wildly back to his father's house; several of the stolen bills were found in the pocket of his jacket.

Owner collected his neighbors, Curesome, Oldboy and Miller; with these and his male slaves, all armed, rode up before Squire Lynch's mansion and demanded the culprit.

Squire Lynch appeared on the threshold. His face was very pale and he held a shot-gun in his hand.

"Don't you come any nearer, gentlemen!" he said.

Colonel Owner raised his rifle to his

shoulder; but Israel stood in front of his host to screen him.

"Stand aside, Captain Johnson! We don't mean any harm to you," commanded Oldboy.

"This is hardly a fair fight," said Israel, coolly.

Squire Lynch used the opportunity which this diversion gave him, to raise his gun and fire.

Colonel Owner fell forward upon his horse's neck. That startled animal dashed away down the red-clay road, dragging his mortally-wounded master, whose foot was caught in the stirrup. There was a stampede of the negroes.

Before Lynch could enter the house, Miller took deliberate aim and shot him through the breast. The squire's life-blood stained his own threshold. That was the end of his bad luck near the Blue Mountain.

Then Oldboy, Miller and Curesome rushed into the house, tracking blood up the stairs, and seized Dal Lynch. Fear of death was written on the boy's face; yet, as he was being hurried out, he caught sight of Israel and cried:

"If I had done what you tole me ——"

They took him away into the forest on the mountain-side. Where justice is uncertain, punishments are excessive.

Israel's preparations had been made in advance, and he now in turn mounted his horse and rode away from the ill-starred house.

The subsequent history of "Americus City" may be given in a very few words.

After the death of Owner and Lynch, Oldboy came to the front, laid out streets and pressed the enterprise as well as he could. A large brick jail was erected upon the central square; but nothing further was accomplished.

No "citizens" offered themselves. The place had acquired an evil name.

To-day it is as Horace Penman saw it. Squire Lynch's house is a dismal ruin, and only three or four wretched hovels, occupied by still more wretched, shiftless folk (enough however to supply the jail with an occasional prisoner) mark the spot and offend the eye.

As for the railway, the war came to postpone industrial projects; and after the war came a new generation of legislators who had never interested themselves in this route.

As for the surviving projectors, Miller had been killed while fighting bravely at the head of his regiment, at the battle of Bull Run, by a sergeant of Company ——, Connecticut volunteers. This sergeant's name was Ezekiel H. Perkins. Mr. Penman was first-lieutenant in the same company. Oldboy and Curesome had lost their wealth in losing their slaves.

CHAPTER XI

 LITTLE-USED road, a mere "track," led from Americus to the foot of the Blue Mountain. There it turned aside, turned to the westward, as though to avoid crossing unhallowed territory.

Israel followed this road to the turning and there, unaffected by those scruples which had actuated other travelers, struck right through the woods toward the summit.

At the base of the mountain were pine, gum and oak trees—pines predominating. Further up the slope these gave place to a magnificent growth in which deciduous trees were the more numerous.

The fauna also changed. During the first fifteen or twenty minutes of ascent, there was an abundance of animal life. Rabbits, lizards, snakes, birds of all kinds, startled by this intruder, sprang or crawled or flew away before him. Above, all became silent. Either such creatures as these were not there, or they were hidden and did not show themselves.

But the most notable change was in the character of the soil and undergrowth. Red clay and white sand, white sand and red clay,—bare, save here and there a tuft of spear-grass—had been the story. Now a dark, rich mould gave nourishment to flourishing rhododendrons and laurels and azaleas and columbine. Vines clad the stately trunks of giant trees with soft verdure,—vines like great cables, like threads of silk, like a mistress, strangling with her passions and exactions yet caressing with the tendrils of her pretty graces.

This change from barrenness to fertility became more marked at one point. It was not as though a line had been drawn or a wall raised between a garden and a desert—the transition was less sharply marked than that—yet at this point Israel said: Here begins the peculiarity of this mountain. Below this there is nothing good for me.

Then he became conscious of a great heat and heaviness in the air. This effect might be due partly to the absence of the sounds of animal life and to the dense foliage, intercepting all motion of a breeze;

but not entirely to these causes. The warmth seemed to steal or steam out from the black earth,—to proceed from the mountain itself in part and not merely from the sun.

Israel advanced through this semi-tropical belt until he arrived at its upper boundary. Here the line of verdure was even more distinctly marked, contrasting strangely with the scant and hardy growth which clothed the bleak rocks of the windy summit.

"So then," he said, "this famous 'thermal-belt' stretches along the whole mountain side, girdling it, naturally enough. It is the result of reflection from the southern plain, the direct rays of the sun and protection from northern winds: these three combined. No mystery about it whatever. . . . And yet the place does seem more than naturally quiet and more than naturally hot."

Through the more practicable upper spaces above the thermal belt, with that lightness of heart which rewards the mountain-climber when he reaches the purer, rarer atmosphere on the heights, Israel made his way joyfully. He had planned his course so as to reach the falls at the foot of the first cascade, and already the sound of rushing waters came to his ears through the stillness.

"Now here," said he, pausing and looking down upon the great forest which stretched away to meet the horizon, "if one were a hermit, here would be a good spot for a house."

"I 'lowed it wor pretty nigh right," said someone close behind him.

Israel turned like a flash in the direction from which the voice proceeded and cocked his gun.

"Don't shoot, stranger, don't yer now. I 'low there's plenty ter eat onter this mounting without yer eatin' me." This was said in a persuasive, wheedling way.

The speaker was the type of the North Carolina mountaineer, but with all the characteristics exaggerated. His body was even longer and leaner, his trousers scarcely occupied by his thin shanks, his shoulders even more slouched, his face more sallow and more expressionless, his hat-brim wider. At the same time there was a certain sly, observant look scarce perceptible in his eyes, as he leaned against the half-decayed trunk of an oak tree and waited for Israel to recover from his surprise.

He looked as though he would willingly wait and observe for a hundred years.

"How did I pass you by without seeing you?" Israel demanded.

"I 'lowed ye wor studyin' about something mighty earnest."

"I thought there was no one on the mountain."

"I live hyah."

"How long?"

"I disremember."

"Oh, come! About how long?" cried Israel, raising his voice.

"Waal, sence ye wor hyah before"——

"I have never been here before."

That sly look in the mountaineer's eyes became more distinct as he explained: "Ye come from yon side, 'tother side, over the top of this mounting."

"Bah! I tell you I never saw you before in my life."

"Ye wouldn't hev seen me this time ef I hedn't spoke," the mountaineer said; then adding: "An' I wouldn't hev spoke ef I hedn't knowed ye by that thar mark onter yer cheek."

Israel controlled his anger sufficiently

to ask: " How long ago was it that you saw me?"

" I tol' you I disremember. Erbout sixty or eighty year, 'peers ter me."

"Crazy," said Israel, half aloud; then contemptuously: " Next time I pass, don't you dodge behind trees. Just let me hear you speak, or I may shoot you like a rabbit!"

So Israel turned on his heel and walked away towards the falls.

He arrived at the foot of the first cascade, as he had intended. Standing there and looking up, he could see how the water poured over the cliff, at first in a solid mass, then was torn into shreds, then these into drops, and these drops subdivided into fine spray. It fell so softly and was so tempting! He put off his clothes and stood under this bath; then plunged into the deep pool which received all the water and held it for a moment, whirling around and foaming, before it took the second leap downwards.

Emerging from this delicious bath, he saw through the rank growth the roof of a building within stone's-throw.

He could scarcely trust his eyes.

" That was not there a moment ago!"

he exclaimed. "But, pshaw! I passed that crazy beast of a mountaineer without seeing him: why not fail to discover a house? I don't recognize myself in this. . . . But I am no worse than my ancestor with his story of a sleeping figure in the cave, who had not been there when he went in."

In a moment he was dressed; then he forced his way through the tangled underbrush to the house.

This might have dropped from above or sprung up from the soil; for there was no clearing about it. It was built of unhewn logs, like the trunks of the surrounding trees except for being laid horizontally.

The mountaineer sat in the doorway, waiting and observing as before.

Israel went straight up to him and told him that, as he meant to pass a few days on the mountain, for the sake of the game which he supposed must be very abundant, he would be glad of this shelter.

He neither would have consented to receive, nor did he receive, a refusal.

Such was the spirit in which this strange association of Israel with the mountaineer began: the former contemptuous and domineering, the latter watchful and apparently passive.

But in the course of the very first day there came a change. It is our privilege to follow this change both in its outward manifestations and as a secret growth within the minds of the two actors.

In the course of the first day which they spent together, Israel began to take an inexplicable interest in this uncouth companion. When he had ascended the mountain, his mind had been filled with one thought and one desire—to find the ancient mine; now, in spite of himself, this man claimed a share in his thoughts and desires.

Israel was as quick to form determinations as he was resolute in executing them. No sooner, therefore, had he realized the fact just noted than he decided that this man's presence was not purely accidental. Presently he acknowledged to himself that this interest in the personality of an unattractive being was absorbing into itself his eagerness to possess the treasure. Then he saw that this man was to be his instrument or agent.

We may quietly reason this out and find that his conclusion was theoretically just; but Israel's inference was immediate, he trusted it and acted upon it.

In this connection it is to be noted also that the mountaineer did not remain entirely passive.

There is apparently a sentiment of hospitality, and at least a very slight sense of the duties of a host which cannot be eradicated from the breast of that social animal, Man.

This recluse, then, showed an unexpected promptness in calling Israel's attention to the sights of the mountain. He began to tell his guest that this climate and soil were especially favorable to one variety of fruit which was, indeed, produced elsewhere, but nowhere in such perfection. A single, but especially fine and beautiful, specimen was now to be seen. Would Israel like to go a short distance to enjoy it?

The two went together down the mountain to the lower boundary of the thermal belt. There grew a superb magnolia tree, towering above its fellows and conspicuous from afar, with its dome of dark green, glossy leaves, "thick inlaid" with great starry flowers whose fragrance made the still air heavy with sweetness.

"Thar, onter yon side, 'tother side," drawled the guide.

Israel's curiosity was thoroughly aroused and he went alone to the farther side of the magnolia, while the mountaineer stood watching him.

There, close before his face, hanging from a blossom-laden branch of the magnolia, was the body of Dal Lynch.

"Ernother one is a-ripening onter this mounting," said Israel's host.

But the mountaineer did not allow his hospitable cares to interrupt habitual occupations. So, for instance, Israel observed him heaping dried leaves and twigs upon a large ant-hill, swarming with these busy workers; then kindling this nicely laid fire and watching the destruction of the ant-community with silent satisfaction.

Upon inquiring the cause of this proceeding, Israel learned that his host devoted a large portion of each day to the extermination of animals of all kinds. He hoped in time to enjoy a rare pleasure in being the only remaining living creature upon the Blue Mountain.

Israel gave him the name Guardian from the following circumstance:

He had the habit of sitting where the stream issues from the mountain side,— sitting motionless, muttering to himself, but refusing to speak to Israel when at that spot.

Israel recalled the legend heard from the Indian chief and began to invest this homely figure with a web of romance. There was a certain majesty in the Guardian's bearing while he sat there so quietly. If this was lent him by his surroundings, at least it was borrowed majesty, and not something meaner.

This impression Israel tried to laugh at in order to cure the fancy by laughing.

"The source of this stream of sparkling water," he said, speaking to himself, "is perchance that fountain of immortal youth which the first adventurers who came to America believed in so firmly. This dried-up nondescript is then all that is left of the last Indian Prince, or say a disguise which he has assumed for my amusement. Has he put away my ancestor—(Curesome says he did not die)—stowed him away in the cave somewhere? That would be a happy thought! The old gentleman would wish to die, yet find himself kept provokingly young by the virtue of this fountain!"

But the laugh was not very merry and the fancy remained in all its force. Here was a new sensation for Israel. This being, in his inscrutableness and savage independence, was the first he had ever met whom he must acknowledge to be in any sense superior to himself. This feeling was quite as unbearable as was the restraint imposed by the presence of the mountaineer at the very point where Israel's long search was to terminate. He was in the way and must be removed.

And yet it seemed that he would in some manner aid Israel to discover the treasure. How? How could he be at the same time an obnoxious impediment and the very agent of the discovery?

"Very simply," Israel replied to his own question. "The discovery is bound together with his death."

CHAPTER XII

THUS it seemed to Israel that as the inconvenience of the Guardian's presence increased and became oppressive, a certain fearful suggestion became more distinct, took definite shape in his mind and insisted upon being felt and heard at all times.

The image of death was everywhere—in the stillness of this desolated forest, in the ambiguous words as in the long fits of silence of this man of the Blue Mountain. It became familiar, and it was no longer shocking when it had become quite familiar.

Was this mysterious being deliberately educating Israel to become his murderer? Whether with design or by accident, everything he said or did contributed to the murderous resolve steadily growing in Israel's breast.

Of course our adventurer attempted, at first by indirect methods and then by direct questions, to obtain the desired information. In this effort he was foiled by the irritating, stupid silence of his host, who affected not to understand his questions.

Meantime he searched for the legendary entrance to the mine, with as little success.

It could not be the present issue of the stream, for here the stream filled the cavity from which it proceeded.

He conjectured that the underground current had changed its bed and examined the rocks above, below and to a distance on either side of the present cascade.

Diligence and persuasion failing, Israel resolved to try the effect of terror upon the mountaineer.

It was plain to him that his own life depended upon success in this one effort. The fate which had overtaken every creature who had come within the influence of the mountain, or some deadly spirit ruling the territory of the mountain, he felt was drawing near to himself.

His spirit became feverish and he was haunted by strange fancies. Among these the most persistent was that his ancestor had lacked courage and strength to overcome the Guardian and had remained as his thrall upon the Blue Mountain.

So then one day Israel addressed the Guardian who was sitting absorbed in thought at the source of the torrent. Receiving no answer, he seized him by the throat and threatened to wring his neck.

Still no answer.

Then, wild with passion and stung with disappointment, he raised his tormentor bodily above his head and dashed him to the earth again.

The mountaineer lay motionless, but his eyes were open and his lips moved.

Israel bent over him, clutched him with his right hand and with his left pointed over the cliff.

" Tell me what I need to know, or ——"
A terrible gesture filled out the sense.

Then the Guardian said, but without fear, that there was a great treasure very near to them; even as there is such treasure everywhere that men live. There was a great curse, he said, resting upon the possessor thereof,—so fearful a curse that its possession could not advantage any person who retained human affections. By a single act of true generosity the hoard would be sacrificed and lost forever.

He further said that Israel was not yet worthy to possess it, inasmuch as he had still some generosity in his nature. Was Israel ready to commit murder deliberately in order to gain the secret of the treasure?

"Whom should I murder?"

Anyone standing in his way.

"Oh, that is not necessary! There's plenty to eat on this mountain without my eating you, as you yourself said."

The Guardian looked at him long and earnestly; then his head sunk upon his breast and he would speak no more nor raise his eyes from the ground.

"'Deliberately', you dismal fool!" cried Israel. "'Deliberately'! You would have me do the thing deliberately, my fine mummy, my excellent petrified prince! I know a gayly worth two of your deliberatelies. Wait here for me, my lean and drawling bag of bones!" With that he descended to the cabin, shouting aloud whatever came into his mind, for the information of the silent man above.

"I am going for the spade. That will do for both purposes. Jem Davis' spade! You told me how he came to settle on this mountain with his wife and children and buried them all with this spade a few days afterwards. Then he died on the last mound and you took the spade. Here it is. Yes, it is strong and will do for both uses!

"Here I am. Look up! No? Have you anything more to say? Take your own time. There's no hurry. 'Deliberately', you know. That was rather a fine word for a stupid who can't even answer when he's spoken to.

"You do not answer? Well then —— Understand that I am not angry or in the least excited. If you object to the way I propose to do it, please say so now. No? Well then——"

The spade descended swiftly upon the bowed head. Once only.

Half its work was done.

The other half required more time.

Israel drove the spade into the loose gravel which evidently had been brought by the swift current from within the mountain. Below this stratum he found a sufficient depth of earth only in one spot, immediately below a huge boulder forming one side of the aperture which gave passage to the torrent.

"Sit there, old earth-worm", he shouted, propping the body against this boulder, as he had so often seen the Guardian place himself. "Sit there and watch me build a snug little house for you. It shall fit you as a snail-shell fits the snail." And he fell to work with the spade, still laughing and speaking to the dead mountaineer as though the latter could hear and see.

"There now! There is room for your empty head. . . . And that will do for your spindle shanks. . . . One more spadeful for your knob and two for your heels. . . . So"—measuring with his eye the limp figure and the narrow trench he had excavated—"That will fit you better than your skin and last you longer. In you go"—throwing the body into the grave and beginning to cover it with earth.

Only the face remained uncovered when Israel paused in the work and leaning upon his spade once more questioned his victim, who seemed no more inscrutable now in death than he had been in life.

"Last chance, old toad, before I shut you up for good and all! Will you answer now?"

The loosened earth was stirred as though the dead man had essayed to rise. Then the figure sunk as in a quicksand; the countenance with its staring eyes disappeared beneath the water which now burst through the walls of the grave and filled it to the brim; there was a grinding, rumbling sound above.

Israel sprang aside not an instant too soon.

The great boulder beneath which the trench had been dug, thus undermined and deprived of part of its support, broke away from the mountain-side and dashed over the cliff, followed by a shower of smaller stones.

Israel's wild gayety passed all bounds as he watched the course of the avalanche, which carried away the cabin and stormed forwards, downwards, mowing a great swath through the forest until, far below, its rage was spent and all grew still where that gigantic magnolia which bore such awful fruit lifted its pyramid of dark leaves and starry flowers high above the neighboring trees.

He laughed and shouted and waved his arms, encouraging its progress; crying that at last he was alone, that not a sign of life remained upon the mountain and that now the fiend himself dare not come between him and the thing he sought.

Then suddenly it flashed through his brain that he had expected the discovery to be immediately connected with the Guardian's death.

He faced about and saw that the grave was covered by *débris* and that, where the boulder had been, a low and narrow opening gave admission to a gloomy passage which seemed to lead inward towards the heart of the mountain.

He sprang forward quickly, as though fearing it might close again before he could reach it.

Along the bed of the swift stream, the current tugging at his feet to force him back, over the slippery rocks, through the darkness, he rushed along upwards, inwards, shouting above the noise of the torrent a challenge to all the devils to stop him if they could.

Then he reached a point where the stream ceased to be turbulent. It glided along with a pleasant murmur, while the cavern seemed to Israel to become a vast chamber through which his voice echoed; and in reply to his shouting, near voices called back and distant whispers repeated the tone again and again.

"Helloa! Israel-for-Israel!" he shouted.

"Hi, Israel-for-Israel! Ho, Israel-for-Israel! Israel!—srail!——ael! Hi—ael! ——el! Hi—Ho! Heigho!" shouted and laughed and murmured and sighed a chorus of voices, near and distant.

"Israel-for-Israel!" he shouted again with all the force of his lungs. "Here am I, Israel!"

"I! I! I! I! I!" repeated the chorus, in a thousand mocking tones.

"Yes, I!" he cried again. "As often as I choose, I! I! Come and see —— and bring a light from h——, some of you!"

"Here is a lantern, master!"—This voice was not an echo. Someone was standing close beside Israel and holding a miner's lantern in his hand. Its feeble light disclosed features at the same time familiar and strange: they were those of the mountaineer; they were those of the old portrait; they were the features of Gray. Their expression was smiling and servile, and the voice in which this being continued to speak was servile.

"Don't harm me, master; don't you now," he pleaded. "See here, master!" —He held the lantern nearer to the wall of the cavern, which reflected its light from a myriad points with a rich, yellow gleam.

"Gold! gold!—mine and yours," he cried; "for I am your servant, to serve you in all things. Here, master, and everywhere, I am your servant!"

Only the voices of the cavern replied. Dreadful voices, that will not cease to echo night and day in my mind!

Thus began the association of Israel with Gray. Up to this point, every important act in Israel's evil life is as clear to me as though I had been an eye-witness throughout; but from this point onward all is indistinct and uncertain. How could it be otherwise? When selfish strength is joined to diabolical cunning — that undying spirit of darkness which will serve anyone who has conquered the last generous impulse — what hope to trace its course? That wrong which Strength has done, Cunning has concealed.

Conclusion—By Mr. PENMAN

TOWARDS the end of March last, I received a note from Mrs. Eaton requesting me to arrange an interview at my office between herself and Livingstone. I did not feel at liberty to refuse, and no doubt I was moved by curiosity and a desire to be present at a meeting so novel in character.

The interview was accordingly arranged for the thirty-first.

At half-past two o'clock in the afternoon of that day Mrs. Winthrop Eaton entered her old adviser's private office. She had of late showed distressing signs of failing health, and now as she came in I noticed, more than ever before, lines of suffering about her eyes and mouth. But these vanished in the bright smile which lighted up her whole face as she came forward and took the easy chair by the grate, saying:

"Many thanks for your prompt obedience, Mr. Penman."

Then, with an instantaneous change of tone, manner and expression, she continued to speak, as though recurring to a train of thought which had been interrupted by her entrance.

"He has proved," she said, "that a man may do as much evil as he chooses, provided he does it through agents and screens himself behind them, and yet escape punishment entirely. He has proved that the wages of sin is *not* death, but wealth, power, position, the smiles of honest women and the respect of honest men."

"My dear Mrs. Eaton," I said anxiously, "you do not feel well."

"Do not say that—not that!" she exclaimed. "This is what I mean: Israel Slyme, or James Johnson, has taken a new name, and now calls himself Donald Livingstone!"

This assertion she had repeatedly made to me in almost the same terms; I thought it best, however, to urge the objections to this view once more, and said:

"But, my dear madame, Livingstone comes of an old and prominent family, as you know; and he was born in Paris while his parents were traveling abroad ——"

"Yes," she interrupted, with sarcastic emphasis; "and both parents soon afterward died—very opportunely—and the child was brought up by an uncle Andsoforth and an aunt Andsoon, who are also dead. It is a most ingenious story,—so ingenious that I have not been able to prove absolutely that it is untrue, but only that it is extremely improbable. Even if I could, it is not Livingstone's invention, but Gray's."

"But young Israel had such a remarkable face that I am sure I should recognize him, even after these thirty years."

"Not necessarily. Thirty years ago his face was unformed. His coloring and expression and other things which have changed with time were what you would naturally have noticed then."

"But Israel had a peculiar birthmark on his cheek ——"

"Which is covered by a scar, and that scar almost hidden by his beard. But we need not disprove anything! We have only to confront him with the facts. Hardened as he is, he will betray himself in some manner!"

"But," I objected, "such things do not happen in these days—such adventures as you think Israel has had. Besides, Livingstone's own account of the manner in which he gained his wealth is satisfactory, or nearly so. He was in California, looking for an opportunity to make an investment in lands. He stumbled upon a deserted town, which he bought for a mere song. It was a great piece of luck. The site had been well chosen, but the projectors lacked 'push' to carry out what they had begun. Besides, the entire State of California was at that period so attractive a field for enterprise that this one undertaking had been, naturally enough, abandoned when it proved to be difficult. He found by trial that the difficulties were largely imaginary. That was the beginning of his great prosperity."

"Oh, don't you see," she exclaimed, "that this story is a mere invention, suggested by his actual experience at Americus City? It is true that he bought lands in California; but he did not go there until seven years after he left Oskawask, and then his purchases showed him to be already enormously wealthy. When you and Perkins were driven from the Blue Mountain by blood-hounds, Gray told you that his master, Captain Johnson, had just returned from the West. That fixes the date of his California speculations."

A few minutes before three o'clock Livingstone, grave and gracious as usual, entered my office. Mrs. Eaton took no notice of his polite bow, but continued to speak as though he had been present during the foregoing conversation. She addressed herself to him, instead of to me—that was the only difference. She told him that her husband was in great distress. He was earning, she said, scarcely enough to keep a roof over their heads, and he was earning that by efforts beyond mortal strength. He was killing himself by degrees.

This communication she made with such suddenness and force that Livingstone did not venture to interrupt her; and she concluded with a demand, rather than a request, for a large sum of money.

At that point he found opportunity to explain that he was not unacquainted with Winthrop's embarrassment; that he had felt privileged by his affectionate intimacy with her husband to offer him assistance, but that the offer had been most positively refused.

I say that Livingstone found opportunity to make this explanation; but that statement is not accurate. Mrs. Eaton appeared scarcely to note what he was saying. When Livingstone referred to her husband's refusal, she rose from her chair and walked quickly up and down the room several times. I looked at her appealingly, but she ignored my presence.

Livingstone also stood up and began to say that Winthrop's rejection of his proposal should not prevent his serving her in any way in his power. She paid no heed to this, so he ceased speaking, and we were all three silent for a minute or two.

Then she came and stood before Livingstone. Looking fixedly at him, with the strangest expression I ever saw on mortal face, she asked:

"Why?"

"I beg your pardon," he said.

"Why did he refuse?"

"On the ground," Livingstone answered, "that he could give me no security for the loan, and that his pride would suffer if he accepted such a favor from me, upon whom, he said, he had no claim."

"No claim!" she echoed; and then

with inconceivable extravagance and fiery eloquence she charged him with being no less than the most abominable among men.

She said that he offered the revolting spectacle of a brother lifting himself up by the ruin of his own family and standing conspicuously upon the ruins to pose before the world as a benefactor and friend of the poor. She protested against the course which he had been pursuing with reference to his son, Winthrop, saying that he had exposed him to dangers which would have corrupted the heart and ruined the career of any less pure and sturdy nature.

As though utterly at a loss to understand her, Livingstone asked: "For what purpose have I done this?"

"I shall tell you why you have done this thing," she replied. "Inasmuch as Winthrop is your son, he is part of yourself. To just that extent you include him in your self-love. But only a portion of his nature is derived from you. His share of noble impulses keeps you out of possession. If you could destroy the mother's nature in him, your empire over him would become complete."

"Very ingenious and perfectly logical.

Receive my congratulations upon this reasoning, Mrs. Eaton," he said. " But—forgive me if I press the question—to what end all this elaborate and troublesome preparation? What do I mean to do with your husband finally?"

" Mr. Livingstone," she replied, " I know more of your past life than you imagine, perhaps. I know and can prove by what crooked paths you have come to your present position. Do not misunderstand me," she added, noticing that the cynical smile on Livingstone's face changed to a slight frown. "I do not mean to threaten you with exposure. I wish to be perfectly fair and open in my dealings with you and I make no pretense of being able to injure you seriously. You have covered your tracks so well, you have shifted responsibility so dexterously, that it would be difficult if not impossible for anyone to prove in a court of law, or to prove to the satisfaction of the public, which sees and admires only your success, that you are —— what you are. I will not stoop to calling hard names. You have not hesitated to use unlawful and detestable methods,—but indirectly, paying others to run the risks for you and leaving them to their punishment when detected. This you have done, not through cowardice, but knowing that it was the one path by which you could advance always in security. You are no coward: you would have acted for yourself if that had been necessary or best for your interests. In one case it did become necessary, and then you stained your own hand so deeply ——"

"Here is my hand," Livingstone interrupted, drawing off a glove and holding out the right, white and shapely, but evidently very powerful. "What stain is there on my hand?"

"I promised myself not to use harsh terms," said Mrs. Eaton, watching him narrowly. "The man—the victim—was alone, friendless, a hated recluse. I shall not tell you the facts exactly, but I shall suggest them." She began to pace the floor as she spoke, still, however, keeping Livingstone in view.

At first the latter displayed only courteous attention; but as the narrative progressed, when the mountaineer was described, and that horrible fruit which grew upon the Blue Mountain, and the curse with which the possessor of the hoard must be cursed, Livingstone appeared to find in her words a significance at least equal to that which they had in the mind of the speaker. As I watched him it seemed to me that, whereas he had at first desired to appear attentive, he now desired to conceal the extent and intensity of his interest in what she was saying. Finally, when Mrs. Eaton had traced the work of the mountaineer, calling him by all his names in turn—mountaineer, guardian, Israel-for-Israel, Gray—and showing how he had trained the young adventurer to commit murder; when she had shown the treasure-way opened above a grave, and the danger which Israel himself escaped gaining in force as it rushed onward in an avalanche of desolation and ruin; when she spoke then of those mocking voices that would not cease to mock and scoff in the cavern, Livingstone took several steps toward me, his eyes threatening, his whole figure shaken with stormy passion.

"I hold you responsible for this, Mr. Penman!" he cried; but then he checked himself. It was the most sudden transformation conceivable. An instant afterward there was not a trace of emotion in his demeanor. Taking out his watch, "Excuse me for noticing the hour," he said. "Ah! it is later than I supposed; but I am only sorry to be obliged to end my call now. Many thanks for your entertaining conversation, Mrs. Eaton. I have never, upon my word, been so genuinely interested. You have made me forget time and place and myself, even! But indeed you noticed how your invention carried me away. When you speak like that, madame, one believes that fiction is reality, and puts himself in the place of the creatures of your imagination."

A baffled, despairing look had come into Mrs. Eaton's white face, and she was trembling so that I feared she would fall; but with a final effort she replied: "I did, indeed, feel much complimented by your outburst. It was evidently spontaneous and natural."

No sooner had Livingstone gone out than Mrs. Eaton's courage and strength gave place to terror and exhaustion. I did what I could to cheer her, but soon found that she paid no heed to my words and that her condition was rapidly becoming more and more distressing. I made haste, therefore, to convey her to "Westwood," where I left her in the care of her husband and returned alone to Oldhaven.

If my life were not nearing its close— even if I had before me many years—I should never be able to forget the thoughts which filled my mind as I hastened homeward. The scene which I had just witnessed had stirred the fountain of memory to its depths, and things long hidden rose to the surface. Every incident, of which I had ever had knowledge, in the lives of those people who have figured in this history, came back to me then. The whole course of their lives was distinct in my mind; and yet the extravagant and supernatural elements which poor Mrs. Eaton's diseased fancy had introduced seemed not less real, but even more real, than the commonplace portions of their experience. It seemed to me that her version of the story of Israel was valuable, not merely as the photograph of her own mind when trembling on the verge of insanity; but that if she had deliberately chosen to express by way of allegory the essential and central realities of such a nature as Israel's, she could not have done it more significantly; that even if she had misrepresented Livingstone, the individual, she had not misrepresented either the class of adventurers with which she identified him or that spirit of self-seeking which seems to me (an old and timorous Oldhavener) the cancer in our national body; that her feverish imagination had created, in the character of Israel, something more real than any individual: a personified national tendency. She had spoken truth, I admitted to myself; but a truth which sanity refuses to see. The man of sane mind is content with partial knowledge of his associates, and does not seek to discover the awful secrets and the possibilities of evil which are veiled by a respectable exterior. But the veil of discretion had been lifted by the terrible accusation which I had just heard, and for the moment I also believed that the real Livingstone and the real Gray were Beówulf and Grendel—strength and diabolical cunning working together, as Israel had asserted that they might. The real Gray, I said to myself as I drove homeward through the darkness, is not the efficient servant, whose manners are perfect and whose practices are secret. The real Gray is what Mrs. Eaton described: the undying guardian of the hoard, serving in order to retain possession,—the actual owner, whoever may be the temporary possessor, of great wealth employed for selfish purposes.

At the date of this writing, Mrs. Eaton is still confined in a private asylum; but her physicians report great improvement and promise speedy restoration to health and reason.

What is the plain and literal truth in relation to Livingstone? I do not know; for I am incapable of professing to know anything which is not susceptible of positive proof. It seems to me that credence given to that which is not thus susceptible of proof savors of a form of insanity similar to that from which poor Mrs. Eaton is now suffering. But I should like to suggest one or two lines of thought which I myself have pursued in reasoning upon this question. They are these:

Unless Mrs. Eaton had some items of information which she has never imparted to me, it is probable that the suggestion of the murder originated and was elaborated in her own mind. What I had told her about Americus City, the resemblance between the man whom we saw on the mountain and Gray, the name Johnson, the physical peculiarities of the mountain itself—these particulars would hardly have been shaped and combined into such a story unless the germ of the suggestion had been in her own nature. Our opinions of others reflect our own essential character. It is an awful thought that the germ of murderous impulse is hidden in every heart—even beneath the tenderest and purest bosom. *Humani nihil a me alienum puto.*

That instinct which leads one back to one's early home, in the desire to end life where it was begun, would account for Livingstone's return, if he is the lost Israel Slyme; but he certainly would not have returned to his old home without first destroying every trace of his course which could lead to his identification. If, therefore, he is the same individual, no person will ever know it. If Mrs. Eaton had appealed to him as a stranger or mere acquaintance, he would doubtless have responded according to her wish; for it is not a generous act when Mr. Livingstone gives. It involves no sacrifice. But she compelled him to refuse her demand when she claimed it as of right. To have given after that accusation would have been to plead guilty.

But Livingstone interests me less than Gray. Israel, or Livingstone, will die and carry with him his secrets into the grave. Gray—the real Gray—will not die.

THE END.

www.ingramcontent.com/pod-product-compliance
Lightning Source LLC
Chambersburg PA
CBHW022144300426
44115CB00006B/339